イギリス英語の

悪口雑言
あっこうぞうごん
辞典　True English

アントニー・ジョン・カミンズ　［著］
Antony John Cummins

三澤快枝　［訳］
Yoshie Misawa

東京堂出版

まえがき

Introduction

著者より *Author's Note*

　舞台は始まろうとしていました。コメディアンが琥珀色のスポットライトに照らされ，クラブの暗い客席では観客の期待が高まっていました。その中にあって私はいつしか舞台のことも飲み物のことも忘れ，考え事をしていました。そのとき私は本書を出版しようというオファーを受けていたので，舞台どころではなく，自分がこれから乗り出そうとしている仕事と冒険のことでどうにも頭が一杯だったのです。けれども私の明るいはずの未来には暗い影がさしていました。疑いという影です。東京の至る所で見た夥しい数の英語の本の洪水。掃いて捨てるほどあるイディオムとスラングの本，山のようなCDや目をひくようなイラストや表がふんだんに掲載された本が頭をよぎり，私の不安を募らせました。この本が今までにあったどの本ともあまりにも違いすぎてとても売れそうにないと，この本を出版しようとしなかった出版社もあったことを思い出し，私はますます不安になっていきました。

　私の集めた言葉は本当に何かの役に立つのだろうか？

　こんなに汚らしくて，不快で，無作法に吐き出された反吐のような言葉の数々。英語のなかの屑のような言葉，ただそれだけだ！　私の輝かしい未来は不安と敗北感でほとんど焼き尽くされそうでした。あのごまんとある英語の本に，このうえ付け加える価値のある一冊なんて，この私が一体どうやったら書けるんだろう。

そのとき爆笑が私の耳に飛び込んできました。忘れていたコメディアンが観客をどっと沸かせたのです。突然，青天の霹靂のように私は衝撃を受けました。それは客席を沸かせた彼の言葉でした。それはまさに私がほんの数時間前に書いた言葉であり，あまりにも不快なためにゾッとして書くのをためらった言葉でした。さらに次から次へと言葉が私を襲ってきました。まるでそのコメディアンがその日私が書いた章を読んでいるのかと思うくらい，立て板に水のように私の言葉を繰り出してはあてこすりに満ちたギャグをとばしていました。それはほんの少し前に私が日本の読者に警告したばかりのものだったのです。

その夜の余興が始まりました。何人もの芸人が並んで舞台に上がり，5 分ずつ持ちネタを披露し，観客に投票してもらうのです。彼らは一人ひとり全く違っていて，スタイルもバラバラでした。それでもたった一つだけ彼らを結び付けていたものがありました。彼らは間違いなく私が書いた言葉を使っていたのです。だれも知りたがらないし，そんなものを書いた私の本は日本の書店の片隅でほこりをかぶって売れ残ってしまうかもしれないと，ついさっきまで思っていた言葉の数々でした。でもそうではなかった！　その言葉はここで生きていました。クイーンズイングリッシュも，スラング一覧表も，手垢のついたイディオムもこの舞台にはない。本質的に下品で，当てこすりに満ちた汚くて暗い言葉，これが英語の真の姿の一面なのです。この本は書店に並んでいる他の本とは全く違います。辛辣さや下品さや差別感をまぎらわすPC（＝political correctness：政治的公正さ）もありません。

とにかくお読みいただきたい。きっとこの怪物があなたの英語をあなたがまだ知らないレベルへと押し上げるでしょう。

取り扱い注意！　*Warning*

本書をお読みになる際に，十分注意していただきたいことがあります。本書の内容は実際使われている侮辱的，暴力的，その他いろいろな下品な表現を含んでいます。イギリスはいつも騎士道や威厳をもってあなた

を出迎えてくれる上品な所とは限らないことを覚悟してください。侮辱を受けたり与えたりするようなどぎつい言葉のやりとりが数限りなくあるのです。泣きたくなるような場面もあるかもしれませんが，それが現実なのです。イギリスは厳しい所であり，私たちの使う言葉もまた厳しいのです。私は英語を勉強している多くの日本人と会いましたが，100％間違いなく彼らは言語能力の大きな部分が欠落していました。日本人で私より専門用語をよく知っている人や英語の歴史を私より詳しく知っている人にも会ったことがあります。けれども夜通しカラオケバーや居酒屋で一緒に過ごしているうちに，彼らはきまって私の方に向き直り尋ねるのです。

「君たちの言うことがなぜわからないんだろう？　私は30年間英語を勉強してきたのに，まだ君たちの基本的な会話すら理解できないのか」

それに対して私はいつもこう答えます。

「あなたの使っているのは上等なレベルの英語です。あなたは悪態も理解していないし，私たちの文化的背景の知識もないからです。私たちの低俗な英語は聞きなれないでしょうが，この下等な英語を理解できるようにならなければ，レベルを上げることはできないのです」

ところが，ここで日本人の感覚がものをいいます。彼らは私の言葉に上品に相づちを打つのですが，目を見ると私の言うことを信じていないことがわかります。彼らは英語の秘訣はもっと語句を覚えること，もっと専門用語を覚えること，もっと体裁のいい言い回しを覚えることだと思っているからです。そしてさらに自分のやり方で進んでいくのです。辛くて果てしない苦難の続く道を進んだ結果，どこへもたどりつけないのです。ほとんどすべての英語学習者が同じような道をたどっていると言ってもいいでしょう。

そうならないために本書をぜひ読んでいただきたいのですが，その前に，**著者と出版社は皆さんに厳重に警告いたします。**この本に登場する英語の多くは攻撃的ですので，使えばトラブルになることもあります。使えば侮辱になるということを自覚している場合以外は絶対に使わないでください。各章の中でも必要に応じて注意はしてあります。さらに，

この本の多くの語句はそれぞれ注意書きがつけてありますし，使う場合にはどんな注意をしたらいいのかを説明しています。繰り返し言いますが，くれぐれも注意してください。

学習の仕方　*How to Study*

　英語を勉強するとき，まずしなければいけないことは英語とは何かを理解することです。この段階が，流暢に話せるようになるために克服しなければならない最大の障害と言えます。英語は一枚岩ではありません。つまり明確な境界や明確な法則のある統一された体系ではないのです。日本の人たちは英語という言葉をいろいろな意味で間違って使っています。英語を話せるようになるとはどういうことなのかを画一的に考えるという罠に無意識に陥ってしまっています。英語はそれを話すだれとでも100％コミュニケーションできるようなきっちりした体系ではありません。このことはコンピューターで簡単に確かめることができます。マイクロソフトのワードを開くと英語の種類が選べるようになっています。主な二つはイギリス英語とアメリカ英語ですが，ほかにも標準的なイギリス英語以外の英語を使う人のための英語の設定がたくさんプログラムに組み込まれているのです。

　英語の違いをわかりやすくするために例を挙げてみましょう。90歳のスコットランド人でその地方の豊かな文化や語彙，スラングや歴史を身につけているネイティブスピーカーがいたとします。かたや麻薬の密輸をやっている，イングランドの都会に住む15歳の少年がいたとしたら，彼の使う言葉やアクセント，文法はスコットランド人には全く理解できないでしょうし，その逆も言えるでしょう。この二人はごく限られた基本的なボキャブラリーしか共有していないでしょうし，それぞれに特有の語順，文法的不規則性などの傾向があるでしょう。つまり彼らはほとんど別の言語をしゃべっているといってもよいのです。

　次に，これも大変重要な点なのですが，英語には膨大なボキャブラリーがあるということです。日本の人たちはたいてい間違えた目標を設定

して英語学習をしています。英語学習がスタートとゴールのあるものだと勘違いしているのです。理解度０％からスタートして片っ端から覚えていき，最終的に100％になったときに学習が終わると思っているようです。これは絶対にまちがっています。

　私はネイティブスピーカーであり，いわゆる高等教育も受けていますが，身の回りのボキャブラリーのほんのわずかしか知らないといつも思っています。毎日のように新しい言葉を耳にするので，困って辞書を引くことになります。また私が大学に行っていたとき教授の講義を聴いてもボキャブラリーだけではなく，文の構成もわからないことがよくありました。彼はとても専門的かつ学術的に，まるで書くように話すので，私を含めほとんどの学生が理解できなくて落ち込んでしまいます。しかし，もし彼がたとえばスポーツカー産業で働いていてその専門用語ばかり話すようなアメリカ人の若者と会ったら，彼らはお互いに共通の話題もないでしょうし，まわりの人といつも話しているように話したとしたら25％くらいしか理解しあえないのではないでしょうか。英語のボキャブラリーは世界で最大のものの一つであり，最大の英語の辞書は25巻もあります。本棚に並べたら部屋の端から端まで届いてしまうでしょう。もしこれを読むとしたら，おそらく私が理解できるのはほんのわずかでしょう。私は生まれてからずっと英語を学んでいるわけですが，たとえ千回生きたとしてもすべてを学びつくすことはできないでしょう。そこで，このように膨大な言葉に習熟するにはどのようにしたらよいかという疑問が残ります。まず言語を三つの大きな分類にわけてみましょう。

❖日常的ボキャブラリー　Daily Vocabulary
　drink, eat, run, play, table, door, love, hate など，生きている限り毎日のように使う言葉です。あなたの住んでいる地域で使われているスラングやマスコミなどで日常的に聞いて皆が使っている言葉もこれに含まれます。

❖たまにしか使わないボキャブラリー　Occasional Vocabulary

たまに聞くだけでしょうが，聞けばすぐに意味のわかる言葉です。transplant, hibernation, solar, orbit, manufacture, integrate のような単語です。このような言葉はそれほど日常的に使うわけではありませんが，たいていの人が理解できるものです。

❖専門用語　Specialised Vocabulary

これは特定の分野に特有の言葉で，仕事上の必要から，また個人的な興味から覚えようとして覚えるものです。これには，科学，学問，芸術，ビジネス関係，神秘主義，宗教などなど，さまざまな分野の専門的な用語があります。誤解が生じやすいのがこの種類の言葉です。

　以上のように考えると，皆さんは疑問に思うでしょう。それではなぜ人は互いに理解しあえるのだろう？　なぜなら，人はそれぞれ自分の社会的社交範囲の中でおさまっていて，たいていの人は自分の属する集団から外へは決して出ないからです。

　イギリスでは下層階級や教育のない人は，たいてい最初の 2 種類のボキャブラリーとほんのわずかの 3 番目のボキャブラリーだけしか使いません。彼らは自分にとって社会的に快適な範囲から外に出て，人と会話したりしません。彼らはすべてのレベルで自由に英語を話しているようにみえるかもしれませんが，そうではありません。彼らはアカデミックな講義にはついていけないでしょう。理解できる範囲が限られているのです。

　医師や学者についても同じことが言えます。彼らは自分の社交範囲の人たちとだけ付き合っているので，もしそこから離れて全く違う，たとえば建設作業員や配管工のような社会的地位や職業が全く違う人の中に入ったら，おそらく使われている言葉を理解するのは難しいでしょう。この人たちがもし会話するとしたら自ずと第 1 番目のボキャブラリーと 2 番目のボキャブラリーのうちのいくらかに頼らざるを得ないでしょう。それ以外のものを使えば理解しあうのが難しくなってしまいます。

　そこで私のアドバイスですが，重要なのは第1番目の日常的ボキャブラリーをとにかくスラスラ使いこなせるようになることです。この簡単なボキャブラリーの範囲の言葉を使ってネイティブスピードで会話することができれば，あなたは英語のネイティブスピーカーに近づくはずです。そこから範囲を広げようとすると問題が起こります。ですから早く範囲を広げようとあせらず，まずは範囲をせばめて時間をかけることです。イギリスの下層階級のほとんどの人はこの限られた量のボキャブラリーを使って一生を過ごします。ですからそれだけ重要性があるということです。

　私の友人のカオリさんはこのよい例です。彼女はイングランド北部出身の恋人と6年間暮らしていました。初めて会ったとき，彼女がイングランド北部の英語をスラスラと話したので，信じられないくらい驚きました。彼女は私が会った日本人のなかで最も英会話が上手い人です。第一のボキャブラリーについて彼女はほとんど完璧にマスターしていました。話しているうちに第二，第三の分類にまで及んでくるとだんだんミスをし始めました。彼女の限界はやはりあったのです。だとしても彼女の基本的な英語の理解は素晴らしいものでした。それはほとんどの日本人がやらずに過ぎていってしまうものなのです。

地域的要素　*Regional*

　どの言語にも地域ごとに方言があります。イギリスではそれが顕著です。同じ町でもそれぞれの地域に独自の方言があるほどです。さらにそれぞれ関心事が異なるため，違う語彙を使っているいろいろな人種グループや社会的階級なども関係します。それではどのようにその情報すべてを学べばいいのでしょうか？　無理なのです。絶対にできっこありません。それを解決する鍵は，あなたが理解できない言葉それ自体ではなく，会話の中にあるその言葉以外のボキャブラリーなのです。普段よくしゃべっている仲間以外の人と，たとえばアメリカ映画の話をすると，全く知らない言葉を耳にすることがよくあります。もしその言葉だけ聞

いたらどんな意味か全くわからないでしょう。でも，新しい単語，すなわち文化的背景があったり既成概念を破壊するような言葉は，前後の文脈によって意味がわかります。私が言いたいのはすべての文化の新しい単語を際限なく覚えようとするのはやめて，会話の前後関係から意味をとらえるような練習をする方がいいということです。

文化的要素　*Cultural*

　文化やライフスタイルはあなたのボキャブラリーや理解度を左右します。親友のライアンさんは私の同僚のアメリカ人の英語教師でした。皆さんは私たちが同じ言葉を話していると思われるかもしれませんが，ほとんど同じではあるものの問題はありました。私の友人がイギリスから日本に遊びに来て私の所に泊まったときのことです。ライアンさんも遊びに来て一緒に過ごしたのですが，私たちの会話がわからなかったと後で言っていました。ほとんどの言葉はわかるのですが，意味がよくわからなくなったそうです。これは私たちの育ってきた環境の違いのせいです。反対のこともありました。ライアンさんが子供のころ見ていたテレビ番組の話や彼の世代のアメリカ人なら当然知っている情報についての話をしても，私にはちんぷんかんぷんでした。彼が何のことを言いたいのかが理解できませんでした。

　より話をわかりやすくするために例を挙げると，たとえば90歳のご婦人で生け花と着物が好きなずっと田舎暮らしをしている人がいたとします。かたや，13歳で今どきの漫画やコンピューターゲームの話をしているような男の子がいたとしたら，二人が何かしらの理解を得ようと思ったらごく基本的な日本語だけを使うしかないでしょう。

　このことから言えるのは，あなたもどこの地域の言語を学ぶか決める必要があるということです。日本の人はすべての地域のすべての文化のボキャブラリーを学びたい，すべてを知りたいと思っています。けれども私が自分の文化を理解するためには，これまで生きてきた時間が必要でした。それは皆さんも同じだったことでしょう。それならば，英語を

話しているすべての国の文化を学ぶためには何百回も生きなければならないことになります。それは無駄な努力です。まずあなたが一番好きな文化を選ぶことをおすすめします。イギリスですか，アメリカですか？または英語を使うほかの文化のどれかですか？

　次にするのは，自分の世代を考え，その国や地域でその時代に何が起こっていたのかを追っていくことです。その文化のテレビ番組を見るのもいいでしょう。その社会で起きている出来事を理解したり歴史を勉強したりしましょう。どれか一つの文化にあるスラングを学んだら，次第にマスコミで共有している別の文化を理解するようにしていけばいいのです。たとえばイギリスにはアメリカにない人気コメディ番組やショー番組がありますし，その逆もあるでしょう。どこの英語を話したいのかまず選び，そしてその地域の文化を学びましょう。そうすればあなたは英語の中に足場ができて，それを足がかりにしてさらに学習を推し進めることができます。あなたを勇気づけるような情報があります。イギリス映画がアメリカで公開される場合，もし俳優がスコットランドやアイルランドやコックニーなどのなまりがあると英語の字幕がつきます！また聞くところによると映画の「ハリー・ポッター」にはイギリス英語版とアメリカ英語版があるそうです。これは古いイギリスの言い回しがアメリカの観客に理解できないためです。

　最後に付け加えると，私はテレビは時間の無駄だと考え，約8年はテレビを持たないで暮らしているので，現代のマスコミ文化の情報に疎く，友達と話していると理解できないこともあります。ですからあなたが英語を聞いて理解できなくても，それは英語力の問題ではなく，流行や文化的背景を共有していないからかもしれません。

何を言うかではなくどのように言うか
It's not what you say, it's how you say it.

　最後に声の調子についてのアドバイスをしましょう。日本語では場面によって言うべききまり文句があり，それを言うだけで無難にすませる

ことができるようですが，英語はそうではありません。英語は口調によって意味が大きく変わるのです。最も上品な言葉が口調によっては最も侮辱的にも，最高におもしろい言い方にもなりうるのです。例を挙げましょう。かつて付き合っていたガールフレンドのお祖母さんに二回目に会ったときです。彼女が「おばあちゃん，こんにちは，アントニーを覚えてる？」と聞きました。お祖母さんは大変上品ぶった上流階級の老婦人でしたが，私の方を憎々しげに見ながら毒のある口調で言いました。

「かすかにね！」("Vaguely.")

私はそのとき彼女の首を絞めたい気分でした。彼女の言い方は最悪でした。この場面で，もし彼女が笑顔でそう言って私に興味を示すような質問を続けてくれていたら，私は彼女と喜んで話ができたでしょう。

ですから英語を話すときには，どんな口調で言うかがとても重要だということをよく覚えておいてください。感情をあまり見せない日本的な感覚は少し脇に押しやって，声にもう少し感情を込めてみてください。ただしやりすぎはよくありませんが。

ごく日常的な会話がほとんど理解できて自然な口調で話せるようになったら，あなたがネイティブスピーカーの英語に近づきつつあるということです。

皆さんの幸運を祈ります。この本を読んでイギリスの文化を理解していただくと同時に，イギリスとはどんな所であるか，ほんの一面でもわかっていただければと願っています。

June 1 , 2009

Antony Cummins

目次◉Table of Contents

【第1章】 感情を表す表現

Chapter 1　The Way The English Feel

【第3章】 **体・性・家族**

Chapter 3　Anatomy, Sexuality and Family

> ## 【第4章】 生活・社会
> ### Chapter 4　The Word on The Street

この本をお読みになる前に

Before You Read This Book

　本書は英語学習用ツールの一つではありますが，英語の中で最も俗な言い方や猥雑な表現ばかりを集めています。正しい文法に適っていない言葉遣いがたくさん含まれているとお感じになるでしょうが，実際には，大半のイギリス人が普段100％正しい文法にのっとって話しているわけではありません。本書を読んでぜひともそのことを理解していただきたいので，あえてスペリングや句読点なども実際に使われる形に近く表記してあります。今までご存じなかった肩肘はらない素顔の英語としてお楽しみください。

　なお，本書に出てくるイギリスという言葉は，イングランドあたりを中心としていわゆるイギリス全体を大まかに指すものとお考えください。イギリスには地域によってあまりにも多種多様な方言があり，一様には捉えられないのですが，本書は極力イギリス全土にわたって多くの人が使って言ったり，理解している言葉を挙げるようにしてあります。

アイコンについて

　本書で使われているアイコンは，それぞれの言い方がどの程度受け入れられているか，またどんな場面で使うべきかを示しています。アイコンのついていないものはどんな場合でもごく普通に使う言い方ということです。

　この基準は絶対的なものではないので人によって受け止め方は違うことがあります。あくまでも基本的な目安とお考えください。

絶対に使ってはいけない言い方です。もし使ったら取り返しがつかないくらいの侮辱と見なされるでしょう。くれぐれもご注意ください。

いろいろな人がいる場の会話では絶対に使えません。ごく親しい友達や口の悪い人なら使うかもしれません。

笑っている顔ですが，友達同士なら使えるという程度の言葉ですので注意が必要です。それ以外の人に使った場合は失礼だと思われるかもしれません。たとえ友達同士でも使えるかどうかはその親しさによりますので，よく考えてから使ってください。

どんなときでも使える上品な言い方。文法的という意味ではありません。

専門用語または文法的にも正しい言葉です。どんな場合に使っても問題ありません。

また，[ ]や / は直前の語句との言い換えが可能であることを示します。

第 **1** 章

感情を表す表現

悪態語と侮辱語：基本編

List of Common Swear Words and Insults

　悪態は，間違いなく言語の中の一番汚い低級な部分です。悪態語を持たない文化もあると言われています。悪態という概念そのものがその人々にとってはよくわからないそうです。それではイギリスはどうなのかというと，全く正反対です。悪態は私たちの言葉の非常に大きな部分であり，上流階級からその日暮らしの人に至るまで悪態を全くつかない人はほとんどいません。過去千年とはいかなくても，何百年間もの間ずっと悪態は切っても切り離せない英語の一部なのです。

悪態をつく

　このリストにある語句は本書のほかの項目にも登場します。それぞれの語句にはたくさんの意味があり，そのうちのあるものは他の項目で紹介しています。次に挙げるのは，それぞれの語の基本的な情報です。どの語も日常会話で使われる汚い不適当な言葉と考えられています。

fuck　▷非常に複雑な語であり，別に1節をもうけて説明しています（78ページ）。

　　例 Fuck off!（失せろ！）

shit　▷怒りや不快感を表す言い方。

　　例 That DVD was shit.（あのDVDは最悪だった）

wank　「マスターベーション（をする）」　▷「質が悪い」という意味で形容詞としても使われます。

　　例 I want a wank.（マスかきたい）

☺ **crap** 「できが悪い」

例 This book is crap.（この本はひどい）

☺ **piss** 「小便」 ▷この語はたいへん下品なので，友達同士ならともかく，気を使うべき相手といるときには決して使わないようにしてください。汚い言葉という意味では悪態語の一種です。

例 I need a piss.（小便してえ）

☺ **Piss off.** 「あっちへ行け」

例 Piss off, I hate you.（あっちへ行け，大嫌いだ）

☺ **pissed** 「べろべろに酔っ払っている」 ▷pissを使っているので下品な言い方です。

☺ **bastard** ▷もともとは「私生児，婚外子」を意味していました。今はだれかを侮辱する言い方です。

例 You stupid bastard!（馬鹿じゃないのか！）

🚫 **twat** ▷女性の陰部を意味しますが，人を侮辱するときにも使います。

例 You daft twat.（馬鹿野郎！）

🚫 **cunt** ▷twatと同様に女性の陰部を意味しますが，人を侮辱するときにも使います。

例 You are a cunt.（お前は最低だな）

💣 **fucker** ▷「馬鹿，あほ」という侮辱を込めた言い方です。

例 You stupid fucker.（くそったれ！）

☺ **nob** 「ペニス」 ▷人を侮辱して使います。

例 You nob.（あほう！）

☺ **nob rot** ▷上のnobにrot（たわごと，くだらないこと）を付け加えることにより，相手がひどく不快だということを示しています。

例 You're just a nob rot.（このくず野郎が）

☺ **nob head** 「馬鹿者」「くだらないもの」

例 He's a nob head.（やつは馬鹿野郎だ）

💣 **dildo** 「張り形」「ディルド」 ▷女性のオナニーの道具。人を侮辱するときに使う言い方です。

例 That guy is just a dildo.（あいつは最低のやつだ）

💣 **tosser** 「まぬけ」「愚か者」 ▷toss off はオナニーをすること。tosser は恋人が見つけられなくてオナニーをするしかない人という意味で，そこから馬鹿な人という意味に使われます。

　例 You are such a tosser.（お前はほんとに駄目なやつだな）

💣 **fuckwit** ▷だれかを侮辱する言い方。

　例 What a fuckwit!（馬鹿野郎！）

💣 **cow** ▷女性を侮辱する言い方。

　例 You stupid cow!（このあま！）

カルチャー トーク

　イギリス人はよく互いを侮蔑した言い方で呼び合いますが，変だと思わないでください。親しい友達同士はよくふざけて呼び合います。これには侮蔑の意味はなく，それどころか友情を強めるものです。けれども口調が大いに関係します。口調に悪意がこもっていたり，意地の悪いものだったら本当の侮辱になってしまい，相手を怒らせてしまうでしょう。過去20年間に悪態語の持っていた毒は薄れ，特に意味のないものになりつつあります。労働者階級では，子供や初めて会う人の前でも悪態語を使うのは普通になっています。もしあなたが，いい人，もしくは育ちがいい人だと思われたいのであれば悪態語はおすすめできませんが。

馬鹿だな！

Describing an Idiot

　イギリスにも馬鹿な人が相当います。わざわざこんなことを言うのは変かもしれません。でもイギリス人と言えば，"公園を散歩しては優雅にお辞儀をして挨拶しあう上流階級の紳士や上品な家族"というイメージを漠然と持っている日本人が多いような気がします。

　たしかにそういうイギリス人も一部では残っていますが，それよりイギリス人は今やそれとはかけ離れたイメージで有名です。ご存じのようにヨーロッパではサッカーが非常に盛んで，人々が年がら年中試合を見に行き来しているのですが，そのせいでイギリス人は主にヨーロッパでは全く違う目で見られるようになっています。

　"ビール腹，フーリガン，馬鹿っぽい"
というのがもっぱらのイギリス人の定評です。嗚呼！

「頭が悪い」「抜けている」と馬鹿にする表現

👍 **idiot** 「馬鹿者」

　例 He is an idiot.（あいつは馬鹿だ）

☺ **as thick as two short planks** 「大馬鹿である」 ▷plank は「厚い板」
　という意味です。短いplank を 2 枚重ねるとものすごく厚い（thick）
　板になります。thick にはほかに「馬鹿な，とんまな」という意味も
　あるので，この表現は「大馬鹿である」という意味になります。

　例 He is as thick as two short planks.（あいつは大馬鹿者だ）

☺ **numpty** 「馬鹿な人」

　例 He is a numpty.（あいつは馬鹿だ）

☺ **numb** 「頭が足りない」　▷脳みそに何の感覚もない，つまり何も考えていないということを表します。

☺ **numbskull** 「間抜け」　▷品詞が異なります。上のnumbは形容詞で，numbskullは名詞です。

　　例 She is a numbskull.（彼女は間が抜けている）

☺ **pig thick** 「大馬鹿の」

　　例 They are pig thick.（あいつらは大馬鹿だ）

☺ **not all there** 「馬鹿だ，頭がおかしい」　▷何かが足りないということから，頭がおかしいということを意味します。

　　例 They are not all there.（あの人たち，ちょっとおかしいよ）

☺ **two sandwiches short of a picnic** 「間が抜けている」　▷ピクニックでサンドイッチが足りないような状況，つまり「馬鹿みたい，抜けている」ということです。

　　例 He is two sandwiches short of a picnic.（彼は間抜けだね）

☺ **not a full box of tools** 「間が抜けている」　▷道具箱に足りないものがあるということから，間が抜けていることを意味します。

　　例 He is not a full box of tools.（あいつはちょっと足りないね）

☺ **not the sharpest tool in the box** 「あまり利口でない」　▷sharpには「頭の回転がいい」という意味もあります。

　　That kid is so sharp.（あの子はとても頭がいい）

　　したがって「道具箱の中で一番sharpというわけではない」というのは，「（道具が）鋭利でない」ということと「（人が）利口でない」という二つの意味をかけた表現になっています。

　　例 He is not the sharpest tool in the box.

　　（彼はあまり切れるほうじゃないね）

☺ **have a screw loose** 「頭が弱い」　▷機械にゆるんだネジがあったらその機械は正しく動きません。このことから「頭が悪くてちゃんと働かない」ということを意味します。

　　例 He has a screw loose.（彼って頭が弱いわね）

☺ **village idiot** 「村で有名な馬鹿者」　▷古い言い方です。昔はそれぞ

れの村に尊敬される長老がいるとともに，village idiotと呼ばれる人がいたものです。

例 He is the village idiot.（彼は村一番の馬鹿者だ）

「嫌なやつ」「見下げはてたやつ」と馬鹿にする表現

● **wanker** 「役立たず」 ▷wankは「マスターベーションをする」という意味です。マスターベーションばかりやっていて一人ぼっちで寂しいというイメージで，かっこ悪く頭も悪い人を意味します。

● **tosser** ▷wankerと同じ意味です。

● **tit** 「馬鹿者」 ▷titは本来は「おっぱい」の意味ですが，「馬鹿」という意味でもよく使われます。

● **prick** 「馬鹿者」 ▷「ペニス」という意味もありますが，今は「馬鹿」という意味でも使われています。一般に，ペニスを意味する語はたいてい「馬鹿」という意味でも使われます。

例 They are pricks.（あいつら，あほだぜ）

● **nob** ▷prickと同じ意味です。

☺ **bell end** ▷prickと同じ意味です。

● **dickhead** ▷prickと同じ意味です。本来の「ペニス」よりも「馬鹿」という意味で使われる方が多い語です。

🚫 **cunt** 「嫌なやつ」 ▷本来は女性器の意味ですが，「すごく嫌な奴」という意味でも使われ，卑劣で失礼な人を表します。

🚫 **twat** ▷cuntと同じ意味です。

☺ **nob rot** 「馬鹿者」 ▷性病という意味もあります。次の使い分けに注意しましょう。

　　He is a nob rot.（彼は馬鹿だ）

　　I have nob rot.（私は性病にかかっている）

カルチャー トーク

　馬鹿者は世界中どこの国にも必ずいます。男女を問わず，ときには集団になっていることさえあります。たとえそういう人を目にしたとしても，イギリス人はあくまで表面的には礼儀正しく振る舞おうとするのが普通です。本人の前では感じよく好意的に話しておきながら，陰にまわってあいつは馬鹿だなどと言うことはよくあります。ごく親しい友達が馬鹿なことを目の前でやったというような場合でない限り，面と向かってだれかを馬鹿者呼ばわりすることはまずありません。もし見知らぬ人やよく知らない人に対してそんなことを言ったら相手は侮辱だととるでしょうし，暴力沙汰になる可能性大です。

> You Fucking TOSSER!!!
> You have put Milk in green Tea!!

「おまえはアホか，緑茶にミルクなんか入れたのか！」

「がっかりだ！」
「まっぴらだね！」：不満と拒絶

Expressions of Dissatisfaction and Refusal

　　何かが気に入らないとかやりたくないという気持ちを表す表現は二つ
の種類に分けられます。上品な表現とくだけた表現です。日本で英語を
勉強しているみなさんは，上品な言い方については問題なくできるでし
ょうから，ここでは，もっと気軽な言い方を挙げてみましょう。

不満を表す言い方

☺ **I am not fucking happy.** 「ついてないな」「ひどいもんだな」

　　▷これは普通の文にfuckingを加えて強調しただけですが，下品な言
　　い方になり，気の置けない友達同士でしか使えません。

　　例 I lost my wallet, I'm not fucking happy.

　　（財布なくしちゃった。がっかりだよ）

💣 **That's not kosher.** 「うさんくさい」　▷kosherは「（食べ物が）ユ
ダヤ教の教えに則って準備された」という意味です。ここからこの表
現は「正しくない，違法だ」という意味になります。

　　例 I bought a DVD the other day from the marketplace, it was a
　　fake, it wasn't kosher.

　　（この間マーケットでDVDを買ったらとんだまがい物だったよ）

☺ **What[That's] a crock of shit!** 「くだらない！」　▷何かを不満に
思っているという一般的な言い方。

　　例 I went to see that new film the other day, what a crock of shit!

　　（この間その新しい映画を見に行ったけど，全然良くなかったよ）

☺ **What[That's] a load of wank!** 「ひどいもんだ！」　▷a load of ...

は「大量の〜」の意。wank はイギリスでは rubbish，アメリカでは trash または garbage と同じような意味で，「くず，できが悪いもの」を指します。したがって，この表現は「くずの山だ！」ということから「ひどいもんだ！」という意味になります。なお，wank はマスターベーションを意味することもありますので注意してください。

例 That is a load of wank.（ひどいよ）

I watched that DVD you lent me the other day, what a load of wank!（この間貸してくれた DVD 見たけど最悪だね）

👍 **That sucks.** 「むかつく，最悪だ」 ▷アメリカ英語ですが，イギリスでもよく使われるようになっています。

例 A）I failed my exams.（試験に落ちたよ）

B）That sucks.（最低だね）

😊 **What〔That's〕a bag of shit!** 「最悪だ！」 ▷文字通りには「糞が入った袋」です。すごく不満であるということを表します。

例 A）I have to work overtime tonight.（今夜残業だよ）

B）What a bag of shit!（最悪！）

😊 **What〔That's〕a load of bollocks!** 「最悪だ！」 ▷bollocks は「睾丸」のほかに「うそ，たわごと」を意味し，a load of ... は「たくさんの〜」の意です。品物が気に入らないとか，だれかがうそを言ったことに対し不満があるということを意味します。

例 A）I have to retake my driving test because I didn't park right.（駐車がちゃんとできなかったからもう一回免許のテスト受けなくちゃならないんだ）

B）What a load of bollocks!（ダサい！）

😊 **crap** 「出来の悪いもの」 ▷もとは「ごみ」という意味です。

例 That's fucking crap.（まったく最低だ）

😊 **What〔That's〕a load of crap!** 「たわごとだ！」

例 A）My girlfriend thinks I'm cheating on her.（僕の恋人は僕が浮気をしていると思ってるんだ）

B）What a load of crap!（あほか！）

拒絶を表す言い方

💣 **fuck that** 「まっぴらだ」 ▷「私は断る」ということを表す一般的な言い方。

例 My ex-girlfriend wants me to go round tonight, fuck that.
（元カノが今夜寄ってくれって。願い下げだ）

👍 **Not on your life.** 「まっぴらだ」

例 A）Will you give me a lift to the shop?（店まで乗せていってくれる?）

B）Not on your life.（だめだよ）

👍 **Not on your nelly.** 「とんでもない」 ▷聞き慣れない表現でしょうが，一般的な言い方です。子供に対して「だめ」と言うときに使うことが多いかもしれません。

例 A）Can I stay up late tonight, mum?（お母さん，今夜夜更かししてもいい?）

B）Not on your nelly.（だめよ）

👍 **No chance.** 「無理だよ」 ▷There is no chance I will do that.（そんなことはしないよ）を縮めた言い方。100%の拒絶を表します。

例 There is no chance.（無理だよ）

👍 **No way.** 「だめだよ」 ▷There is no way I will do that.（そんなことはしないよ）を縮めた言い方。100%の拒絶を表します。

例 A）Will you lend me fifty quid; I will give it you back on Friday?（5ポンド貸してくれない? 金曜日に返すからさ）

B）No way.（やだね）

👍 **Not for all the tea in China.** 「絶対いやだ」 ▷この言い方は大英帝国の領土が最大に広がっていた時代に生まれました。中国にはたくさんお茶がありますが，お礼に中国にあるお茶を全部もらったとしても，頼みは聞けないということを意味します。

例 A）Would you like to be an English teacher in Japan?（日本で英語教師になりたい?）

B）Not for all the tea in China.（ありえない）

hell（地獄）を使った拒絶の言い方

　以下の表現はいずれも「絶対にいやだ，だめだ」という意味で用います。12世紀ごろまでは地獄は何層にもなっていて，凍っている場所もあると考えられていました。ダンテが『神曲　地獄篇』を書いたときにも，熱い所だけではなく，凍った地獄のことも書いたのです。しかし後に人々は，地獄は熱い所だと信じるようになったので，以下のような言い方が生まれました。したがって，ずっと昔のイギリスではこのような言い方は意味をなさなかったことになります。

😊 **Not a chance in hell.** ▷「悪魔がいて炎が燃えさかる地獄では生き残るチャンスはない」ということから，相手の頼みを聞き入れるつもりは全くないということを意味します。

　　例 A）Will you make dinner tonight?（今夜，夕飯を作ってくれる？）
　　　　 B）Not a chance in hell.（いやよ）

😊 **On a cold day in hell.** ▷地獄は火が燃えさかる熱い所なので寒いことは決してありません。つまり「絶対にない」という意味です。

　　例 A）Would you like to baby-sit for me tonight?（今夜，私の代わりに子守してくれる？）
　　　　 B）On a cold day in hell.（絶対ムリ）

😊 **Not a cat's chance in hell.** ▷「地獄の熱のため猫も生き残れない」ということから「絶対に頼みは聞けない」ことを表します。

　　例 A）Would you like to be a receptionist?（受付になりたい？）
　　　　 B）Not a cat's chance in hell.（とんでもない）

😊 **Not a snowball's chance in hell.** ▷雪玉は地獄の熱で溶けてしまうので，そこから「頼み事を聞くことは絶対にない」ということを意味します。

　　例 A）Will you grab that drink for me?（あの飲み物を取ってきてくれる？）
　　　　 B）Not a snowball's chance in hell.（いやだね）

😊 **When hell freezes over.** ▷炎が燃えさかる地獄が凍ることはあり

えないので，「地獄が凍るようなことがあれば引き受ける」とは「絶対に同意しない」ということです。

例 A) When are you going to buy me a drink?

（いつ一杯おごってくれる？）

B) When hell freezes over.（ありえないね）

男「電話番号，教えてくれよ」
女「いやよ」

カルチャートーク

　日本では人に対してはっきり断るのをよしとしない傾向があるようですが，イギリスでは断ることは全く問題ありません。笑顔で断ればユーモアをもって受け止められるので大丈夫です。イギリスでは言葉そのものよりも言い方が大切だということを覚えておいてください。けれども上品な席やあまり親しくない人と一緒のときは丁寧な言い方だけを使うようにしてください。

あっちへ行け！

Go Away!

　もめ事は非常に不快なものですが，残念ながら実生活では避けられない問題でもあります。もめ事は必ずしも暴力沙汰になるわけではありませんが，大声をあげたり口論になったりします。あげくの果てには相手に向かって「あっちへ行け」というセリフを吐くことになるでしょう。この節でわかるように，英語で「あっちへ行け」と言うときは，ただGo away! と言うだけでなく，ほかにもいろいろな言い方があります。本節に挙げた言い回しはすべて攻撃的で対立的な場面で使われる言葉ですので，注意してください。このような事態に巻き込まれることはないかもしれませんが，もしかしたら第三者として居合わせたり，映画や本などで見ることがあるかもしれないので覚えておくといいと思います。

　このような言い方を使うとき，前にjustをつけて使うことがよくあります。justの後にちょっと間をおいて言うと，さらに強調されてあなたが感じているいらだちを表すことができます。また，ほとんどの言い方は単独で使われますが，ほかに付け加えることができる場合は文例を挙げてあります。例文を挙げていない言い方は単独で使った方が自然だということです。

一人にしてくれと言いたいときに

🏺 **I don't mean to be rude but please leave me alone.** 「失礼なことを言うつもりはないのですが，私にかまわないでください」　▷これは非常に丁寧な言い方です。丁寧に言うべきときに使える唯一の言い方です。

例 I don't mean to be rude but please leave me alone. You are really annoying me.（失礼なことを言うつもりはないんですが，お願いだから放っておいてもらえませんか。すごく迷惑なんです）

🍆 **Sod off.**「あっちへ行け」 ▷一般的な言い方です。

例 Just ... sod off and leave me alone.
（ちょっと，あっちへ行って。一人にして）

🍆 **Piss off.**「うせろ」 ▷非常に失礼な言い方です。

例 Piss off, you stupid bastard.（どっかへ行っちまえ，馬鹿野郎）

🚫 **Fuck off.**「うせやがれ」 ▷最も失礼な言い方。本当に必要なとき以外使うべきではありません。

例 Fuck off and leave me alone.（あっちへ行け。ほっといてくれ）

😊 **Get out of my sight.**「どこかへ行ってしまえ」 ▷目下の人に使うような言い方。たとえば母親が子供に言ったり，上司が部下に言ったりします。イギリスでは平等の意識が高まっているので，この言い方はあまり使われなくなってきています。

例 Get out of my sight, you fucking idiot.（どっかに行っちまえ，このどあほう）

😊 **Leave me.**「下がりなさい」 ▷古めかしい言い方。通常，地位の高い人が部下に対して言う言い方。歴史物の映画などで，王や貴族が家来に言うのをよく聞くでしょう。

👍 **Please leave me alone.**「放っておいてください」 ▷命令というより嘆願です。気の弱い人が言うような言い方です。丁寧な言葉遣いですが，男性が言えば弱々しいと思われるでしょう。

👍 **Leave me alone.**「放っておいてくれ」 ▷興奮しているので少し頭を冷やしたいというときの言葉。

例 Leave me alone, you nob rot.（ほっといてくれ，馬鹿野郎）

👍 **Get off my back.**「あっちへ行け」 ▷だれかに悩まされているようなとき，私から離れてほしい，いらいらさせるのはやめてほしいという言い方。

例 Just ... get off my back.（いいから，あっちへ行ってくれ）

Get off my case.　「首を突っ込まないでくれ」　▷caseにはいろいろな意味がありますが，ここでは「問題」という意味です。すなわちこの問題をこれ以上話したくない，そっとしておいてほしいということです。

　例 Just ... get off my case.（とにかく，ほっといてくれ）

Back off.　「下がれ」　▷物理的に後ろに下がってほしいと頼んでいる言い方。または，だれかがあなたに質問している件について話し合いたくないと拒絶する言い方です。

　例 Back off, bitch!（ほっといてくれ，このあま！）

Leave it out.　「やめてほしい」　▷迷惑なことをしている人に，やめてもらうために言う言い方です。

　例 Leave it out, will you?（やめてくれる？）

Fuck off or die.　「くたばれ」　▷「あっちへ行け，さもなければ死ね」，すなわち「お前がここにいればぶっ殺してやる」という意味です。これは実際の暴力をちらつかせた非常に強い脅しです。

Get out.　「出て行け」　▷相手に部屋などから出て行ってほしいという言い方。

Move along.　「あっちへ行け」　▷非常に現代的なスラング。

That's it, I've had enough.　「もうたくさんだ」　▷文字通り「もうたくさんだ」という意味と，「もういいから一人にしてほしい」という意味があります。

　例 That's it, I've had enough of this.（それ以上言うな。もうたくさんだ）

Make like a tree and leave.　「あっちへ行け」　▷「去る」の意味のleaveを「木の葉」のleavesにかけた言い方です。「あっちへ行け」という意味の冗談っぽい言い方ですが，口調によっては強い意味合いになります。

Take a hike ...　「どこかへ行ってしまえ」　▷hikeは「歩く」ですから，「歩いてどこかへ行ってしまえ」という意味になります。

　例 Take a hike, bozo.（どっかへ行け，間抜け）　▷bozoは「（無能な）男，やつ，あほう，間抜け」などの意味です。

☺ **Go and take a flying leap off a cliff.** 「消えてくれ」 ▷文字通り
には「崖から飛び降りろ」で，つまり「どこかへ行ってくれ」という
意味になります。これはたとえ深刻なセリフでも面白い言い方をする
イギリス式ユーモアのよい例です。

☺ **Go take a long walk off a short pier.** 「どこかへ行け」 ▷「短い
桟橋をずっと歩いていってくれ」ということから，「どこかへ行け」
という意味になります。これも典型的なイギリス式のユーモアです。

☺ **Feck off.** 「うせろ」 ▷Fuck off. と同じ意味ですが，feck は悪態語
ではないので婉曲的な言い方になっています。

**カルチャー
トーク**

　もめ事には巻き込まれるべきではありません。決して巻き込まれな
いように最大の注意を払ってください。けれどももし巻き込まれてし
まったら，思い出してもらいたいのは，まず口論から始まって，次第
に大声でどなり合うようになり，次に押し合いになって，最後に暴力
沙汰になるということです。この四つの段階のどこででも止めること
はできますし，止めるべきです。逆に，何も手を打たずにエスカレー
トさせてしまうと最悪の事態を招くかもしれません。
　相手を落ち着かせたいと思ったら，ただ
　I don't wish to argue, I think we should just leave it.
　（争いたくはないんだ，やめておこう）
と言って立ち去ってください。

くだらないよ！

Expressions of Dislike

　上品な場面ではイギリス人は日本人と似ていると思います。どちらも何かが気に入らなくてもあけすけに言ったりしません。しかし，ちょっとやそっとでは剝がれないうわべの上品さの下には，あなたがネイティブと親しい友達にならない限り耳にすることのない種類の言い方があります。ただし，相手が親しい友達だと確信できない限り，丁寧な言い方だけを使った方が無難です。「気に入らない」という言い方は，大まかに言ってとても上品なものと下品で汚い表現の両極端に分かれます。中間的な言い方というのはあまりありません。

「気に入らない」の上品な言い方

　何かが嫌いだと言いたいとき，丁寧な会話では，イギリス人はたいてい遠回しの言い方をします。その場合，以下のような言い方をします。はっきり言わなければならないときには先に謝り，済まなそうな口調で言うのが自然です。

👍 **So-so.** 「まあまあだね」
👍 **Erm, it's OK.** 「うーん，いいんじゃない」
👍 **Not so good.** 「イマイチだな」
👍 **Sorry, I'm afraid I didn't like it.** 「悪いけど好きじゃないよ」

カジュアルで失礼な言い方

　「失礼な」とはこの場合，ごく親しい友達との会話で何でも思ったま

ま言えるようなときに使うという意味です。そんなときは標準的な英語はまず使いません。

　失礼な言い方の場合，次のような言葉で強調することもできます。いずれも「とっても，すっごく」という意味です。

・fucking　かなり下品な言い方です。

・so　伸ばして言うと女性的，またはオカマっぽく聞こえます。

・unbelievably

😊 **shit**　「ひどいもの，価値がないもの」　▷かなり下品な語です。

　例 That film was fucking shit.（あの映画はクソだ）

😊 **shite**　▷shit と同じ意味です。

　例 He is shite at football.（彼はサッカーが下手くそだ）

👍 **poo**　▷shit と同じ意味。

　例 The DVD was so unbelievably poo.

　（あのDVDは全くろくなもんじゃなかった）

👍 **plop**　「ひどいもの」　▷ウンチが水に落ちるポチャンという音からきています。子供っぽい言い方です。

　例 That is plop, no doubt about it.（あれはくだらない，間違いない）

😊 **crap**　「ひどい」「価値がない」　▷shit ほどではありませんが下品な表現です。

　例 That bacon sandwich was crap.（あのベーコンサンドは最悪だった）

😊 **wank**　「ひどいもの」「くず」　▷wank は「オナニーをする」という意味の動詞や「オナニー」という名詞として使われます。

　　I had a wank.（オナニーをした）

　また，この語を何かに対する感想を言うときに使うと「とても気に入らないもの，ひどいもの」という意味になります。

　例 That play was so wank.（あの芝居はほんとにひどかった）

👍 **pants**　「ひどい」「役立たずの」　▷文字通りの意味は「ズボン」ですが，「役に立たない，くずの」という意味でも使われます。

　例 I am pants at computer games.（コンピューターゲームは下手だ）

👍 **naff**　「くだらない」「あほくさい」　▷1980年代に流行しましたが，今でも使われています。

例 This is naff, I can't believe I have paid for it.

（こりゃヒサンだな，こんなものに金を払ったなんて信じられない）

👍 **trash**　「くず」「くだらないもの」　▷一般には「ごみ，紙くず」という意味です。「くだらないもの」という意味で使うのはアメリカ用法ですが，イギリスでも使われるようになってきています。

例 Man, do you think the movie was trash?

（ねえ，あの映画はひどかったと思う？）

👍 **garbage**　「くず」「くだらないもの」　▷一般には「生ごみ」という意味です。「くだらないもの」という意味で使うのはアメリカ用法ですが，イギリスでも使われるようになってきています。

例 It's garbage, I would not recommend it.（最悪だよ。すすめないね）

👍 **gash**　「くず」「ひどいもの」　▷もとは「ごみ」という意味で，主に軍隊で使われていた語です。この語は女性器を表すこともあるので注意してください。

例 What a load of gash!（なんてひどいんだ！）

カルチャートーク

　西欧で始まった現代文明は急速に世界中に広がりつつあると思っています。これは使い捨ての文化です。私たちはもっぱら消費者であって生産者ではありません。私たちは自分のまわりの世界が与えてくれるものを当然のように考えて，それに甘えています。もはや自然の美しさに感動しなくなってしまった人も多いのではないでしょうか。もっと楽しい映画が見たい，もっといい音楽が聴きたい，もっと高価な洋服が欲しいといった欲望ばかりで，シンプルなものを愛する気持ちを失い，何に対しても不平を言うようになっています。この世界は今に不平を言う人や不幸せな人だらけになってしまうような予感がします。

「頭にきた！」
Expressions of Annoyance

　金づちで親指を叩いてしまった，宝くじがまたはずれた，家にまた請求書が届いた，こんな些細な出来事が人生にはたくさんあります。そんなとき，どんなに頭にきているか思わず言葉にしたくなりませんか。日本人はあまりしないようですが，イギリスでは日常茶飯事です。不運に見舞われたときやいら立ったときに思わず言ってしまう言葉を挙げてみましょう。

　このような表現はすべて単独で使われるもので，ほかの言葉が続くことはめったにありません。もし言うとすれば当面の問題のことか，人生を呪うような言葉を続けることがあるかもしれません。これらはみな怒りをやや押し殺しつつ，小声で苦々しく吐き出すように言うような言葉です。

「畜生！」「まったく！」「くそ！」などを表す言い方

💣 **For fuck('s) sake!**

😊 **For pity('s) sake!**

😊 **Shit!**

👍 **Sugar!**　▷これはShit! の代わりに使う言い方です。腹立ちを言葉にしたいけれども，上品な会話だったり子供の前だったりして悪態はつきたくないときに使います。

「信じられない！」を表す言い方

👍 **Unbelievable!**　「信じられない！」「うそだろ！」　▷物事がうまく

いかず，運が悪いときなどに使います。

☺ **Un-fucking-believable!**　▷Unbelievable!を強調した下品な言い方です。fuckはとても便利な言葉で，このようにほかの単語の中に入れることができます。

👍 **I can't believe it!**　▷Unbelievable!と同じように使います。

👍 **Sod's law!**　「やっぱりだ！」「ついてない！」「案の定だ！」
　　▷Sod's lawはMurphy's law（マーフィーの法則）とも言い，まるで神に見放されたように物事がすべてうまくいかないという経験からきたユーモラスな法則です。典型的な例は，「バターを塗ったトーストが床に落ちるときは必ずバターの面が下になる」（The bread never falls but on its buttered side.）というものです。

☺ **Just my sodding luck!**　「ついてないなあ！」　▷これはつきがなくて物事が全然うまくいかないときに使います。

● **Just my luck!**　▷上に同じです。

冒瀆的な言葉

「くそっ！」「畜生！」「ばかな！」などの意味を表す冒瀆的な表現には次のようなものがあります。

☺ **In the name of Christ!**　▷「キリストの名にかけて！」ということで，キリストに助けを求める言い方です。

💣 **Fucking hell!**　▷hellは驚きやショックを表す感嘆詞として使われます。fuckでそれを強調しています。

☺ **Jesus Christ!**　▷キリストに助けを求める言い方です。

☺ **Mother of God!**　▷聖母マリアに助けを祈願する言い方です。

☺ **Bloody hell!**　▷昔からの言い方で，明らかにby Our Lady in hellが転訛したものです。Our Ladyは聖母マリアのことです。

👍 **Ruddy hell!**　▷冒瀆的な言い方を避けたるために上の言い方を簡略化したもの。

👍 **For Pete's sake!**　▷由来はわかりませんが，考えられるのは聖人ペ

テロへの呼びかけでしょうか。

👍 **God!** ▷神に祈りを捧げたくなるような状況で口にしたことからきたのでしょう。いまでは怒りの表現になっています。

カルチャートーク

　イギリス人の感情表現はどちらかといえば抑え気味です。アメリカ人の方がずっと感情を表に出すと思いますが，それでもイギリス人は日本人よりはもう少し感情を表現するような気がします。この節に挙げた言葉は，腹が立ってはいるが，イギリス人の有名な不屈の精神を失わずにそれを表現したいというようなときに人々が口にするのを聞くことでしょう。

　冒瀆的なフレーズは今ではほとんど本来の「冒瀆的」な意味合いはなくなっています。50年前には神を冒瀆するような言葉を言うことは社会的に許されませんでした。今では気楽によく使われるようになっています。ただしイギリスには敬虔なキリスト教信者も多くいますので，注意しなければなりません。彼らにとってはここで挙げたような言葉は大変に罰当たりな言葉です。だれも侮辱しないような状況であることが大切で，近くにお年寄りや十字架を身につけた人がいる場では冒瀆的な言葉を口にしないように注意してください。絶対にしてはいけないことは，教会の中でGodやhellという言葉を使って怒りを表したり悪態をつくことです。

　最後に，Godという単語を書くときは，キリスト教またはユダヤ教（一神教）の神をいうときはGodと大文字にして，その他の宗教（多神教）の神を指すときにはgodと小文字にします。

冗 談 だ ろ

You're joking.

　イギリスに行ったら大笑いしている人をよく見かけることでしょう。みんなよく大っぴらに大声で長々と笑います。ビールのジョッキを片手に陽気に笑うイギリス人はごくありふれた光景です。バイキングはいつでも，死ぬときでさえ笑っていたと言われています。もしかしたら，それが現在まで千年間続いてきたのではないでしょうか。あるいは笑いがイギリス人の生活で大きな部分を占めているのには，ほかに理由があるのでしょうか？

「冗談でしょ」と念を押したりする表現

You're kidding.　「冗談でしょう」　▷一般的な言い方です。

　　例 A）I'm going to live in Japan for a year and teach English.（日本に 1 年間住んで英語を教えるんだよ）

　　B）You're kidding?（冗談でしょ？）

　　A）No, I leave on September the 9th.（いや，9 月 9 日に出発するよ）

Are you taking the piss?　「冗談なの？」　▷冗談なのか本気なのか聞くときの言い方です。ただし，まじめな口調で言うと違うニュアンスが出てきて，だれかがあなたをこき使おうとしているときや値段が高すぎるときなどに，「冗談だろ，本気で言っているんじゃないだろうな」という意味で使います。

　　例 A）Can I have another cigarette?（たばこもう 1 本くれる？）

　　B）Are you taking the piss?（冗談だろ？）

Fuck off.　「冗談だろ？」　▷この表現はいろいろな意味になりますが，

ふざけた感じで言うと「冗談だろ？」という意味になります。その場合，言葉を長めに発音して笑顔で言います。言い方を間違えると失礼になることもあります。また上品な会話や年配の人や子供の前では絶対に言わないように気をつけてください。

> 例 A) You owe me a drink, it's your round.
>
> （今度はお前が一杯おごる番だぞ）
>
> B) Fuck off!（ふざけんなよ）

☺ **Piss off.** 「冗談だろ？」 ▷Fuck off. と同じ意味です。

> 例 A) I have just won the lottery.（宝くじが当たったよ）
>
> B) Piss off!（冗談だろ）

👍 **Are you joking?** 「冗談でしょ？」 ▷文字通りには，冗談なのか本気なのか聞くときの表現です。けれどももし真面目な顔でこれを言うと，相手の要求が無茶だとかあなたの許容範囲を超えていると思っているという意味になります。

> 例 A) I'm pregnant, darling.（ねえ，妊娠したわ）
>
> B) Are you joking?（冗談だろ？）

👍 **I'm only joshing.** 「冗談だよ」

> 例 A) Really are you pregnant?（ほんとに妊娠したの？）
>
> B) No, I'm only joshing with you.（うそ，冗談よ）

☺ **shits and giggles** 「冗談」

> 例 A) Why did you do that to him?（なんで彼にあんなことをしたの？）
>
> B) I'm only having shits and giggles, that's all.（ほんの冗談だよ，それだけ）

👍 **You having a laugh.** 「冗談でしょ？」 ▷相手に本気なのか聞くとき，または相手の要求が無理だと思うときに使います。

> 例 A) I want to be a ballet dancer.（バレーダンサーになりたいんだ）
>
> B) You having a laugh.（マジかよ？）
>
> ▷イギリスでは男性のバレーダンサーはゲイを連想させます。

👍 **(be) pulling your leg** 「冗談を言う」「からかう」 ▷一般的な言い方です。

例 A）All the work you saved on the computer has been deleted.
（君がコンピューターに保存したもの，全部消えちゃったよ）

B）Really?（ほんと？）

A）No, I'm only pulling your leg.（うそ，冗談だよ）

take the mic 「からかう」 ▷一般的な言い方です。これはコックニーなまりの押韻俗語（Cockney rhyming slang）の take the mickey bliss からきていて（bliss は piss と韻をふんでおり，mickey はペニスを表す俗語でもあります），1930年代から使われているといわれています。

例 A）Are you taking the mic?（冗談だろ？）

B）No, I mean it. All the files on the computer has been deleted.
（いや，ほんとにファイルが全部消えちゃったよ）

(be) having you on 「からかう」

例 A）I'm having you on, honest, it's a joke.（ちょっとからかっただけ，ほんとに冗談だよ）

B）I don't believe you.（信じられない）

😊 **Ha, ha in your face.** 「ワーイ，ざまあみろ」 ▷いたずらをしてう
まくいったときなどに，相手に言う言葉です。

例 I won that game, ha, ha in your face.

（このゲームは僕の勝ちだ，ざまあみろ）

**カルチャー
トーク**

　イギリス人はよくいたずらをやりますし，いたずらをされても皆た
いてい怒ったりしません。4月1日はApril Fools' Dayとしてよ
く知られています。この日は後腐れなく互いにいたずらをしあう特別
な祭日ですが，いたずらは正午までにやらなければいけないとされて
います。正午を過ぎてからいたずらをすると，こんどは逆にやるべき
ときにやれない人だとあなたが馬鹿にされてしまいます。

　いたずらされたときにいい反応をする人をgood sportといいます。
これはスポーツやスポーツマン精神とは関係なく，いたずらされても
あまり気にしない「気のいい人」のことです。

　私がやったいたずらで，以前友人のアランの車の鍵を拝借して彼の
車を動かしてしまったことがあります。それから鍵を戻しておいたの
ですが，彼が車を取りに行ったとき，てっきり車が盗まれたと思い，
みごとにだまされました。後で私のいたずらだったことがわかったと
き，彼は実にさっぱりとしていてgood sportでした。

失敗した！

Mistakes

　人はだれでも失敗します。これは人間にとってごく当たり前のことなのですが，英語には失敗したという意味を表す失礼で下品な言い方がいくつもあります。イギリスでは，1 回の失敗なら大丈夫，同じ失敗をもう一度したらただ運が悪かっただけ，でも 3 回やったらそいつは馬鹿だという不文律があります。

「失敗した」というときに

mess up　「失敗する」　▷mistake という語を使わずに「失敗した」と言う最も丁寧な言い方。

　例 I think I just messed up.（失敗しちゃったみたい）

fuck up　▷「失敗」「失敗する」という意味の一般的な言い方ですが，fuck という語を使っているので上品な会話では使えません。

　例 That was a complete fuck up.（あれは全くの失敗だった）

　She will fuck up if she does not listen.

　（彼女は人の話を聞かないと失敗するだろう）

　I have totally fucked up.（私は完全に失敗した）

balls up　「失敗」「失敗する」　▷balls は男性の睾丸の意であり，理由はわからないのですが，睾丸を表す語は「失敗する」という言い方によく使われます。

　例 It was a balls up.（あれは失敗だった）

　I have ballsed that up, sorry.（ミスしちゃった，ごめん）

drop a bollock　「失敗する」　▷bollock も男性の睾丸のことです。

　　例 I have forgot the keys to open the office up, I have dropped a
　　　bollock.（オフィスを開ける鍵を忘れちゃった，失敗したよ）

☺ **make a prick of oneself**　「失敗する」　▷英語ではdo a mistakeと
　は決して言わず，make a mistakeと言うように，失敗したという表
　現ではmakeがよく使われます。prickもやはり男性器を表します。

　　例 He is going to make a prick of himself.（彼はへますするだろう）
　　　She made a prick of herself.（彼女はしくじった）
　　　They are stupid; they are making pricks of themselves.
　　　（彼らは頭が悪いからきっとやりそこなう）

👍 **make a booboo**　「失敗する」　▷それほど一般的ではなく，子供や
　女性が使う言い方です。boobooにも「睾丸」の意味があります。

　　例 Ooops, I made a booboo.（おっと，間違えちゃった）

💣 **make a fuck up**　「どじを踏む」

　　例 Pete made a fuck up of our friendship.
　　　（ピートは友人関係をぶち壊した）

💣 **screw up**　「失敗する」　▷やや下品な言い方。

　　例 We have all screwed up once or twice in our lives.
　　　（私たちはだれでも人生で一度や二度，失敗をしたことがある）

👍 **soz mate**　「ごめんよ」　▷sozはsorryの意味の大変カジュアルな言
　い方です。主に男性がよく使います。

　　例 Soz mate, I didn't meant to spill your tea.
　　　（悪い，お茶をこぼすつもりじゃなかったんだ）

**カルチャー
トーク**

　　私が日本のある大手の英会話学校で働いていたときのことです。私
は休みの日だったのですが，私が働いていた学校で，ある日，鍵を持
っていて開けるはずだった受付の女性が30分遅れてしまい，生徒が
中に入れないということがありました。彼女は自責の念にかられて土

下座して謝ったそうです。これを聞いたとき私は大変ショックを受けました。確かに彼女の落ち度ではありましたが，土下座するほどのこととは思えません。イギリスで，もし土下座して謝れと女性に言ったとしたら，平手打ちされたとしてもおかしくありません。もし私がその場にいたら何としてでも彼女にそんなことはさせなかったでしょう。

　これは極端なエピソードですが，謝るという行為についての文化の違いを感じた思い出がもう一つあります。

　まだ日本に来て間もないころ，同僚の外国人講師たちと渋谷のクラブに行きました。中はかなり混んでいて，私は人波であふれているダンスフロアを眺めていました。その時モヒカン刈りでイギリス国旗を体中につけたパンクスタイルの日本人がやってきました。まず頭に浮かんだのは「トラブルが来たぞ」ということでした。私はけんかが始まるのではないかと思い，彼をずっと見ていました。イギリスではパンクのイメージは暴力とけんかであり，行儀の悪さと酒はつきものです。ポップスをかけているクラブにパンクが来たとなれば，必ず一騒動あるはず。案の定，彼は気持ちよさそうにいすに座って眠っていた酔っ払いにぶつかってしまいました。ほんのちょっとうっかり当たっただけだったのですが，その人を起こしてしまったことに気づいたのでした。私は思いました。大変だ，きっと酔っ払いを殴るに違いないぞ。ところが次の瞬間どれだけ私が驚いたことか，若者はきちんと頭を下げてその男に謝り始めたのです。起こされた方も頭を下げて謝罪を受け入れました。私はあっけにとられてしまいました。私にとってこれは非現実的な出来事でした。

　イギリス社会ではこのような小さな出来事は気にも留められないか，ごく軽くその場しのぎに謝るだけで堅苦しい謝罪などしません。ですからもしイギリスに行ってあなたが当然真剣な謝罪があってしかるべきだと思うことがあっても，そうならないからといって驚かないでください。たとえばただ肩をすくめて "Soz mate." と言えばそれで十分だと思っているのです。また謝るときには言葉そのものよりも口調が大いに関係します。もしあなたがささいなことで大げさに謝ったら，たぶん相手は気まずい思いをするでしょう。

それは言いすぎだ!

Arguments

　口論と白熱した議論との違いは紙一重で，その境界線を越えて相手を怒らせてしまうことはよくあります。

　この節ではどのように口論するかではなく，口論を友好的なレベルにとどめて侮辱やけんかにエスカレートさせないようにするための言い方を紹介したいと思います。

口論になったときに役立つ表現

This is getting out of hand. 「収拾がつかなくなってきた」 ▷事態が行き過ぎて，敵対的になってしまったり，あなたが望んでいるような友好的な討論ではなくなっていると言いたいときに使います。

I don't mean to offend you. 「あなたを怒らせるつもりはない」 ▷相手を怒らせるつもりはなくて自分の言いたいことを伝えたかっただけだ，というときの半ば謝る言い方です。

Keep it friendly. 「友好的にやろう」 ▷口論している人たちや自分が口論している相手に，境界線を越えないで友好的な議論にとどめようと注意する言い方。

This is not an argument but a heated debate. 「これは口論ではなく白熱した議論です」 ▷議論と口論の境目ぎりぎりまできてしまっているけれども，まだ友好的な議論であるとして安心させる言い方。

I think that's a bit much. 「それは言いすぎだと思うよ」

You are out of order. 「きみは言いすぎだ」

We will have to agree to disagree. 「意見が合わないということで

意見を一致させよう」　▷結論が出ない口論を終わらせる古典的な言い方。どちらも違う見方をしているのでお互いに合意することはないから，これが解決できない口論だということに合意するということ。

**カルチャー
トーク**

　皆さんも次のような駄じゃれを聞くことがあるかもしれません。
　「議論する」という意味でdebateという言葉が使われることがあります。また大勢で何かをすることを表すmassという言葉があります。そこでmass debateというと「大勢の人でする議論」ということになりますが，これはmasturbate（マスタ　ベ　ションをする）と音が似ています。
　ですからもしだれかが，
　　Let's have a mass debate.（みんなで話し合おう）
と言うと，あらぬ意味に受け取る人がいるかもしれません。
　またmasticate（噛む）とmasturbateはとても音が似ていますし，orgasm（オルガスムス）とorganism（有機体）も似たような音なので，よくジョークで使われます。たいていこのようなしゃれは高校生くらいで卒業しますが，大人の会話でもたまに聞くことがあるかもしれません。

がんばれ！

Energetic Expressions

　パブで友達同士がオレンジ色の暖炉の火に照らされてテーブルを囲み，ビールやリンゴ酒を飲みながら笑いあうとき。あるいはサッカーをやったりトランプをやったり，コンピューターゲームなどをして過ごすのはだれにとっても心温まる時間です。けれどもそのうち興奮してきて，勝負に熱が入ってしまったら，彼らの口からどんなボキャブラリーが飛び出すのでしょうか？

興奮したときの一般的な表現

　エネルギーや興奮を表現したいとき，思わず叫んでしまうような表現の例を挙げてみましょう。だいたいゲームとかスポーツ，団体競技などをやっているときに言うことが多いでしょう。

●**Come on!** 「しっかり！」「がんばれ！」 ▷サッカーファンがひいきのチームの応援で叫ぶときなどによく使われましたが，今では勝負のかかったどんな場面ででも仲間や自分を応援するときに使われています。

●**Here we go!** 「さあ，いくよ！」 ▷自分や仲間が行動を始めるとき，たとえばビールを飲むとかゲームや競争を始めるときなどに叫ぶ言い方です。

●**Let's go!** 「始めよう！」「さあ行こう！」 ▷勝負を始めるとき，またはどこかへ出発するとき使います。

●**Yes!** 「そうだ！」 ▷興奮したときに口にする一般的な感嘆語です。

●**Yeah!**「そうだ！」「イェーイ！」　▷興奮したときに叫ぶ一般的な言い方で，yes が転訛したものです。

●**Oh yeah!**「オー，イェーイ！」　▷興奮したときに叫ぶ一般的な言い方。上に同じですが，oh によってさらにパワーが上がっています。

●**Good morning, Vietnam!**「いくぜ！」　▷ロビン・ウィリアムズ主演のアメリカ映画（「グッドモーニング，ベトナム」，1987年公開）のタイトルからきています。興奮していることをコミカルに表す言い方です。

勝負事で興奮したときの表現

　次に挙げるのは，親しい友達とたとえばトランプやコンピューターゲームなどで勝負しているときに使うような言い方です。勝ったり興奮したときに言うことが多いでしょう。

💣**Fucking dead right!**「まったくそのとおり！」　▷自分が100％正しい，あるいは相手の言うことに同意するという意味です。ふつうの会話で相手に同意するときにも使えますが，その場合声の調子を下げて使います。

☺**Ya mam.**「ざまあみろ」　▷your mum（＝mother）を短くしたものです。この言葉が使われ始めたときは，相手の家族に対する侮辱で暴力沙汰になりかねない大変失礼な言い方でした。今では「こっちの方がお前より上だよ」ということを意味するだけの面白い言い方になっています。けれどもこの表現は気をつけて使いましょう。これを互いに言い合えるのはごく親しい友達だけです。友達との親しさがどの程度なのかを見極めた後で使ってください。確信が持てなければ使わないでください。

●**Ya mom.**　▷Ya mam. のアメリカ英語の用法。

☺**In ya face.**「ざまあみろ」　▷アメリカで1970年代にいろいろなスポーツで使われ始めた言い方です。自分の方が勝負に勝ったから黙れという意味です。

😊 **In your face.** ▷上の言い方のイギリス版です。yourをよりはっきりと発音します。全体的にゆっくり言います。

👍 **Too right!**「まったくそのとおり！」 ▷自分の言ったことや主張が完全に正しいということ。

👍 **Going down!**「くたばれ！」 ▷これは自分が勝者として勝ち上がり，相手は敗者として敗れ去るという意味です。

👍 **Read them and weep.**「おまえの負けだ，思い知れ」 ▷もともとはトランプ遊びからきています。あなたが持ち札をテーブルに広げ，その札を見てあまりによい手だと知った相手が賭けた金をなくしたことで泣くだろうということです。いろいろな勝負や議論で，相手に勝ち誇るときに使います。

　これらの言い方は全部，ただ何もつけずそのまま言うようなタイプの言葉で，文法にかなった文章になるようなものではありません。どれもゲームや友人同士の口論などが白熱したあげく，自分の勝ちだと興奮して叫ぶ言い方です。あなたが使うときは一緒にいるのが本当に親しい人だけで，気分を害する人がいないと確信できるときだけにしてください。

　また，英語では何を言うかではなく，どのように言うかが大切だということをくれぐれも忘れないでください。これらの表現を使うときは，怒ったように言うのではなく，とにかく陽気に言うことが大切です。そうすれば緊張した雰囲気にならずにすみます。そして親しみを込めて言いたいと思ったら，相手の肩に手を置いて笑顔で言いましょう。ただし，大きな声で言うのはかまいません。

カルチャー
トーク

イギリスでは日本の皆さんの感覚からすると抵抗を感じるくらい感情を表すことは珍しくありません。何かを伝えようとするとき，どのくらい強い感情を持っているかを表すのはとても大切なことです。群衆に溶け込んで彼らのまねをして，同じような感情になろうとしてみてください。

また，英語では一つの単語の意味が変わるだけで，決定的に意味が変わってしまうことがあります。単語の語尾のトーンを変えるだけで皮肉や怒りや侮辱へと劇的に状況が変わってしまうのです。とはいえ，イギリス人は，アメリカ人が興奮してこうした言い方を使っているのを聞くと，あまりにも熱狂的でうんざりしてしまうこともあります。

いい度胸だ！

Nerves

　度胸がいいとは，勇敢であること，困っている人を助けること，立ち上がって，肉体的，精神的，あるいは魂にふりかかる苦痛に耐える勇気を持つことです。

　英語では，「勇気がある」という意味を表す言葉は，いい意味でも悪い意味でも使えます。日本語では，悪い意味で「勇敢だ」という言葉を使うことはないようですが，英語では同じ言葉が否定的，または肯定的，どちらの場面でも使えるのです。どちらの意味で使われているかは前後関係や文脈から判断することになります。

　ここではbraveの代わりに使える表現をいろいろ挙げてみましたが，その中で「厚かましい」という悪い意味でしか使わない言葉はgallとaffrontだけで，それ以外の言葉は「勇気がある」というほめ言葉にも「ずうずうしい」という悪口にもなります。

　ほかの本ではあまり見ない言葉もあります。

「度胸」「勇気」を表す表現

nerve 「度胸」「勇気」 ▷古典的な語です。

例 You're going to do a bungee jump, you have nerve.

（バンジージャンプをするなんて，度胸があるよね）

bottle 「度胸」「勇気」

例 She's got bottle wearing a skirt like that in an area like this.

（こんな場所でそんなスカートをはくなんて，彼女ずいぶん怖いもの知らずだな）

例 You have some bottle going on that ride; I'm too scared of heights for that. （あの乗り物に乗るなんて度胸があるね。私はあんな高いところだめだな）

例 You have some fucking bottle talking to me like that you piece of shit!(俺にそんな口を利くとはたいした度胸だな，このあほんだらが！)

👍 **guts** （恐怖などに対する）「**勇気**」「**根性**」 ▷ guts は本来「腸」という意味で，腹にもっている，恐怖に打ち勝ってやるべきことをやる根性のことです。

例 If you do that you will have to have some guts.

（それをやるならガッツを持たなきゃいけないよ）

👍 **face** 「**度胸**」「**ずうずうしさ**」 ▷人と対決するときは相手と面と向かうということから，face があるとは度胸があるという意味になります。顔を合わせず陰で悪口を言うのは直接対決する勇気がないということになります。

例 He's got some face showing up like this.

（こんなふうに姿を見せるとは彼は度胸がいい）

👍 **brazen** 「**度胸がいい**」「**ずうずうしい**」 ▷否定的な意味でよく使われます。

例 They are a bit brazen shouting their mouths off like that. （あんなふうに大きな声でどなるなんて，あの人たちちょっと厚かましいよね）

例 Sandy is being very brazen today.(サンディ，今日はやけに勇敢だな)

例 That girl is far too brazen for my liking, her boyfriend should put her on a leash. （あの娘はじゃじゃ馬すぎて俺の好みじゃない。カレシがちゃんとつないどかなきゃだめだ）

👍 **brass** 「**度胸**」

例 Can you believe the brass of him, asking such a question to her?

（あんな質問を彼女にするなんて，あの人を食ったような態度，信じられる？）

例 Wow, he has brass, look at how high he can climb.

（うわっ，根性あるな，見てみろよ，あんなに上まで登れたぞ）

例 What a dickhead, he had brass, thinking he could tell me what to do, fucking idiot!（あのアホ，俺に指図なんかしやがった。馬鹿野郎！）

👍 **brass neck** 「度胸」

例 I've got enough brass neck to do that.

（それをやるだけの度胸はあるよ）

👍 **gumption** 「積極性」「元気」「度胸」　▷たいていは自分ではなくほかのだれかの行為に対して使います。「ずうずうしい」というやや否定的な意味合いでもよく使われます。

例 He had some gumption when he hit that other guy for next to nothing.

（何でもないようなことであの男を殴ったなんて彼は傍若無人だ）

👍 **gall** 「度胸」「厚かましさ」

例 I can't believe you have the gall to say that to my face.

（私に面と向かってぬけぬけとそんなことを言うなんて信じられないわ）

😊 **spunk** （困難に立ち向かう）「勇気」「元気」　▷ほかにも「精液」「カリスマ性」などの意味があるので注意が必要です。アメリカでの方がよく使われています。

例 She has got real spunk; I'd love to go out with her.

（彼女，本当に元気だね。デートしたいな）

😊 **balls** 「根性」　▷balls は「睾丸」という意味ですが，have balls で「勇気がある，向こう見ずだ」という意味になります。

例 She's got balls!（彼女は根性があるね！）　▷この場合女性に対しての言葉ですが，侮辱しているのではなくほめています。

👍 **affront** （憚らず公然とする）「侮辱」「無礼」

例 Last week, Bryan had the affront to tell me to turn my music down.（先週ブライアンが僕に音楽の音を下げろとしゃあしゃあと言いやがった）

👍 **bravado** 「からいばり」「無鉄砲な勇気」　▷ややコミカルな語です。

例 Military boys always have loads of bravado.

（軍人はいつもからいばりばっかりだ）

☺ **balls of steel**　「ど根性」　▷文字通りの意味は「鉄の金玉」。勇敢で，硬派で，タフな男について使います。

🈘 I'll do it, I've balls of steel.（俺はやるぞ，根性だ！）

**カルチャー
トーク**

　a stiff upper lip（引き締めた上唇）とはイギリスでよく使う言い方で，イギリス紳士の心得です。臆病風に吹かれると上唇が震えだすので，唇を引き締めてぶるぶる震えさせないようにする，つまり勇気を持ってということです。すべてのイギリス紳士はどんなときも上唇を引き締めなければならなかったのです。

　とはいうものの，今はそうではありません。イギリス紳士は絶滅種となりつつあり，騎士道や英雄的行為はもはや過去のものです。今は法律がすべてをコントロールしています。襲われている人を助けようとして手を出せば，逆に自分が罪に問われて刑務所に入る羽目になるかもしれないのです。

　私は以前，女性が男に顔面を殴られたのを見かけたことがあります。それを止めようとして車から飛び出したら，友人たちに止められてしまいました。かかわると面倒なことになるし，男がナイフや銃を持っているかもしれないというのです。結局，最初に女性が男性を殴って，彼は一度だけ殴り返したということがわかったので，やっと納得して立ち去ったのですが，今でも私はイギリスの男がどんなに堕落してしまったか忘れることはできません。

さあ行こう!

Let's go!

　「さあ,出かけよう」と呼びかけるときにいろいろな言い方があります,それぞれ多少ニュアンスが違います。たいていは陽気で元気がいい言い方なのですが,それでも少し違いがあるのです。

　次に挙げる言い方はすべてそのまま何もつけないで使います。どこかへ行こうとか,違う場所に移ろうというときの言い方です。

「出かけよう」と呼びかける表現

☺ **Let's haul ass.** 「急いで行こうぜ」　▷下品な言い方です。arse ではなく ass という語を使うため多少アメリカっぽい雰囲気があります。haul ass で「さっさと出かける」という意味です。

👍 **Move it out.** 「次に進め」「出発しろ」　▷これは命令ですが,let's を前に入れると「～しましょうか」という婉曲な言い方になります。

👍 **Let's march.** 「行きましょう」　▷古い語感と軍隊を思わせる響きがあります。家を出たりレストランを出るときなどに親が子供に言ったりします。

☺ **Shall we sod off?** 「行こうよ」　▷sod off は go away「立ち去る」という意味です。この場合,陽気な口調で疑問形で言います。そうしないとだれかを不愉快にさせるかもしれませんので気をつけてください。

👍 **Let's ride em cowboy.** 「出かけよう」　▷アメリカ英語です。おそらくはアメリカのテレビ番組でカウボーイが馬に乗って町を出るときに使われた言い方でしょう。

👍 **Off we go.** 「さあ行こう」 ▷非常に陽気な言い方です。

👍 **Let's ride.** 「出かけよう」 ▷移動手段が馬だった時代にできた言い方です。

👍 **Shall we make a move?** 「次の場所に行きましょう」 ▷make a moveはある場所から次の場所に移るということです。

👍 **Shall we move on?** 「次の場所に行きましょう」

👍 **Shall we push on?** 「次の場所に行かないと」 ▷pushには困難を克服してがんばるという意味合いがあり，「何とかして次に行きましょう」と義務感を伴った言い方です。

👍 **We better get a move on.** 「もう行かないと」 ▷遅れるので急いで行こうという意味です。

カルチャートーク

　これらの言い方はイギリスの有名なpub crawlのとき，よく耳にします。pub crawlとはパブをはしごすることです。次々といろいろなパブに行っては酒を飲み，もう飲めなくなるまで続けます。月曜の朝，日曜にpub crawlをした同僚の話を職場で聞くことがよくあるはずです。pub crawlで有名な町もあり，これらの町にある店ではpub crawlのための地図やルート図を売っていることもあります。私はマンチェスター育ちなのですが，マンチェスターにはEccles（エックルズ）という地区があり，ここは1マイル四方あたりのパブの数がヨーロッパ一多い所だと言われています。余談ですが，Ecclesはecclesiastical（教会の，聖職者の）という語を短くしたものです。よりによってこれだけ酒場のある所にこの名前とは！

　とはいえ，イギリスのパブは今や廃れつつあります。パブの廃業はどんどん加速しています。私が知るだけでも何百ものパブが閉められていますが，新たに開業したパブは見たことがありません。パブ文化はもはや廃れてきていて，もうすぐ消えてしまうでしょう。パブの占めていた社交の中心という役割は家で楽しむ娯楽やレジャーへと移りつつあります。

ついてるね！

Luck

　運に恵まれて神の恩寵を受けるとか，あるいは運が悪く不思議な力があなたに振りかかるとか，そんな運や魔力は現代社会には居場所がありません。昔のやり方は新しいものに駆逐され，コンピューターとインターネットが新しい人間性の一部となっているのですから。

　ところが，英語はいまだに昔の名残をたくさんとどめています。運や魔力は英語の中で生きているのです！

幸運を表す表現

lucky 「幸運な」　▷幸運であることを表す基本的な表現。

　例 You lucky devil!（おまえ，ついてるな！）　▷devil はここでは「やつ，人」という意味ですが，その人の幸運がまるで悪魔の力でも借りたかのようにすごいものだというニュアンスになります。

good luck 「幸運」

jammy 「運がいい」

例 You jammy git!（いいな！）▷git は「役立たず，間抜け」の意味。

lucky bastard 「ついている人」　▷すごく幸運なことがあった人をいう言い方。

　例 He is one lucky bastard.（彼はすごくついてるよ）

have the luck of the Irish 「ついている」　▷これはアイルランド人が魔法を使い，自然の力をコントロールできると信じられていたことから生まれた言い方です。アイルランドは魔法の生きている場所と思われていて，アイルランドの人たちは大変運がいいと思われていま

した。

例 I can't believe you won, you must have the luck of the Irish.

（お前が勝ったなんて信じられないよ。ついてたね）

👍 **marked by God**　「神が味方している」　▷これはもう古くさい言い方ですが，たまに耳にすることがあるかもしれません。神があなたの祈りを聞き届けてくれた，つまり神があなたに味方してくれるおかげで物事がうまくいくという意味です。

例 She must be marked by God to have such luck.

（そんなに運がいいなんて，彼女には神様がついているよ）

👍 **joucy**　「運がいい」　▷最近できた言葉で，語源や正しい綴りははっきりしません。話し言葉だけで使われていて，幸運なことを表します。

例 You joucy bugger!（おまえはついてるな！）

🙂 **jammy sod**　「ついている」　▷すごく幸運なときの感嘆する言い方。

例 Jammy sod, I wanted to get a date with her.

（いいな，僕も彼女とデートしたかったよ）

🙂 **lucky sod**　「すごくついている人」

例 My father is a lucky sod.（私の父はすごくついてる）

😊 **lucky streak**　「幸運が続くこと」

例 Since Christmas I have had nothing but a lucky streak.

（クリスマスからずっとつきまくってるよ）

👍 **streak of luck**　「幸運が続くこと」

例 What a streak of luck I am having!（なんて幸運続きなんだ！）

幸運を表すものやお守りのいろいろ

● **horse shoe**　「蹄鉄」　▷蹄鉄はイギリスでは幸運のシンボルです。

● **silver**　「銀」　▷銀は幸運のしるしではありませんが，邪悪なものから守ってくれる力があると言われています。そのためホラー映画にもよく出てきます。

● **black cat**　「黒猫」　▷黒猫は幸運だと思われるときと不運だと思われるときがあります。どちらが正しいかはよくわかりません。

● **crucifix** 「はりつけの像，十字架」 ▷キリスト教で力と保護のシンボルです。

● **pentagram** 「五芒星形」「ペンタグラム」 ▷魔術のシンボルであり，邪悪なものと考えられていましたが，魔術の研究が進んで，だんだんお守りと考えられるようになってきています。

● **four-leaf clover** 「四つ葉のクローバー」 ▷幸運のシンボルです。

● **hawthorn** 「サンザシ」 ▷キリストが十字架にかけられたとき，冠にされた植物で，お守りになると言われています。

不運を表す言い方

🍶 **unlucky** 「不運な」 ▷不運を表す一般的な言い方。

🍶 **bad luck** 「不運」

例 What rotten bad luck!（なんてついてないんだ！）

👍 **cursed** 「呪われた」「たたられた」 ▷いつも運が悪いような人に使います。

例 I feel that I am cursed.（きっと俺は呪われてるんだ）

👍 **damned** 「信じられないくらい運が悪い」

例 With luck like yours you must be damned.

（ほんとに信じられないくらいついてないね）

👍 **unlucky streak** 「不運なことが続くこと」

例 What an unlucky streak I'm having!

（なんでこうついてないことばかりなんだ！）

👍 **streak of bad luck** 「不運なことが続くこと」

例 You are having a streak of bad luck.（つきに見離されてるね）

不吉なアイテム

● **black cat** 「黒猫」 ▷幸運のシンボルとしてみられることもあり，どちらが正しいのかよくわかりません。

● **inverted crucifix** 「逆さ十字架」 ▷悪魔や邪悪なもののサインです。

● **inverted pentagram** 「逆さ五芒星形」 ▷五芒星形はかつては邪悪

なものと思われていましたが，今はお守りになっています。それを上下逆さまにしたこの形は悪魔を表し，昔から悪魔を連想させる動物であるヤギに似ていると言われます。

**カルチャー
トーク**

　イギリスでは運がいいことはある種の力だと今でも考えられています。運，不運が現実にあるのかという疑問が取り上げられるのは哲学的な議論でだけです。ほとんどの人は，幸運というパワーがあると信じていますし，「一寸先は闇」の世の中で切実に実感できるものと考えています。イギリスでもどんどん昔の迷信や伝統は消えつつありますが，それらを残していこうと活動している団体もあります。

INVERTED CRUCIFIX

HORSE SHOE

FOUR LEAF CLOVER

INVERTED PENTICLE

PENTICLE

素晴らしい！

Expressions of Liking

　いろいろなことに対して感想を求められることがよくあります。日本の人たちと話していると，「よかった」という感想を言うのにgreatやfantasticばかり使う人がよくいますが，ほかにもまだまだたくさんの言い方があります。ぜひ覚えてあなたのボキャブラリーを増やし，状況に合わせて自然に答えられるようにしましょう。

強調する語の使い方

　後に挙げるgreatやそれに類する言葉は単独でそのまま言えば大丈夫です。ただし，文章にするなら次のような強調語を入れるのが普通です。

❖上品な会話での強調語
● **absolutely**
● **unbelievably**
❖気楽な会話での強調語
● **completely**
● **so**　▷使うときには気をつけてください。男性がsoを伸ばして言うとおかまっぽく聞こえます。
● **fucking**　▷かなり下品な語です。
● **totally**　▷これはアメリカ用法ですが，イギリスでも使われるようになっています。

　強調語を使うのは，強調する必要があるからだということに注意してください。たいしてよくもないことに対して強調語を使うのは不自然に

聞こえます。強調語を使うときは文法が正しくなかったり，文章が少し
変だったりしますが，前にも述べたようにイギリス人はいつも 100％正
しい文法で話しているわけではありませんし，ときにはスラングが全く
規則に反していることもあります。

「素晴らしい」を表す言い方

great 「素晴らしい」「よい」 ▷ごく一般的で基本的な語です。スラ
　ングがふさわしくないような上品な会話で最も使われる単語です。

mint 「とてもよい」 ▷北イングランドでよく使われる言い方ですが，
　世界中の英語圏のどこでも通用します。これは骨董の世界に起源があ
　る言葉で，何か古いものを買ったり見つけたようなとき，その状態が
　いいことを，

　　　It's in mint condition.（新品同様である）
　と言います。その工芸品がミントのように新鮮である，つまり未使用
　で古びていないということです。ここからmintは「非常によい」とい
　う意味で使うようになりました。

　例 The film was fucking mint.（あの映画はものすごくよかったよ）

lush 「素晴らしい」 ▷これは最近よく使われるようになってきた言
　葉です。イングランド南部でよく使われますが，だんだん広く使われ
　るようになってきています。

　例 I had a sandwich for dinner, it was lush.
　　　（夕食にサンドイッチを食べたけどおいしかった）

fantastic 「とても素晴らしい」「すごい」 ▷greatより程度が上で，
　「とても素晴らしい」という意味の強い表現です。

　例 I say, this wine is fantastic.（ほんとにこのワインは素晴らしいよ）

wonderful 「とてもよい」「素晴らしい」 ▷スラングではなく，非
　常に上品で好ましい表現です。

　例 The show was wonderful.（あのショーはすごくよかった）

buzzing 「ジンジンくる」 ▷1990年代にドラッグ文化とレイブ（屋
　外や特別な会場で行われるダンスのイベントやパーティー）の流行と

ともにはやった語です。ドラッグをやったときの，頭の中が「ブーンとうなっている（buzzing）」ような感じを言い表しています。今やレイブはほとんど廃れてしまいましたが，この言葉だけは残っています。今ではほとんどドラッグを連想させることはありません。ですから使ってもかまいませんが，もしドラッグをやっている人との会話だったら，彼らはおそらくドラッグについてこの言葉を使うでしょう。

例 I am completely buzzing.（最高の気分だよ）

☺ **wicked** 「素晴らしい」 ▷wickedは本来「悪い，よくない」という意味なのでこれは矛盾した使い方ですが，1980年代に「素晴らしい」という意味で使われるようになりました。おそらくは食べ物からきている使い方だと思われます。体に悪い食べ物の代表といえば，たとえばチョコレートやケーキのようにたいていだれもが好きな甘い物です。そのためwickedであるものは素敵なものとなったのではないか，というのが私の推測です。一般的にはなぜwickedがよい意味で使われるようになったかはわかっていません。この言葉はイギリスの文化に浸透してきて，今や酒のブランド名にまで使われるようになりました。

例 That was so wicked.（あれはすごくよかった） ▷この文は文脈次第で，「悪かった」という意味にも，「すごくよかった」という意味にもなります。

☺ **way out** 「ふつうじゃない」 ▷1960年代のヒッピー革命のときに現れた言い方です。よい意味で「普通ではない」ということを表します。

例 This music is way out man.（この音楽は斬新だねえ） ▷この文は今の英語では時代遅れですが，音楽ファンやヒッピーなら今でも使うかもしれません。

☺ **groovy** 「素晴らしい」 ▷これも1960年代のヒッピー革命のとき生まれた語。grooveには「ダンスをする」という意味もあり，当時の音楽の好みを表しています。groovyは，本来は「ダンスするのにいい」という意味だったのですが，音楽に限らず「素晴らしい」という意味を表すようになりました。

例 Groovy!（いいね！）

👍 **splendid** 「素晴らしい，見事な」 ▷greatの意味でかなり上流階級っぽい語。どんな種類の会話ででも使えますが，上品な会話で使われることが多いでしょう。

例 That was absolutely splendid, thank you for a wonderful evening.（本当に素晴らしかったです。すてきな夜でした，ありがとう）

👍 **spectacular** 「目を見張るような」 ▷greatより程度が上です。

例 The dinner was unbelievably spectacular.

（ディナーは間違いなく素晴らしかった）

😊 **top** 「最高の」 ▷最近の言葉です。順位が最高ということから，その分野で超一流ということを意味します。

例 Your car is top.（君の車，最高だね）

👍 **terrific** 「すごい」 ▷greatの意で一般的に使います。「とても感心した」という意味です。

例 Terrific, I'm glad we can agree on that.

（すごい，意見が合ってうれしいよ）

👍 **triff** 「すごい」 ▷terrificを縮めた語。

例 Triff mate, just triff.（すごいねえ，とにかくすごいよ） ▷これは二人の人が同意している場面です。

👍 **fabulous** 「素晴らしい」 ▷greatの意で一般的な語。中流階級や上品な人たちがよく使います。

例 Absolutely fabulous, simply smashing!

（本当に素晴らしいよ，すごいの一言だ）

👍 **fab** 「素晴らしい」「すごい」 ▷fabulousを縮めた語。

例 The ride was fab.（あの乗り物は最高だったよ）

😊 **fan-dabi-dozi** 「サイコーだ」 ▷イギリスで80年代にテレビで人気があったthe Krankies（スコットランドのコメディ・デュオ）がはやらせた言葉です。標準的な言葉ではないので，友達同士なら使えますが，上品な会話では使えません。

👍 **brilliant** 「素晴らしい」 ▷greatの意味で一般的な語です。

例 She was so brilliant, I couldn't believe it.

（彼女はすごくすてきで信じられないくらいだった）

👍 **brill** 「すごい」 ▷brilliantを縮めた言い方です。

例 Brill mate!（よくやったね！）

👍 **cool** 「すごい」「かっこいい」 ▷アメリカ英語ですが，イギリスに上陸してそのまま使われるようになっています。greatの意味で標準的な語になりつつあります。

👍 **ace** 「素晴らしい」 ▷トランプでエースは優れているために，素晴らしいという意味になりました。

例 That was totally ace.（あれはピカイチだったよ）

👍 **unbelievable** 「すごい」「素晴らしい」 ▷「信じられない」という意味ですが，この場合「信じられないくらいよい」という意味です。

例 That is just simply un-fucking-believable.（あれは超すげぇよ）
　　　▷fuckingはこのように他の語の途中に入れて意味を強調することがあります。

👍 **smashing** 「素晴らしい，決まってる」 ▷これはsmash（粉々にする）の派生語ですが，greatの意味で使われるようになりました。

**カルチャー
トーク**

　イギリス人は皮肉な（sarcastic）ことで有名です。英語のネイティブでない人にとって皮肉（sarcasm）はユーモアの中で最もわかりにくい表現の一つでしょう。皮肉は言葉づらで理解するものではないからです。面白くするための気の利いた言い回しがあるわけではなく，それを言うときの声の調子が重要です。

　たとえば，あなたがすごく出来の悪い映画を見てその映画がひどいということがだれの目にも歴然としているとき，皮肉な答えではこうなります。

　　A）Did you like the film?（あの映画，よかった？）

　　B）It was fucking mint.（全く最高だったよ）

　これをまったく気持ちを込めないで退屈そうな調子で言えば，だれにでも皮肉だということがわかります。

　ただし，皮肉が嫌いな人もたくさんいて，次のようなフレーズを耳にすることもあります。

　　Sarcasm is the lowest form of wit.

　　（皮肉はウィットの最低の表現だ）

　それに対して皮肉な人はこう答えるでしょう，

　　But the funniest.（でも一番笑える）

と。

第 **2** 章

ことば・表現

スピード

Speed

　英語を勉強している皆さんは反対語をたくさん覚えるでしょう。big（大きい）と small（小さい），little（小さい）と large（大きい），straight（まっすぐな）と round（丸い），そしてもちろん fast（速い）と slow（遅い）も。

　ここで取り上げたいのは，スピードが速いというときに fast を使うことはあまりないということです。英語には fast を使わずに速さを表す表現がたくさんあります。

速さを表す表現のいろいろ

🖓 **rapid**　「速い」「急な」　▷一般的言い方。

　　例 My Internet connection is rapid.（インターネットの接続が速い）

🖓 **quick**　「速い」「迅速な」　▷一般的言い方。

　　例 You made the breakfast quick.（あっという間に朝ごはんができたね）

🖓 **quick-footed**　「足が速い」　▷もともとは走るのが速い人を意味しましたが，頭の回転が早い人の意味でも使われます。

　　例 You got here fast; you must be very quick-footed.（着くのが早かったね。すごく足が速いんだね）

🖓 **like a bat out of hell**　「すばやく」「猛スピードで」　▷直訳は「地獄から飛び出してきたコウモリのように」です。Bat out of Hell はポップス史に残る有名な曲のタイトル（アメリカのロック歌手ミートローフの曲，邦題「地獄のロック・ライダー」）でもあり，おそらく英語で最も有名なイディオムの一つですが，歌が先かイディオムが先か

はよくわかりません。

例 I ended up in a club full of gangsters; I was out of there like a bat out of hell.（やくざだらけのクラブに入ってしまうはめになって，脱兎のごとく飛び出した）

👍 **light-footed** 「身軽で足が速い」

例 You surprised me, you are very light-footed.

（びっくりしたなあ，何て足が速いんだ）

👍 **Speedy Gonzales** 「スピーディー・ゴンザレス」　▷アメリカの有名なアニメ Looney Tunes（日本では「バッグス・バニー・ショー」などの番組名で放送された）のキャラクターで，メキシコ一足が速いネズミの名前です。1980年代にとても人気がありましたが，今は下火になっています。25〜30歳くらいの人は足の速い人をいうのによく使います。

例 All right, Speedy Gonzales, slow down.

（大丈夫だよ，スピーディー・ゴンザレス，落ち着いて）

👍 **lightning fast** 「すばやい」「電光石火の」　▷lightning は「稲妻」の意味。

例 That game installed lightening fast.

（そのゲームはあっという間にインストールできた）

👍 **faster than a speeding bullet** 「弾よりも速く」　▷ご存じ「スーパーマン」のキャッチフレーズ。

例 He drives faster than a speeding bullet.（彼は猛スピードで運転する）

👍 **faster than a speeding train** 「列車より速く」

例 She runs faster than a speeding train.（彼女はものすごく足が速い）

👍 **(be) bombing it** 「猛スピードで突っ走る」　▷この表現は必ず be bombing it という形で使われます。爆発的なスピードがあること。

例 Here comes my brother, he's bombing it down the road.

（ほら弟が来た，すごい勢いで走ってくるよ）

👍 **(be) tearing it up** 「猛烈な勢いで進む」　▷あまりにも速いので道路を切り裂く（tear it up）くらいだということ。この表現も be tearing it up の形で使われます。

　　例 My cousin is tearing it up in his car.

　　　（いとこがすごいスピードで運転している）

👍 **screaming**　「すごい速さで」　▷コーナーを回るとき車のタイヤがキィーッと音をたてる様子から。

　　例 I came screaming round the bend.（いらいらしてすごい速さでやってきた）　▷round the bend：頭にきて，気が変になって，逆上して。

👍 **hell for leather**　「猛スピードで」「全速力で」　▷「とても速い」というときの古めかしいイディオム。

　　例 They were having sex and he was going hell for leather.

　　　（セックスをしていたとき彼はすごく急いでいた）

👍 **ripping**　「（引き裂くような）すごい速さで」　▷これも必ず ripping という形で使われる表現。速すぎて何か裂いてしまう（rip）という意味です。

　　例 When my friend Darren entered the cheese rolling competition he came ripping down the hill.（友人のダレンがチーズ転がし競走に参加して，丘からすごい速さで転がり落ちた）　▷cheese rolling competition は英国グロスターシャー州ブロックワースのクーパーズ丘で毎年 5 月に行われる伝統的なお祭り。

👍 **slow down to a gallop**　「ギャロップまでスピードを落とす，遅くする」　▷何かをやるのが速すぎるという意味でユーモラスに用いられるイディオムです。ギャロップは馬の一番速い走り方です。それよりも速いというのは可能な範囲を超えているのでスピードを落とした方がいいということになります。

　　例 Slow down to a gallop and tell me all from the beginning.

　　　（少し落ち着いて始めから話して）

👍 **like hellfire**　「とても速く」　▷hellfire はキリスト教からきた表現で，罪を犯した者が罰として焼かれる「地獄の業火」のことです。地獄の苦しみはすぐにあなたのもとへやってくるということですが，今では宗教的意味が失われ，単にとても速いという意味で使います。

例 They were running like hellfire. （ものすごく速く走っていた）

👍 **like a rocket** 「ロケットのように」

例 He types as fast as a rocket. （彼はものすごく速くキーボードを打つ）

▷この文ではas fast as a rocket（ロケットくらい速く）という表現に変わっていますが，意味は同様です。また，この例文は英語として意味をなしていません。この文を文字通りの意味にとるとロケットに手があってキーボードを打てることになってしまいます。この場合のロケットは単にスピードが速いことを表す比喩的表現なのです。ネイティブ・スピーカーのようになるためには，文法的に完璧になる必要がないというよい例です。

👍 **whiz(z) by** 「ヒューッと鳴る」「シュッと飛ぶ」　▷「ヒューッ，ブーン」とうなりをたてて空中を速く飛ぶ音からきています。

例 A wasp just came whizzing by my head.

（蜂がブーンとすごい速さで頭のあたりに飛んできた）

👍 **supersonic** 「超音速の」「すごく速い」

👍 **quick-witted** 「頭の回転が速い」「機転のきく」

「遅い」と言いたいときの表現

　「速い」に比べて「遅い」ことを表す英語の表現はそれほど多くありません。速さに比べたら遅いというのは並外れたことではないからでしょう。これらの言葉が生まれた当時のイギリスの生活は本当にのんびりしたものでした。車も電車も機械的なものは何もなかったのです。こういうものが生活の中に入り込んできたために，速さを説明するのにさまざまなものを使った描写が必要になりました。

　さて，現代ではコンピューターがますます使われるようになっています。それにつれて遅さを表す言葉もさらに生まれてくるでしょう。なぜなら遅いコンピューターというのは問題であり，問題は必ず話題にのぼるものだからです。

👍（be）**ambling along**　「ゆっくりと進行する」　▷もともとは「ゆっくり歩く」という意味から。

　　例 A）How is your manuscript coming along?（原稿は進んでる？）

　　　B）It's ambling along.（なかなかはかどらないよ）

　　　▷これも文法がいつも正しく使われているわけではないことを表すよい例です。amble は「のんびり歩く」という意味ですが，原稿は歩くことができません。けれどもこの文はそう言っているのです。

👍（be）**bobbing along**　「うろうろして遅くなる」　▷bob は「上下に動く，揺れる」ということ。あてもなく水の上を漂っているということから。

　　例 A）How is your business going?（仕事はどう？）

　　　B）Oh, it's bobbing along.（手間取ってるよ）

👍（be）**chugging along**　「バタバタ（シュッシュッポッポッ）と音を立てながらのろのろ進む」　▷古くて遅い蒸気機関車から。

　　例 This computer is so slow it's just chugging along.

　　（このコンピューターはすごく遅くてのろのろだよ）

👍（be）**plodding along**　「ゆっくり進む」「とぼとぼ歩く」　▷ゆっくり歩くという意味から。

カルチャートーク

　イギリス文化は他の先進国と同様にかなりスピード優先なのですが，私が埼玉，千葉，東京で働いていた経験から言って，日本の都会生活ほどスピードが速いものはないと思います。私たちは自分のしていることをよく考える暇もなく，あまりにもせわしなく生活しているのではないでしょうか。おそらく反省したときには手遅れなのかもしれません。有名なイギリスの物語「ウサギとカメ」the Tortoise and the Hareは，私たちが犯しそうな過ちを見事に指摘しています。

　カメとウサギが競走して，最初のうちはウサギが全力疾走し，カメはただゆっくり歩いていました。ところがウサギはすぐ飽きてしまい，間違いなく勝てると油断して寝転がって休んだら寝入ってしまい，何時間も寝てしまいました。するとゆっくりだけれども真面目なカメが先にゴールしてしまい，ウサギががっかりしたという話です。

　この寓話はイギリス文化の中でいろいろなときに取り上げられますが，特に有名なのは1980年代にやっていたキャドバリー社のチョコレートキャラメルのCMで，セクシーなウサギのキャラクターが30秒ほどこのお話を聞かせるというものでした。

「はい，チーズ！」：写真を撮る

Taking a Picture

　日本で写真を撮ってもらおうとするといつも「チーズ」と言うように言われるのですが，これを聞くたびに私はいたたまれなくなります。「チーズ」なんて私の祖母くらいしか言いません。イギリス人は写真を撮るとき「チーズ」と言いあっていると日本の人は思っているようですが，それは昔の話で，私の祖母の時代のことです。

　イギリスでも写真を撮るときには，にっこりさせるために必ず何か一言言いますが，その言葉は状況によって変わります。

お年寄りに言う場合の表現

　お年寄りの写真を撮ってあげたり，お年寄りに写真を撮ってもらうときは，一般に，

👍 **Cheese.**

と言います。

見ず知らずの人，またはそれほど親しくない人に言う場合

　見知らぬ人に写真を撮るように頼まれた場合，次のような言い方があります。

👍 **Ready ... 1, 2, 3.** 「いきますよ……１，２，３」
👍 **Smile.** 「笑ってください」

親しい友人や恋人の場合

　親しい友人や恋人の場合，セックスに関する品の悪いことやおもしろいことを言います。その例はあまりにもありすぎて決まり文句としては挙げられないのですが，たいていはその日にあったことを冗談にしたり，セックスに関するジョークを言ったりするとだれでも笑顔になります。子供や知らない人が一緒にいる場合には，そのとき自分たちがいる所の地名を言ったり，そのとき自分たちがやっていることを言ったりします。

　その場で思いつくままに言えばいいのですが，たとえばこんな感じです。

　　例 Everyone, ready ... Manchester! 「皆さん，いきますよ……マンチェスター！」

　　Look this way ... bollocks! 「こっち見て……キンタマ！」

　　Everyone smile ... big tits! 「みんな笑って……デカパイ！」

四 文 字 言 葉 — fuckという語

The F word: Fuck

　私が日本で英語教師をしていたとき，日本のみなさんはよく辞書で調べたすごく難しくて見栄えがする言葉や，抽象的でほかの生徒に説明するのが難しい言葉，また時にはあまりにも漠然としていてネイティブの私でさえ意味がよくわからない言葉を使って，なんとか私を感心させようとしていました。けれども複雑な言葉を使わずに，簡単な言葉を正しい語順で言う方が英語はうまく聞こえます。ネイティブをうならせるにはこの方がずっと効果があるのです。

　英語の中で一番難しい言葉は何かと考えてみたことがあります。私だけでなく同僚の英語教師も同じ意見でしたが，英語の中で最も難しい言葉はtheとfuckの二つだという結論に達しました。fuckという語に捧げた歌を歌った有名なコメディアンがいます。その歌詞はインターネットで広まっています。ここでは彼が使った説明を分類して挙げてみましょう。けれども，文法的な分類もしているので，多少わかりにくい部分があるかもしれません。この語をマスターする一番いい方法は，文法ではなく，それを使っているまわりの人たちから学ぶことなのですが，とりあえず手始めとしてはよいでしょう。

　なお，the F wordという言い方があります。これはfuckを表す婉曲な言い方で，やむをえずfuckという語に言及する場合に，fuckの代わりに使います。

fuckをセックスに関して使う場合

❖他動詞として

例 David fucked Sue.（デイビッドはスーとセックスした）

❖自動詞として

例 Sue fucks.（スーはセックスが好きだ）

Noriko is fucking beautifully.（のりこはセックスがとてもうまい）

▷このbeautifullyは「うまく」という意味です。

She fucks like a goddess.（彼女はセックスがうまい）

fuckを強調語として使う場合

例 Who the fuck were you talking to?

（お前は一体だれと話していたんだ）

What the fuck do you want?（一体どうしたいんだ？）

I don't give a fuck.（私は全然かまわない）　▷not give a fuckは「まったくかまわない，どうでもいい」という意味です。

fuckingを強調語として使う場合

❖形容詞として

例 Takeshi is doing all the fucking work.

（たけしはこのものすごい仕事を全部やっている）

How many fucking times do I have to tell you?

（一体何回言ったらわかるの？）

You fucking idiot!（馬鹿野郎！）

❖副詞として

例 Noriko is fucking gorgeous.（のりこはものすごく魅力的だ）

He's fucking disgusting.（彼はまったくひどい奴だ）

Steven eats too fucking much.（スティーブンはやたら食べ過ぎる）

I don't understand what you fucking mean?（あなたが一体どういうつもりなのかわからない）　▷もっとわかりやすく言ってもらいたいということです。

I just don't fucking like it.（まったく気に入らないね）　▷強い不満を表します。

❖単語の中に挿入して

　fuck という語はほかの単語の中に挿入することができます。その語に注目してもらいたいということや，特に思い入れが強いということを表します。ただし挿入する単語は 2 音節以上でなければなりません。

例 un-fucking-believable（ほんとに信じられない）

　　woopy-fucking-doo（やった，すごいぞ）

　　vio-fucking-lin（ヴァイオリン）

fuck のその他の使い方

例 I got fucked at the shop.（その店でぼったくられた）

　Oh, for fuck's sake!（冗談じゃないぜ！）　▷うまくいかなかったときに落胆や狼狽を表して使います。

　I am so fucked now.（お手上げだ）

　It was fucked up.（まったくめちゃくちゃだった）

　You don't want to fuck with me, mate.（俺を怒らせないようにしろよ）

　What a fuck up!（大失敗だ！）

　Why don't you just fuck off somewhere else?

　（どこかへ行ってくれないか？）

　Just fuck off, you tit.（あっちへ行け，馬鹿野郎）

　Fuck off!（うせろ，くたばれ）

　アメリカには相手に中指を立てて侮辱や攻撃を示すジェスチャーが
あります。これはイギリスでも使われますが，イギリスにはそのほか
にも指を使ったジェスチャーでより攻撃的なものがあります。手の甲
を相手に向けて二本の指を顔の前で立てて見せるしぐさです。これは
一本指よりずっと攻撃的であり，Fuck off.（うせろ）という意味に
なります。このサインの由来はフランスとイギリスの間の有名な戦争
にあります。イギリスの弓の射手はヨーロッパ中で恐れられていまし
た。彼らは非常に熟練していて無敵だったため，イギリスが帝国を築
くことができたのも彼らのおかげだと言われています。高貴な騎士で
はなく下層民である射手によって多くの戦いに勝利したのです。そこ
で敵は射手を捕らえると，彼の右手の人差し指と中指を切り落として
イギリスの陣地に送り返しました。二本の指を切り落とされた射手た
ちは役に立たないばかりか，彼らを養うために国はお金を払わなけれ
ばならなかったのです。

　私のアメリカ人の友人はこれを知らず，まったくこのジェスチャー
を気にしていませんでした。私は日本人が数を数えるたびに私に二本
指を立ててみせるので，その都度，少しカチンときていましたが，あ
るときそれに気づいた人にどうかしたのかと聞かれました。そこで私
は日本人が 2 以上の数を数えるたびに「あっちへ行け」と言われて
いるような気がすると説明したことがあります。みなさんがイギリス
へ行ったら，写真のために「ピース」とポーズをとるときや，数を数
えるとき，知らないうちにだれかを侮辱しているかもしれないので気
をつけてください。

上品ぶった言い方

Sounding Posh

　英国紳士のシルクハットとステッキや，霧のロンドン市街，ワイングラスをチンと合わせる音。これがイギリスの上流階級のイメージでしょう。これはもう過去のものになってしまいましたが，言葉にはいまだに決まり文句として残っていて，自然と上流階級を思い浮かべる表現があります。このようなボキャブラリーを使うと，育ちがよく教養もある上流階級の人という印象を与えます。

　このようなボキャブラリーは上流階級をステレオタイプ化しているものでもあります。マスコミは上流階級の人々をこのような決まり文句で固定観念化しているわけです。しかし，現実にそういう人たちがいないわけではありません。実際，私はこれらの言葉すべてを上流や中流階級の人たちが使うのを聞いたことがあります。ただ，それはコメディアンが特権階級の人をまねるときに使う言葉でもあります。もしあなたがイギリスの上流階級出身でなかったら（本書を読んでいるということはそうではないということでしょうが），場違いで馬鹿げて聞こえてしまうので，あまり会話で使わない方が無難です。もし友達に冗談で上流階級の人のまねをして言うのだったら，笑わせるような口調で言った方がいいでしょう。もしあなたが特権階級の出身だとしても，これらの言い方を使いすぎるのはやはりおすすめできません。私は丁寧な話し方は大切だと思いますが，これらの言葉はあまりにも含みが多すぎる言葉なのです。

上品さを表す表現のいろいろ

● **golly gosh** 「おや，まあ」 ▷驚きやショックを表す言い方。golly も gosh も god の婉曲語。

  例 A) I have bought a new car.（新しい車を買ったよ）
    B) Golly gosh, that's fantastic.（へえ，すごいね！）

● **jolly good** 「よろしい」 ▷同意を表して使います。

  例 A) I have started university.（大学に入学したよ）
    B) Jolly good.（それはよかった）

● **jolly good show** 「でかした」「よくやった」 ▷たとえばだれかが泥棒を捕まえるところを見たとしたら，上流階級の人ならこう言うだろうと思われている言い方です。

● **what-o** 「やあ」「おやおや」 ▷これは声の調子によっていろいろな意味で使われます。ショックや驚きを示したり，何かに注意を向けたり，挨拶として使われることもあります。実際に使われることもありますし，上流階級を表す決まり文句として使われることもあります。

  例 What-o, old chap!（やあ，こんにちは）

● **charmed** 「（お会いできて）うれしい」 ▷正式な挨拶や人に紹介されたときに言う言葉です。

  例 Charmed.（お会いできてうれしいです） ▷女性が使います。
    Charmed I'm sure.（お会いできてうれしいのは間違いないですね）
    ▷I'm sure をつけると嫌みなニュアンスが含まれます。

● **one** 「私」 ▷自分のことを言うときに，I の代わりに使われます。

  例 Does one really have to go and see the opera, it's such a bore.
    （本当にあのオペラを見に行かなければいけないだろうか，あんなに退屈なものなのに）

● **I say** 「ねえ」「おい」「あのね」 ▷ショッキングなことや論議を呼ぶようなことを話すときに使います。また，命令，依頼，宣言をするときなどにも使われます。

  例 I say, what do you think of that woman there, she is rather spiffing don't you think?

（ちょっと，あそこの女の人をどう思う？　すごくいいと思わないか？）

● **spiffing**　「すごくいい！」「そうしよう！」　▷同意を表したり，何かがとてもよいことを表すときに使います。

　　例 Oh, I say your new car is spiffing.

　　（わあ，君の新しい車はすごくいいね）

● **chaps**　「君たち」　▷上流階級の男性がほかの男性たちに呼びかけるときに使う言い方です。

　　例 Ok, chaps, shall we go?（それじゃ君たち，出かけようか？）

● **old chap**　「君」　▷上流階級の男性が親しい友人に呼びかけるときに使います。

　　例 I say, old chap, you are looking a little dogged.（やあ，君は少し具合が悪そうに見えるよ）　▷この dogged は unhealthy（不健康な）という意味。

● **rather**　「確かに」「もちろん」「とても」　▷驚きや同意を表す感嘆語として使ったり，very の意味で使ったりします。

　　例 I say, you look rather dashing tonight.

　　（おや，今夜はすごくかっこよく見えるよ）

● **Tally ho!**　「さあ，行こう」　▷Let's go. と同じ意味です。

● **champers**　「シャンパン」　▷上流階級が使うくだけた言い方。

　　例 Oh, the champers in this restaurant is terrible.

　　（ああ，このレストランのシャンパンはひどいな）

● **Good day.**　「こんにちは」「さようなら」　▷形式ばった挨拶です。

　　例 Good day, sir.（さようなら，失礼します）

● **darling**　「あなた」「君」　▷上流階級の女性がほかの女性に対して，または上流階級の男性が妻に対して呼びかける言い方。

　　例 I say, darling.（ねえ，ちょっと）

● **awfully**　「とても」　▷very の代わりに使われます。

　　例 This film is awfully boring.（この映画はひどく退屈だ）

● **How frightful!**　「何てひどいんだ！」　▷いやな気持ちや不快感を表すときに使います。

例 A）I had my car stolen the other day.（この間，車を盗まれたんだ）
　　B）How frightful!（何てひどい！）

● **marvellous**　「素晴らしい」

例 This caviar is bloody marvellous.
（このキャビアはまったく素晴らしい）

● **dashing**　「よい」「元気がよい」「粋な」

カルチャートーク

　上流階級の典型的なイメージはもはやシルクハットと燕尾服のロンドンの紳士ではありません。いまやRange Rover（レンジローバー）を運転し，ヨットを持っていてフェンシングとアーチェリーをたしなみ，競馬を見るのが好きで郊外に住んでいるハンサムな男性や女性というイメージです。彼らは高価な酒を飲みラグビーをやり，ジーンズやスーツジャケットやポロシャツなどを着ます。また，上流階級の娘といえば車やポニーを買ってもらっては

　Daddy bought me a new car.
　（パパが新しい車を買ってくれたの）

というような若い女の子のイメージが頭に浮かぶのですが，彼女たちは実際に存在しています。彼女たちはdaddy's girlと呼ばれています。社会的地位がとても高い家に生まれた彼女たちは，男性はもちろんのこと，女性も憧れるような高嶺の花です。

　ところで，mummy's boyという言い方がありますが，これは全く違う意味で，階級とは無関係です。mummy's boyは，母親のそばから離れず，全然男性的でない人を指します。

古英語
Old English

　神秘と冒険と魔法の国，騎士が乙女の名誉をかけて戦い，紳士が葉巻をくゆらせブランデーを片手に当時の最新の哲学を語り合った所，古きイングランド。現代ではかろうじてその痕跡をとどめているだけですが，時々会話のなかに昔の名残が感じられることがあります。それはたいてい次のような言葉遣いをしたときです。このような表現は，お笑いの中とか会話でわざと時代を感じさせたいときしか使わないのですが，皆さんが想像する以上によく使われているのです。

　昔使われていたのは Old English（古英語），または Middle English（中英語）と言われるものですが，今の英語とは全く別の言語といっていいほど違うもので，研究しようとしたら一生かかってしまいます。これから挙げるのは本当の Old English とは違うものも多いのですが，私たちが時代がかった言い方だと思っているものです。

古英語の表現

● **ye**〔jíː〕「汝は」　▷you の古語，あるいは the の古語として使われます。これは Old English の中で使うとしたら一番手っとり早い単語です。

　例 Ye have no faith in me!（おぬし，私を全然信じておらんな！）

● **ye old**「由緒ある」　▷店などが昔からあって歴史があると感じさせたいときに使います。これは古い町の何百年もあるパン屋やパイの店などの看板によく使われています。

　例 Ye Old Pie Shop

Ye Old Bakery

Ye Old Barber Shop

● **fair maiden** 「うるわしの乙女」 ▷騎士は竜から乙女を救い出すというイメージがあり，この乙女たちは処女で美しいと相場が決まっていました。今では男たちがふざけて自分の恋人や妻や友達を fair maiden と言ったりします。これには二重の意味合いがあって，その女性が純粋で美しいというだけでなく，言っている本人も騎士道精神がある勇敢な男だというわけです。

例 Come, fair maiden, let's go to the ball.

（お嬢様，舞踏会に行きましょう）

● **varmint** 「悪党」「やくざ者」 ▷友達同士などの間で使われることが多く，けんかを売っているようなニュアンスがありますが，コミカルで昔風の響きがあるため，言われた方も笑ってしまうでしょう。

例 You damn varmint, you have stolen all of the pizza!

（何て悪党なんだ，ピザを全部取ったな！）

● **scoundrel** 「悪党」「ろくでなし」 ▷varmint と同じような響きがあります。

例 You filthy scoundrel, you have used my DVDs again!

（この汚らわしい悪党，俺のDVDをまた使ったな！）

● **You, sir, ...** ▷文のはじめの呼びかけです。けんかを売っているようなイメージですが，今では笑わせようとして使うこともあります。これで始めたら，この後にはたいてい非難する言葉が続きます。

例 You, sir, have insulted me.（こら，侮辱したな）

● **Damn you sir** 「こら」「おい」 ▷だれかが何か悪いことをしたときや紳士的ではない振る舞いをしたときに使います。これもコミカル

Ye Olde（＝Old）Vic
（Vic は Victoria を縮めたもの。ヴィクトリア女王治世当時に創業したパブの看板）

でフレンドリーなニュアンスがあります。

例 Damn you sir, you have done a foul deed.

（おいこら，ずるをしただろう）

古語を使ったイディオム

　これらのイディオムはイギリスでは日常会話で使っているものですが，日本ではあまり知られていないと思います。私が教えるまで日本人が使っているのを聞いたこともありません。

●**full tilt** 「**全速力**」「**全力**」　▷tiltは騎士が馬上槍試合を行うとき，二人の間にある仕切りのことです。馬上槍試合はtiltingと言われることもあります。go full tiltは「全速力で走る，全力でやる」という意味になります。

例 I was late for work so I had to drive at full tilt.（仕事に遅れてしまったので，フルスピードで運転しなければならなかった）

●**to the hilt** 「**徹底的に**」　▷hiltは剣の柄のことです。「柄まで」ということは，剣を相手の体にできるだけ深く刺すということで，そこから「できる限り，徹底的に」という意味になります。また，この表現は性的な意味でも使われます。ペニスを剣になぞらえ，女性の体の中にできるだけ深く入れるという意味になります。

例 I havc bccn shopping and we are now stocked up to the hilt.

（買い物したからもう買い置きがいっぱいだよ）

●**hung from the yardarm** 「**のっぴきならない**」　▷昔のイングランドの海軍に由来するイディオムです。当時の船は帆船で，マストにはyardarm（帆げた）が横に渡されていて，これで帆を支えていました。船乗りが処刑されるとき，彼らは帆げたに吊るされたといいます。そこからこのイディオムは「事態は深刻である」という意味になります。

例 If Mother catches you eating all the ice cream, you will be hung from the yardarm.（お前がアイスクリームを全部食べてるとこお母さんに見つかったら，大変なことになるぞ）

●**keel haul** 「ひどい目に遭わせる」　▷これも海軍からきているイディオムです。keel（竜骨）は，船全体の底の中心を船首から船尾まで貫いている船の背骨に当たる主要な部分です。haul は「引っ張る」という意味です。keel hauling は，だれかの手足を二本のとても長いロープにくくりつけて船の脇に吊るし，反対側の甲板から引っ張り上げるという刑罰です。犠牲者は船底の下をくぐって反対側の甲板に引っ張り上げられるわけですが，船底はカミソリの刃のように鋭いフジツボに覆われており，それが肉を切り裂き，また竜骨を越えるときに背骨が折れることもあります。そこからこの表現は「ひどい目に遭わせる」という意味で使われるようになりました。

例 If we don't meet our monthly targets, we will be keel hauled.（もし月間目標に届かなかったら，大変なことになるな）

カルチャートーク

　日本にいたとき電車の中でよく見た光景です。仕事帰りのビジネスマンが別れのあいさつをするとき，よくふざけて敬礼をすることがありますよね。これを見るたび私は，もし彼らが敬礼の起源を知ったらきっと驚くだろうと思って思わずにやりとしたものでした。
　起源は中世と言われています。騎士はこれから戦うというときに兜の面頬を開けてお互いの顔を見せ合いました。これは戦う相手に自分の顔を見せるのが騎士道精神にかなっているとされたためでした。これが敬礼の起源です。現代の敬礼は軍隊によって異なり，それぞれ形や敬礼をする速さまで細かく決められています。
　敬礼のほかに欧米的なあいさつに握手がありますが，その起源は暗いものでした。握手はふつう利き手，つまり多くは右手で行いますが，これは剣を抜く手でもあります。剣を抜く方の手を握っている限り攻撃できないので安心できる，つまりあなたを殺すつもりはないというメッセージだったと言われています。

英語の方言と地域や国の ステレオタイプ

Regional Expressions

　イギリスは一つの国であり，そこに暮らしているのはみな同じイギリス人だと思っている日本人が多いかもしれませんが，実際のイギリスは，ほとんど別々の国といっていいほど異なる歴史を持つ四つの地域（イングランド，ウェールズ，スコットランド，北アイルランド）の連合王国なのです。そのうえ多くの移民労働者も加わって，イギリス諸島にはものすごくいろいろな人々が住んでいます。

　本節ではそれぞれの文化が他の文化の人々からどのようにステレオタイプとして考えられているか，そして各地域の出身者がいかにも言いそうだと思われている言葉を挙げていきます。

　ここに挙げた言葉は地域や人種をネタにした冗談を言うときに使われるような言葉です。これを読めばその手のジョークを耳にしたとき理解できるようになるでしょう。このような言葉は，たいていは笑って聞き流されると思いますが，人種差別につながるような表現もあるので，絶対に自分では言わないようにしてください。みなさんが使うことはないだろうという前提でアイコンはあえてつけてありません。相手や状況によってはたいへん侮蔑的になりますから，原則として使うのは避けた方が無難です。

イギリスの各地方の典型的な表現

　ここに挙げたボキャブラリーは，いろいろな地域の人々がどんなことを典型的に言うと思われているかというイメージであり，実際にそう言うわけではありません。ここに挙げたような言い方はステレオタイプを

示しているだけです（なかには本当に言うものもあります）。［　］の中の言葉は発音しやすい方法を示しています。これらの言葉は文法的に正しい文章になっているわけではなく，ただそれぞれの方言を表現しただけのものです。

❖ウェールズ人

　ウェールズ人は田舎者と見られており，『指輪物語』（*The Lord of the Rings*）に出てくるホビット（Hobbit）はウェールズ人がモデルだと言われています。ウェールズ人をからかうときよく持ち出される典型的なイメージは羊とセックスしている寂しい農民です。

● **ehhhhhh boio**［aaa-boy-o］　▷典型的なウェールズ人の挨拶だと思われています。

● **yaki-dar**　▷この地域のものと考えられている典型的な言葉。

❖イングランド人

　古典的なイングランド人の男は帽子とステッキを持った紳士です。

● **what-o**　▷この地域に典型的と思われている言葉。上のehhhhhh boio，yaki-darと同じく，特に意味はありません。これらは，たとえば名古屋の方言をからかって「おみゃー」「えびふりゃー」と言うような言葉なので，ジョークのネタでしか聞かないようなものです。

● **jolly good**　▷イングランド人が同意するときに言うだろうと思われている言葉。

● **tally-ho**　▷「さあ行こう」と言うときのステレオタイプな言い方。

❖ロンドンっ子

　ステレオタイプは，平たい布の帽子をかぶり，茶色の古スーツを着て，帽子をやたらに触ってはうなずく人です。

● **All right governor**［gov-na］．　▷ステレオタイプの挨拶。

❖バーミンガムの人

　イングランドのバーミンガム出身の人はBrummyと呼ばれています。ものすごくゆっくりしゃべるというイメージです。

●**All right.**　▷ものすごくゆっくり発音する。

❖リバプールの人

　リバプール出身の人はScouserと呼ばれています。ありがちなイメージは始終泥棒する人。

●**Eh-eh calm down.**　▷直訳すると「えっ，えっ，落ち着いて」。これはHarry Enfield（ハリー・エンフィールド）というテレビのコメディー番組で有名になり，今ではリバプールと言えばこの言葉が連想されます。

❖マンチェスターの人

　マンチェスターの出身者はMancと呼ばれます。イメージはサッカーファンかインディーズ音楽の愛好者。

●**All right, our kid.**　「わかったよ」　▷our kidは自分の兄弟姉妹を指すイングランド北西部に特有の言い方です。

❖スコットランド人

　Scottishと呼ばれています。赤毛でキルトを着ていて，大柄で力が強いイメージです。

●**Hock-I-da-new**　▷この地域特有の言葉。

●**aye**　▷eyeと同じ発音です。スコットランド人が同意するときに，よくこう言います。

❖アイルランド人

　アイルランド人（Irish）は小柄で黒い髪で，緑色の服を着ているイメージです。けんかっぱやくて，とても酒好きだと思われています。

●**Ohhh be Jesus.**　[O-Be-ji-su-sue]　▷アイルランド人がびっくりしたときに言う言葉として考えられています。

外国人に関する表現

　ごく親しい友人や仲間内でなら以下に取り上げるような言い方が普通に使われることもあります。しかし日本人がこのような言葉を使ってし

まうと，まず不自然だし，誰かを不快にさせてしまう可能性が大いにあ
ります。ですから，いかなる場合でも絶対に使わない方が賢明です。も
し，だれかが悪気なくこういうことを言う場面に遭遇したら，ほほえむ
ぐらいにとどめておいてください。

❖パキスタン人

　イギリスにいるパキスタン人は，交差点に店を持っているとよく言わ
れます。これはPaki shops（失礼な言い方です）とかcorner shops（使
って大丈夫です）と言われています。

●**bud bud ding ding**　▷インド系の言葉がそう響くことからきてい
　ます。

●**var-ding ding**　▷上に同じです。

❖中国人

　中国人はフィッシュアンドチップスの店を経営しているイメージです。

●**ha-saw**　▷これは中国語がそう聞こえると思われているためです。

●**Sore finger?**　▷白人のイギリス人が中国人と話をするのはフィッ
　シュアンドチップス店が多いのですが，そこで

　　　Salt and vinegar?（塩と酢はかけますか？）

　と聞かれるときになまりが強くて，

　　　Sore finger?（指が痛い？）

　と聞こえることからきています。

❖日本人

　日本人のステレオタイプのイメージと言えば，ビジネスマンで，たく
さん写真を撮り，女性は着物を着てすり足で歩くと思われています。

●**ha-saw**　▷中国語と同じですが，日本語を表す場合はより低い声で
　言います。日本人のまねをするときは早口でのどに引っかかったよう
　な声で訳のわからないことを話します。

❖東南アジア系の人

　タイ人，ベトナム人など東南アジア系の人のありがちなイメージは，

性転換した人か，娼婦か，金持ちの男と結婚してイギリスに来たという
ものです。

● **Ping pong!**　　▷タイ語をまねたもの。

● **Me love you long time, 5 dollar.**　　▷直訳は「イッパイアイシテア
ゲルヨ，5 ドルデアソバナイ？」。戦争映画『フルメタル・ジャケット』
(*Full Metal Jacket*) からきた，よく知られている言い方です。

**カルチャー
トーク**

　イングランド人として率直に言うのですが，私たちは周りのすべて
の地域の人々に，おそらくは正当な理由で嫌われています。イングラ
ンドには大変暴力的で血なまぐさい歴史があります。決して人のよさ
で世界最大の帝国になったわけではないのです。何百年もの迫害の結
果，今もイングランドは周囲の人々から嫌われています。フランス人，
ウェールズ人，スコットランド人，アイルランド人は，ほとんどの人
が程度の差はありますがイングランド嫌いであると言えます。ときに
はまったく深刻ではなく冗談のタネにされるほど他愛ない場合もあり
ます。たとえば私は反イングランドふきん，反イングランドTシャツ
を見たことがあります。

イングランド北部の
方言について

Me-Our-My

　「私の」という所有を表す正しい言い方はmyです。けれどもイングランドにはmyの代わりにourやmeを使う方言があります。

　この章でmeとourがmyの代わりにどのように使われているか説明しましょう。これらはイングランド北部では普通に使われている言い方なのですが，皆さんは使わないようにしてください。これらはQueen's Englishにかなった言い方ではなく，時には見下されます。けれども前書きでも述べたように，そもそも本書が生まれた理由はQueen's English（またはBBC English）と言われる英語を話している人はそれほど多くないという事実そのものなのです。BBC English とはかつてBBC（British Broadcasting Corporation）がQueen's Englishを話す人だけを採用していたためこう呼ばれるようになりました。

[例1] お兄ちゃんはどこ？
　正しい文法にかなった英語では
　　Where is my brother?
となるでしょうが，myの代わりにmeを入れて
　　Where's me brother?
と言うことができます。そしてbrotherをour kidに変えることもできます。meとourを同時に使うことはできないのでこうなります。
　　Where is our kid?

［例 2］ それは私の夕食です。

　　正しい文法にかなった英語は

　　　That's my dinner.

となるところですが，dinner を tea に代えて

　　　That's my tea.

と言うこともできます。そして my は me になります。

　　　That's me tea.

［例 3］ 私が住んでいる地域は危険なところです。

　　正しい文法にかなった英語は

　　　It's a dangerous place in the area where I live.

となるところですが，dangerous は a bit dodgy と言い換えることがで
きます。

　　　It's a bit dodgy in the area where I live.

　　さらに in the area は round に置き換え可能であり

　　　It's a bit dodgy round where I live.

となります。

さらに where I live すなわち neighbourhood は our end とも言えるので

It's a bit dodgy round our end.

となります。

カルチャートーク

　イングランドの北部と南部の間には現在も大きな溝があります。今までも対抗意識はありましたし，これからもおそらく続くでしょう。北部のアクセントで話すことは下層階級のすることと見られていましたし，クイーンズイングリッシュは貴族階級のものと考えられていました。ただ，この区別は少なくなってきていて，テレビの司会者も今では全国各地から出てきています。けれどもまだ亀裂があるところもあります。軍隊がそうですし，イングランド南部の上流階級，さらに中流階級はひときわ頑固で，彼らがイングランド北部の英語を毛嫌いしているのは確かです。私はこのアクセントのおかげでこれまでどれだけ苦労してきたかわかりません。

　イングランド北部の英語を使うことにより与える印象はよくないために，これを使うことはおすすめしません。それでも南部だけを旅行し，そこの人たちだけと話し，イングランド南部で作られた映画しか見ないつもりなら別ですが，イギリスの人口の50％が話すことを理解するためだけとしても，このような話し方も理解しておいてほしいと思います。

階級制度

The Class System

　イギリスには三つの世界が存在します。まるで魔法の世界のように，同じ場所に同時に存在している 3 層の世界です。この三つの世界は物理的には同じ場所に存在しているのですが，交流するのは時々開く不思議な入り口を通してだけです。ここで違う世界の住人とたまには会話をすることもあります。この状況は非常に複雑なのですが，本章ではこれら三つの社会がどのように作用しながら共存しているか説明しましょう。

　子供のころ，私たちは，欲が深くて高い税金をかけては庶民の怒りをかう悪い王子と戦うロビンフッドのディズニー漫画を見て育ちました。このほかにも城に住む王や王子，莫大な富を持つ男爵や伯爵，馬に乗って悪者と戦う騎士などの昔話があります。それ以外はごく少数の金持ちの商人と，畑で一日中働いてわずかな賃金をもらうその他大勢の農民からできている世界でした。イギリスでは何が変わったのでしょうか？ほとんど変わってはいません！　私たちは貴族や王子，王女，そして忘れてならないのは女王が今も城や邸宅に住んでいる国に生きているのです。騎士（ナイト）もまだいます。でも今は戦士ではなく，チャリティー活動をたくさんする人であるとか，有名なスポーツ選手や映画スターに，女王が騎士の称号を与えます。しかし，ある調査によると，近年騎士の称号を与えられた人の90％が時の政府に100万ポンド近く寄付をした人たちだったことがわかっています（今では女王がだれに称号を与えるかを政府が決めるのです）。

　また，畑で働いて高い税金を払っていた農民たちはどうなったのでしょうか？　もちろん今でも存在します。今は畑で働くのではなく，コー

ルセンターや会社で一日中働き，やっと生活できる程度の貯金をするために生きているわけですが。高い税金はどうなったのでしょうか？　それもまだあります。所得が35000ポンド以下なら20%，それを超えると40%もの税金がかかっているのです。

　政府は階級制度の存在に言及されるとあからさまに隠そうとしたり，啓発しようとしています。当局は階級制度が過去のもので，すべての人は同じ権利を持っていると言うでしょうが，これは全くの間違いだと断言できます。階級制度は昔と同じように今も存在します。確かに投票権はだれにでもありますが，候補者は同じようなことを言い，当選すれば何も変えない人たちばかりで，選択の幅は限られています。イギリスは急速に自分の法律で自分の首を絞めつつあります。

　各階級について説明する前にまず言っておきたいのは，それぞれの階級にははっきりとした境界線があるわけではないということです。それはむしろなだらかな曲線のグラフのようになっています。社会の底辺にいるその日暮らしの人々から始まって上に向かって曲線を描き，下層階級から上層労働者階級，下層中流階級，上層中流階級へと続いていき，最後に貴族階級という非常に高い壁が立ちはだかり，その頂点が女王陛下です。

　この原則にはたくさんの例外があり，全部論じようとすると本一冊になってしまうので，ここでは概要だけを述べたいと思います。

階級

lower-low class	下層労働者階級
low class	労働者階級
upper-low class	上層労働者階級
lower-middle class	下層中流階級
middle class	中流階級
upper-middle class	上層中流階級
aristocracy	貴族階級

下層階級または労働者階級

　この階級が人口の大半を占めています。彼らは中流階級の下で，事務員，清掃員などいろいろな仕事につき，生活費や住宅ローンを払い，老後の蓄えをするために賃金を得ています。1000年前からずっと何も変わっていません。唯一変わったのは生活水準で，今の方がよくなっていると言われています。だれもが休暇に出かけ，コンピューターを持ち，お金の余裕が昔よりはできました。

　これは議論の余地がある大変複雑な問題なのですが，ここでは簡単に，イギリスにはまだ大変貧しい人々がいると言っておくのがよいでしょう。生きていくだけでもぎりぎりの貧困に喘ぎ，死ぬまでそれが続くという人たちが現在もいます。また，快適に生活している人々もいますし，やる気を出してこの階級から脱出しようとする人もいます。しかし一般的に下層階級にはあまり「明日」を考えられない人が多いのが現実です。やる気に乏しく，自分を取り巻く世界や自分が持っているチャンスにも気づかない人が大勢います。犯罪の多くはこの階級から生じると言ってもよいでしょう。本書に収録したような下品な英語もこの階級から出ているものです。けれども彼らは人口の最も高い割合を占めているのですから，この種の英語はきっと耳にすることでしょう。

中流階級

　中流階級は定義が簡単です。お金を持っている，医者，聖職者，弁護士，外科医などの専門職やエリート会社員（単なる事務員ではない），または事業経営者などです。けれども中流階級の生活をするためには十分な収入があり，中流階級の地域に住み，子供を中流階級の学校に入れ，中流の車を持ち快適な生活をする必要があります。たいてい子供は大学まで進み，学費は親が払います。労働者階級の子供は，もし大学へ行きたければ奨学金や政府のローンを借りて行くのです。労働者階級では中等教育が終わるとすぐ仕事につく人がほとんどで，中流階級や大学教育に嫌悪感を持ってさえいます。

　下層階級出身者のなかには中流階級に入れるほど経済的に豊かな人も

います。けれども下層階級の育ちであるため下層中流階級の下につくことに甘んじています。私の両親は戦後の荒廃した地域で労働者階級として育ちました。二人とも工場で働き，そこで出会い，私が生まれ，私は完全に労働者階級の地域で育ちました。その後，両親は離婚しそれぞれ再婚しました。母は金持ちのビジネスマンと結婚し，今は上層中流階級のライフスタイルで暮らしていますし，父も事業を始め，やはり上層中流階級程度にまで収入は上がりました。けれども彼らは本当の中流階級を欺くことはできません。私は両親とともに中流あたりにいるわけですが，彼らは中流の生活が身の丈にあっていません。しっくりなじんでいないのです。会話の話題や服のセンスやマナーで，明らかに下層階級出身だとわかってしまいます。

　もとの階級を本当に抜け出すには三代かかると言われています。次の階級との間には境界線が存在します。特に貴族階級との間には大きな壁があります。そこはもはや金があまりものを言わない世界です。あなたは最も大金持ちのスポーツ選手や，映画スター，ポップスの伝説的スターになることはできるかもしれません。イギリス女王より金持ちになることもできるかもしれません。しかし，貴族階級の一員ではないのです。あなたは女王陛下が許可しないかぎり，永遠に上層中流階級にとどまるのです。

貴族階級または上流階級

　これこそ曲線のいきつくところです。上流階級側から手を差し伸べられないかぎり通ることのできない関門です。お金を積んでもチケットは買えません。家系だけがこの地位に必要なのです。

　高貴な家系は1000年にわたり存在しています。これは爵位で成り立っている世界です。生まれと王室の指名によってのみ与えられる称号です。イングランドのピーク地方にCavendish（キャベンディッシュ）家という貴族の邸宅があり，だれでも訪れることができます。15ポンドで家の中を見て回ることもできます。お金が贅沢に使われており，彼らがどのように暮らしているか，前述の魔法の入り口から別の世界をチラ

ッと見られるのです。700年以上にわたり富を享受してきた貴族の邸宅なのですが，彼らはあなたが理解できないライフスタイルを持っています。職を確保する心配もなく，起きて仕事に出かけなくてもよく，老後どうやって暮らしていくかも心配しなくてよく，ただ莫大な富と称号がもたらす特権で快適な生活を送るだけなのです。私はいままでに二人貴族に会ったことがあります。それだけです。たった二人だけです！　私はチャールズ皇太子に会ったことがあります。また，自分の敷地で野外映画会を催した貴族にも会ったことがあります。彼がその会を催したのです。これが私の人生において上流階級とかかわったすべてなのです。

　イギリスには三つの世界があり，それらはめったに交わることはありません。けれども貴族の世界は終わりに近づいています。女王は長い間，新たに爵位を授けておらず，最近世襲制の称号を受けたのは，唯一の女性首相だったマーガレット・サッチャーの一族だけです。貴族は急速に没落しつつあり，財産もなくなってきている家もあります。だから屋敷を公開したり，敷地で映画会をやったりするのです。彼らは大地主でしたが財産はどんどん縮小しています。いつかは女王の一家だけが称号を持つ日がくるかもしれません。が，それはいずれにせよ数百年後のことでしょう。

　忘れていた地位がもう一つありました。騎士<ruby>騎士<rt>ナイト</rt></ruby>です！　騎士は階級制度のなかでは異色の存在であり，中流階級でも上流階級でもありません。Sir（サー）の称号を持ちますが，爵位はありません。片足を中流階級に，片足を貴族階級に置いて，この二つを結ぶ橋のように存在しています。

ネットの造語と
ネット掲示板略語

Leetspeak(1337) and Bulletin Board Shorthand

　コンピューターは私たちが暮らしているこの世界の顔をすっかり変えてしまった道具であり，現代の最大の発明品の一つであることは間違いないでしょう。さらにコンピューターは英語に多大な影響を与えています。15年前まではだれも聞いたことがなかったような言葉が大量に流入してきて，今やコンピューター用語はこれまでにないほど増大しています。若いコンピューター世代は自分たちの使う言語を部外者が全く理解できないようなものに変えてしまっています。

　新たに英語に仲間入りしている主な語句はleet（1337）（またはleetspeakとも呼ばれます）と掲示板略語です。leetはeliteが転じてできた語であり，よくアルファベットを数字や記号で表記するのが特徴的です。これによるとlは1，eは3，tは7で書き換えられるので，leetは1337になります。これはコンピュータープログラマーやユーザーが秘密の会話をするために作った暗号っぽい言語です。

　もう一つは掲示板略語です。これはインターネットフォーラムや掲示板で使うとき書き込みやすいように頭文字をとった略語（acronym）です。

　leetspeakと掲示板略語をこの節では一緒に扱っています。実際この二つははっきりと区別されているわけではありません。それぞれ別々の人たちが使っているということではないのです。コンピューターに習熟している人ならどちらもすべて使っているでしょう。また，これらは文法的な文ではなく，ただそのままの形で使われます。

ネットでよくみかける表現

- **lol**（または **loal**） ＜ laugh out loud 「爆笑」

- **pwn3d** ＜ pawned 「やっつけた」「やられた」 ▷ owned と同じ意味ですが，故意にスペルを変えています。「支配する」という own の原義から pwn はオンラインゲーム用語で「やっつける，ぶっ殺す」という意味で使われています。pwn3d はその過去形または過去分詞形に当たります。

- **chwn3d** ＜ chowned ▷ pwn3d と同じく owned の変形したもので，「やっつけた」，「やられた」という意味です。

- 😊 **wtf** ＜ what the fuck 「なんてこった！」「チクショウ！」

- **uber** 「超いい」「最強」 ▷ ドイツ語で super の意の語。

- **ha ＞＜ 0rz** ＜ hackers 「ハッカー」

- **r0 ＞＜ rz ur b0 ＞＜ 0rz** ＜ rock your boxes ▷ box は箱，つまりコンピューターの意味。「お前のコンピューターを揺する」とは「勝負はこちらの勝ちだ」ということ。

- 😊 **cba** ＜ can't be arsed ▷ 何かをしたくないという意味のスラング。

- **tbh** ＜ to be honest 「正直言って」 ▷ 他の人が賛成しないようなあなたの正直な意見を言うときの決まり文句。

- **omg** ＜ oh my god 「なんてこと！」「ひどいや！」「どうしよう！」

- **afaik** ＜ as far as I know 「私の知る限り」 ▷ 自分が知る限り正しいと信じている情報を言うとき使います。

- **imho** ＜ in my honest opinion 「正直なところ」

- **afk** ＜ away from keyboard 「席を外します」 ▷ 文字通りの意味で，キーボードの前から離れること。

- **brb** ＜ be right back または bathroom break 「ちょっと席を外します」「トイレタイム」

- **lmao** ＜ laugh my arse off 「爆笑」

- **rofl** ＜ roll on the floor laughing 「爆笑」 ▷ 直訳すれば，床に転げ回って笑うという意味。

- **n00b** ＜ noob または noo-B 「新入り」 ▷ newbie という単語を

表し，発音も同じようにします。初心者のことをやや馬鹿にした言い方です。

●**flame**　「炎上」　▷leetspeakや略語ではありませんが，これは他者を中傷するために意図的に行うネット上の攻撃です。さらにflame warというネット上の激しい論争になることもあります。

●**ffs**　＜　for fuck sake　「チクショウ！」「あきれた！」「冗談じゃない！」

**カルチャー
トーク**

　イギリスの教育界では憂慮される事態が起こりつつあります。高校の試験でコンピューター略語やＥメール略語で書かれた解答用紙が提出されるようになっているのです。私たちは新しい英語の出現を目撃しているのでしょうか？

宗教的な言葉

Religious Words

　英語の中で宗教的な言葉と言えばキリスト教に関する言葉ですが，イギリスではキリスト教の人気が次第に衰えてきています。この節に出てくる言葉にはかつてはとてもさまざまな意味と力があり，大変重大に受け止められていました。けれども今やだんだん冒瀆的な意味はなくなりつつあり，ほとんどの人に受け入れられています。今では時代遅れになっているものもありますし，しょっちゅう耳にするものもあります。いずれにせよ英語のネイティブと親しく話すようになれば，必ずどこかで聞くものばかりです。

　ただし，あくまで相手や状況によっては使ってはいけないことがあります。アイコンはつけてありませんが注意してください（カルチャートーク参照）。

宗教に関連する表現のいろいろ

●**Jesus Christ**　▷ショック，驚き，怒りなどの感情を表す言い方で，いろいろな意味になります。どんな意味で使われているかは会話の前後関係によって，またそれを言う口調（これが重要）によってわかります。

　例 Jesus Christ, look at the size of that!

　　（うわーっ，あの大きさを見てよ！）

●**Holy Mary**　▷Jesus Christ と同じように使います。Mary はイエス・キリストの聖母マリアです。人は何か救いを求めてこの言い方を使います。そこから，意見を言うときに感情を込めるために使われるよう

になりました。やはりその意味やどんな感情が込められているかは口調によって表します。

例 Holy Mary, what is she wearing!

（まったく彼女は一体何て格好をしているの！）

●**Holy Mary mother of God** ▷これも Jesus Christ や Holy Mary と同じ使い方です。何かに驚いたりショックを受けたときに使われます。

例 Holy Mary mother of God!（何てことだ！　信じられない！）

●**I swear, in the name of Jesus Christ** ▷swear にはいろいろな意味がありますが、ここでは「誓う」という意味で、「神の名にかけて誓う」ということです。ですからこの言い方は、自分が言おうとしていることは絶対に真実だということを意味します。

例 I swear, in the name of Jesus Christ that I did not know she was lying.

（彼女が嘘をついていたなんて、絶対神にかけて知らなかったってば）

●**by all the saints** ▷Jesus Christ などと同じように単独で使うこともできますし、後に文を続けてショックや怒りを強調するためにも使われます。もともとの意味は証人として聖人すべてを呼び出してもいいくらいだということですが、今はその意味は忘れられ慣用句として残っています。ただし最近の若者には Jesus Christ を使う人が多く、この言い方はあまり使いません。

例 By all the saints, I would never have believed you.

（私だったらあんたの言うことなんか絶対に信じたりするわけなかったわ）

●**in the name of Christ** ▷これも神の名を呼んで救いを求めるということから、いろいろな感情を表すことができます。たいていは怒りや腹立ちなどを表します。

例 In the name of Christ, will you wash the dishes?

（お願いだからお皿洗ってくれる？）

●**in the name of God** ▷上に同じ。

例 In the name of God, will you be quiet?

（後生だから静かにしてくれる？）

●**in the name of all that's holy** ▷不信を表すことが多いのですが，他の表現と同様に感情によって意味も変わります。

㋕ In the name of all that is holy, will you trust me!

（お願いだから信じてくれる？）

●**holy shit** ▷shit は神聖であるはずがないのでこれは大変おかしな表現ですが，実際に使われる言い方です。たいてい驚きやショックを表します。

㋕ Holy shit, that is mint.（すげえ，かっこいいな）

●**bloody hell** ▷地獄は苦痛と血の場所ですが，この bloody は血とは関係ありません。bloody は by our lady が転訛したものです。by our lady は古い言い方で今はだれも使いませんが，our lady とは聖母マリアのことです。bloody hell という言い方はふつう怒りやショックを表しますが，その意味は口調で変わります。

㋕ Bloody hell, what a beautiful woman!（驚いた，なんて美人なんだ！）

●**hell's bells** ▷地獄で鳴っている大きな鐘のことだと言われています。驚きを表す言葉。

㋕ Hell's bells, he is huge.（すごい，彼はばかでかいね）

●**fucking hell** ▷怒りを表す言い方です。fucking は強調に使われています。

㋕ Fucking hell, shut up.（いいから黙れ）

●**by Christ** ▷これも神への祈りです。いろいろな意味で使われますが，自分の願いを強調するときによく使われます。

㋕ By Christ, I wish he was my boyfriend.

（どうにかして彼が恋人になってくれないかなあ）

カルチャー トーク

　このような言葉は宗教に由来しているので，使ってよいときと使うべきでないときがあることに注意してください。

　まず何よりも年配の人がいる場では使わないようにしましょう。キリスト教は近年急速に衰えてはいますが，年配の人の中には今でも非常に信心深い人たちがいます。さらに日本では十字架を身につけるのはファッションですが，イギリスでは十字架は今でも信仰が篤いことを表します。

　また，教会では決してこのような言葉や（あなたが聖職者でないかぎり）hellという言葉を言ってはいけません。聖職者であってもこのような言葉は90％使わないでしょうし，宗教的な言葉を悪態や驚きの言葉で使うことは神への冒瀆ですから絶対に禁物なのです。もう一つ，教会の中では帽子をとるようにしてください。参考までに，教会には武器を持って入ってはいけないことになっています。これは人々が武器を携帯していた当時にできた決まりです。

第 **3** 章

体・性・家族

疲労と空腹

Tiredness and Hunger

　ここでは，会話の中で満腹だとか空腹だとか，疲れていると言うとき
によく使われる言い方を紹介します。このようなことを話題にしない方
がいいという場面は普通の会話ではまずありません。たとえば日本では
上司にあなたの身体的な欲求を言うことは不適切かもしれませんが，イ
ギリスではたいていの場合，たとえ上司に対しても自分が空腹だと言う
のは問題ありません。

　ただし，この節に出てくる言い方は自分のことを言う場合にだけ使う
方がよいでしょう。もし話している相手が親しい友達だったら，相手の
ことを言うのもかまわないでしょうが，それほど親しくない人に対して
「疲れているように見える」などと言うと大変失礼になります。テレビ
や映画に出ている人やその場にいない人のことを言うのを耳にすること
はあるかもしれません。

疲れている

🫗 **tired** 「疲れた」「眠い」 ▷疲れていることや眠いことを表す一般的
　な言い方。

　例 I am so tired. （とても疲れた）

🙂 **knackered** 「へとへとだ」 ▷もともとはセックスでへとへとに疲
　れたという意味ですが，今では50歳以上ぐらいの人だけが性的な意
　味を連想します。現在ではtiredの意味で広く使われています。

　例 I was up all night, I am so knackered. （徹夜したからくたくただ）
　　　▷このsoはfuckingと言い換えることもできます。

☺ **cream crackered** 「へとへとだ」 ▷knackered と語尾の音をそろえた言い方。

例 I was up all night, I am cream crackered.（徹夜したからぐったりだ）

💣 **fucked** 「疲れた」 ▷fuck は本来は「セックスする」の意味。fucked は「疲れた」のほかに，「ドラッグや酒に酔っている」「解決できない問題がある」「壊れている」などの意味にも使います。

例 You look fucked.（ひどい顔になってるよ）

☺ **wasted** 「疲れた」「弱った」 ▷これも会話の前後関係によっては「ドラッグや酒に酔っている」という意味になります。

例 I have been awake for hours, I am so wasted.（ずっと起きてたからへばっている） ▷ここでも so を fucking と言い換えることができます。

👆 **spent** 「疲れきった」「消耗した」 ▷人気映画シリーズ『オースティン・パワーズ』（*Austin Powers*）から使われるようになりました。

例 And I'm spent.（もうだめだ）

☺ **buggered** 「くたくただ」 ▷bugger には「アナルセックスをする」という意味もあるので注意。

目が覚めている

🧪 **wide awake** 「パッチリ目が覚めている」 ▷エネルギッシュな感じがする語。

例 I can't get to sleep, I'm wide awake.
（パッチリ目が冴えて寝られないよ）

👆 **wired** 「バリバリ元気だ」 ▷エネルギッシュな感じがする語。
例 I am wired and ready to go.（すごく元気だから出かけられるよ）

空腹だ

🧪 **starving** 「すごくお腹が空いている」
例 I haven't eaten for hours, I'm starving.
（ずっと食べてないからお腹がすいた）

👍 **starvin marvin** 「すごくお腹が空いている」

　　例 I have been on a diet, I am starvin marvin.

　　（ダイエット中だからお腹ぺこぺこだ）

👍 **famished** 「すごくお腹が空いている」 ▷famine（飢饉）から派生
した語。

　　例 That boy looks famished.（あの子はひどくお腹が空いているようだね）

👍 **wasting away** 「げっそりしている」 ▷空腹のためやせ衰えるとい
う意味。

　　例 Why don't you eat something? You are wasting away.

　　（何か食べたら？　げっそりしているじゃない）

🚫 **I'm as hungry as an Ethiopian.** 「エチオピア人のように空腹だ」

　　▷1980年代にエチオピアの貧困と飢餓がしばしば報道されたことから。

　　例 I just had sushi, but I'm still as hungry as an Ethiopian.

　　（すしを食べたけどまだお腹がすいているよ）

👍 **I could eat a horse.** 「腹ぺこだ」 ▷イギリスでは馬は食べません。
「馬でも食べられそうだ」とは空腹のあまり何でも食べられるという
意味になります。

　　例 I could eat a horse I'm that hungry.

　　（馬でも食べられるくらいお腹が空いている）

👍 **I'm chewing my arm off.** 「腹がぺこぺこだ」 ▷自分の腕でも食べ
てしまいたいくらい空腹だという意味です。

　　例 If they don't serve the food soon I will eat off my arm.

　　（すぐに食事を出してくれないと，自分の腕でも食べてしまいそう）

満腹だ

👎 **bloated** 「満腹だ」

　　例 I've just had Christmas dinner at Steven's house and I'm bloated.

　　（スティーブンの家でクリスマスディナーを食べて満腹だ）

👎 **full** 「満腹だ」 ▷もう食べられないというときの最も普通の言い方
です。

例 I think he's full.（彼は満腹だと思うよ）

👍 **stuffed**　「満腹だ」

例 You look stuffed.（満腹みたいだね）

👍 **ready to explode**　「お腹がはち切れそうだ」

例 I just had sausage and I'm ready to explode.

（ソーセージを食べたばっかりでもうこれ以上食べられない）

👍 **(I've) had my fill.**　「十分いただきました」　▷「満腹になったのでもう結構です」という言い方です。

例 No more thank you, I've had my fill.

（もう結構です。十分いただきました）

👍 **(be) going to vom**　「吐きそうだ」　▷vom はvomit（吐く）を縮めた言い方です。

例 I have had three slices of chocolate cake and I'm going to vom.

（チョコレートケーキを三切れも食べたからお腹いっぱいで苦しいよ）

カルチャートーク

　日本では「眠い」と「疲れた」ではまったく違う意味になりますが，イギリスではsleepyとtiredは多少の違いはあるものの，実際はどちらもほぼ同じ意味で使うことができます。逆に，正確な意味で使いたいときは説明が必要かもしれません。

　要するにsleepyとtiredは，日本人は区別して使わなければならないと思うでしょうが，イギリスではどちらの意味でどちらの語を使ってもかまわないのです。

あざや障害

Spots and Deformities

　人の体は残酷なものです。子供は体の障害をからかいの的にするので，子供時代がいじめで暗いものになることもあります。この節にあるボキャブラリーのほとんどは非常に差別的ですので，どんな場合でも絶対に使ってはいけないものです。しかし子供と接することがあれば，たぶんどこかでこれらの言葉を耳にするでしょう。みなさんも知っておけば，その場にいる大人が子供になぜ悪い言葉を言ってはいけないかと叱るのか意味が理解できるようになるでしょう。

あざ，ほくろ等に関する表現

spots 「吹き出物」 ▷湿疹やにきびなどを指す，カジュアルで差し障りのない言い方。

　例 Your face is covered in spots.（顔中吹き出物だらけだよ）

pimple 「吹き出物」 ▷年配の人がよく使います。

　例 You have a small pimple on your neck.
　（首に小さな吹き出物ができてるわよ）

(be) growing another head 「吹き出物ができかかっている」 ▷吹き出物ができる様子を「head（頭）ができる」ととらえた，冗談めかした言い方。

　例 Oh my God! You look like you are growing another head.
　（大変だ。吹き出物ができてるみたいだよ）

black head ▷黒い点のようになっている吹き出物。

　例 Your cheeks are full of black heads.（ほっぺたが黒いぶつぶつでい

っぱいだよ）

🍶 **acne** 「痤瘡<rt>ざそう</rt>」「にきび」　▷大量の吹き出物を表す専門用語。疾患の一種。

　　例 Steven has very bad acne.（スティーブンはにきびがひどい）

👍 **yellow head**　▷膿がたまっている吹き出物。

　　例 That's disgusting; you have got the biggest yellow head I've ever seen.（うわっ，ひどい。見たことないくらい大きい吹き出物ができてるよ）

🍶 **birthmark** 「生まれつきのあざ」

　　例 She has a birthmark on her temple, but it's not very obvious.

　　（彼女はこめかみにあざがあるけれども，それほど目立たない）

🍶 **mole** 「ほくろ」

　　例 I want my mole removed.（ほくろをとりたいな）

手足を失う

🍶 **amputee**　▷手または足を失った人をいう医学的で差し障りのない言い方。

　　例 I saw an amputee this morning, he had no left arm.

　　（けさ左足のない人を見た）

😊 **peg leg**　▷片足の人をいう戯言的な言い方。pegは「木製の義足」の意で，義足をつけた海賊を連想させます。

　　例 Hey! Peg leg, where is your parrot?（よう一本足，オウムはどこだい！）

障害について

　ここに挙げる言葉は学校の校庭で聞く類のもので，大変に失礼で否定的な言葉と考えられています。けれどもすでに述べたように子供は残酷なもので，これらの言い方はすべて今でも耳にするのです。

　以下の表現は完全に差別的で失礼なものです。ただし，これらの語は障害を表すものではあるのですが，ほとんどの場合，障害者に向けてというより，若者や子供たちが互いを馬鹿にし合うとき使うような言葉で

す。ちなみに，fuck という語も若い世代ほど非常に頻繁に使う（両親に聞こえないところでですが）ので驚かれるかもしれません。

🚫 🥄 **spasticated** ▷かつては発達障害を表す医学用語でしたが，しばしば差別的に使われたため，今日では節度のある会話では決して使いません。現在は代わりに disabled を使います。

🚫 **spastic** 「とろい奴」「のろま」 ▷spasticated を短縮した言い方。大変ネガティブな言葉です。
  例 You fucking spastic.（馬鹿野郎）

🚫 **spaker** ▷spastic と同じ。
  例 You can't even kick the ball straight, you fucking spaker.（ボールもまっすぐ蹴れないのか，馬鹿野郎）

💣 **mongoloid** ▷医学用語でしたが，しばしば差別的に使われたため今日では節度のある会話では決して使いません。かつては「蒙古症」と呼ばれていたものですが，人種差別的であるため現在正式には発見者の名をとってダウン症（ダウン症候群）Down syndrome と呼ばれています。ただし差別語または悪態語としてはこの言い方はまだ残っています。
  例 You got your homework wrong, it was simple, you are a fucking mongoloid.（宿題を間違えたんだ。簡単だったのに。馬鹿だな）

💣 **mong** ▷mongoloid を短縮した語で，大変失礼な言い方。
  例 Mong! You dropped my sandwich.
  （馬鹿野郎。おれのサンドイッチ落としやがって）

💣 **mongified** 「間抜けな」 ▷mong から派生した語。
  例 That guy is shit on this game, he is mongified.（あいつはこの試合でひどかった。間抜けだ）

💣 **chicken wing** ▷鶏肉の「手羽」の意で，障害がある短い腕のこと。

💣 **window licker** ▷障害者がミニバスに乗って日帰り旅行に出かけるのをよく見かけます。障害のため窓に寄りかかっていることが多く，まるで窓をなめようとしているように見えることから。

💣**elbow kisser** ▷麻痺のため腕がうまく使えず，自分のelbow（ひじ）をなめたりキスしようとしているように見えるということから。

*

これらの言葉を会話で使ったとしたら必ず気分を害する人がいます。繰り返しになりますが，絶対に使わないでください。ここに挙げたのは皆さんがなかなか知る機会がない英語のもう一つの側面を知っていただくためです。どうぞ理解するだけにとどめておいてください。

障害に関する言葉でもっとも不快だと感じるのはどんな言葉か？　という調査をBBCが2003年に行なっています。2053人の回答者（約18％が障害者）がもっとも不快と答えた言葉を多い順に並べると次のようになります。

1	Retard	5	Special	9	Wheelchair-bound
2	Spastic	6	Brave		
3	Window-licker	7	Cripple		
4	Mong	8	Handicapped		

本節で取り上げた言葉がいくつも含まれていて，それらがいかに不快で侮辱的だととらえられているかおわかりいただけると思います。その半面，とくに障害のある人たちはspecial, brave（勇敢な），handicappedなどのような"気を使った"言い方をされることに対しても不快感を抱いていることがわかります。相手への敬意がなければ言葉だけ取り繕っても無意味だということにつきるのでしょう。それにしても本書で繰り返し警告しているように差別的，侮蔑的な表現を避けなければならないのは言うまでもありません。

では，もし実際に障害について話をする機会があったら，どんな言葉を使えばいいのでしょうか。参考までに，障害のある人のことを言うときに用いられる一般的な表現を以下に挙げておきましょう。

●**person〔people〕with disabilities** 「**身体障害者**」 ▷ごく一般的に使われる言葉です。また，身体障害について，mobility impaired（運動機能障害のある）という表現が用いられることもあります。視覚障害はblindのほかにvisually impaired，聴覚障害はdeafまたはhard

of hearing などの言い方も使われます。
- **disabled**　▷上に同じです。
- **differently abled**　「異なった心身能力を持った」　▷disabled（能力が欠けている）という言い方をやめ，障害を前向きにとらえようとした表現です。
- **physically [mentally] challenged**　「身体／精神に障害がある」▷challengedは「努力を要する，恵まれない」という意味です。やはりdisabledやhandicappedという否定的な表現を避けるために考案された言い方です。
- **wheelchair user**　「車椅子利用者」　▷これまで使われていたwheelchair-bound（車椅子に束縛された，車椅子生活の）という表現は否定的であるため，現在ではこの言い方が使われます。

　そのほか，

　　He has paraplegia.（彼は対麻痺がある）

のように具体的に障害名を挙げる言い方も用いられます。慢性疾患による障害がある場合はchronically ill（慢性疾患がある），または単にdisabledと言うことが多いでしょう。「認知障害がある」はcognitively disabled,「自閉症の人」はa person with autism,「アスペルガー症候群の人」はa person with Asperger's syndromeといいます。

カルチャートーク

　日本で教えていたときに，主に若い人たちでしたが，よく吹き出物やにきびについてお互いに言い合ったり，顔のあざやほくろのことを尋ねたりしているのを見ました。イギリスでは人のあざや吹き出物などのことを口にすることは失礼この上ないことであり，気がつかない振りをするのが普通です。もしこういった話題をだれかが持ち出したとしたら，部屋全体が気まずい空気になってしまうでしょう。

トイレの話

Toilet Language

　　トイレといえば孤独とプライバシーの場所ですが，最近のイギリス人にとってはそうではなさそうです。というよりそうではない方向へ変わりつつあるというべきでしょうか。以前はイギリスでもトイレや排泄に関する話はタブーでしたが，最近ではどんどんあけすけになってきています。イギリスの文化やマナーが悪くなってきたと嘆く人がたくさんいますが，排泄に関してこれだけ多くの言葉があることもその証_{あかし}なのかもしれません。一般的にはトイレに関する話をするときイギリス人は気を使って話していると言えるのですが，最悪の場合は覚悟しておいてください。あまりの言葉遣いにあきれてしまうかもしれません。

大便の言い方のいろいろ

defecate 「排便する」 ▷「排泄する」という意味の上品で標準的な言い方。

bodily waste 「排泄物」「老廃物」 ▷「排泄物」を表す広く使える語で，上品な会話で用いても大丈夫ですが，トイレに行きたいというときには使わない方がよいでしょう。

shit 「大便」「くそ」 ▷「大便」の一般的で下品な言い方。

poo 「うんこ」 ▷子供に言うとき，または子供が使う言葉。ガイジンは日本人が『クマのプーさん』（Winnie-the-Pooh）と言うとおかしくなります。Poo san は Mr. Shit（ウンコさん）と言っているように聞こえるのです。

crap 「くそ」「排便」

例I'm having a crap!（ウンチが出そう）

👎 **plop** ▷「ウンチ」の意の俗語。「ポチャン」という水の音からきています。

😊 **dump** ▷「大便」の一般的な言い方。

😊 **turd** ▷「大便」の一般的言い方。

😊 **rabbit droppings** ▷硬くてウサギの糞のように小さくころころした便のこと。

🍶 **diarrhea** 「下痢（便）」

😊 **ring of fire** ▷辛いカレーなどを食べて排便をするとスパイスがring（ここでは肛門の意）を通るとき焼けるように痛いことを表します。「金環」「環太平洋火山帯」の意もあります。

😊 **flock of sparrows** 「下痢（便）」 ▷直訳すると「群れスズメ」。これはスズメの群れが木から一斉に飛び立つイメージから生まれました。下痢便が肛門から出るときの液体の中の小さいツブツブの感じがスズメの群れを連想させます。

😊 **pebbledash the bowl** 「下痢をする」 ▷pebbledashは家の外壁の仕上げ工法で，小石を高圧エアーで建物の外壁のモルタルに埋め込みます。下痢のときの音と便器（the bowl）に残る便の状態が似ていることから。

😊 **submarine** 「くそ」 ▷便が便器に落ちると水の中に沈んでいくため。

😊 **Richard III [the Third]** 「くそ」 ▷リチャード3世（Richard the Third）は昔のイギリスの国王ですが，turd（くそ）と音が似ているため代わりに使われる言葉遊びです。

小便の言い方いろいろ

🍶 **urinate** ▷「小便をする」の標準的な言い方。

😊 **piss** 「小便（をする）」 ▷一般的な言い方。

😊 **slash** 「放尿」「小便をすること」 ▷一般的な言い方。

😊 **leak** 「小便」 ▷水漏れからの連想で，一般的な言い方。

👎 **shed a tear for Nelson** 「小便をする」 ▷ホレイショ・ネルソン

(Horatio Nelson) 卿はトラファルガー海戦で勝利した有名な提督で，イギリス史上大変人々に愛されている人物です。このイディオムは港に近い地域でよく使われているものです。「彼を悼んで涙を流す」というのが文字通りの意味ですが，もちろんここでは悼んでいるわけではありません。

☺ **leak the lizard**　「小便をする」　▷lizardは「とかげ」ですが，この場合は「ペニス」を表し，「ペニスから水を出す」ということです。

👍 **drain the pipes**　「小便をする」　▷「パイプの水を排出する」という言い方ですが，もちろんあなたの持っている生理的な排水システムを言っています。

👍 **empty my bladder**　▷bladder（膀胱）を空にするという文字通りの意味です。

嘔吐する

🍶 **vomit**　▷上品で標準的な言い方。

🍶 **projectile vomit**　「勢いよく吐く」　▷口から吹き出すような嘔吐を意味する標準的な言い方。

👍 **throw up**　「吐く」「もどす」　▷「嘔吐する」の一般的な言い方。

👍 **blow chunks**　▷「嘔吐する」意のアメリカ英語。

👍 **spew**　▷「吐く」「もどす」意の一般的言い方。

👍 **vom**　▷vomitを縮めた言い方。

表現のいろいろ

　これらの語句はたいてい自分のことを言うのに使われるのでIで始まります。だれかが他の人の排便の欲求について話すということはふつうないでしょうから。次に挙げる文例はわかりやすいように，使われるべき文の形式で分けてあります。

　I need/want a shit/poo/plop/dump/turd/Richard III [the Third]/crap.（ウンチがしたい）

I need/want to defecate.（大便がしたい）

I need/want a leak/piss/slash.（おしっこがしたい）

I need/want to urinate/shed a tear for Nelson/leak the lizard/empty my bladder/drain the pipes.（おしっこがしたい）

I need/want to vom/vomit/projectile vomit/throw up/blow chunks/spew.（吐きそうだ）

My shit was like rabbit droppings/（a）flock of sparrows.（ウサギのウンチみたいだった／下痢だった）

I have diarrhea/pebbledashed the bowl.（下痢です）

I have（a）ring of fire.（お尻が痛い）

カルチャートーク

　前述のようにイギリス人の上品さは低下してきているのですが，教養のある人は上品な言葉遣いをしますし，トイレに関する直接的な言葉を上品な席で使ったりはしません。トイレに行きたいという上品な言い方をいくつか挙げておきます。

wax my moustache（男性）

powder my nose（女性）

I'm going to the bathroom.　▷bathroomはトイレの意味にも使えます。toiletという直接的な言葉を使いたくないときに。

I'm going to the rest room.　▷これは主にアメリカで使われる表現です。

　それでも最初に言ったとおり，たとえ女性でもこの節にあるようなはしたない言葉を使うこともありますので，くれぐれも驚かないようにご用心ください。

男性の体

Male Body Parts

　女性の場合，胸，性器，尻という三つの性的な部分それぞれに数多くの言葉が存在しますが，男性についてはほとんどペニス，陰嚢，睾丸に限られています。男性が自分たちの体で話題にするほど関心があるのはそれくらいなのでしょう。私は男なので男性が使うこの種の言葉しか耳にすることがありません。性的な関係にでもないかぎり，異性と性器について会話することはまずないからです。

　イギリスの女性たちが私の知らないどんなボキャブラリーを持っているのか私も知りたいところです。

ペニスを意味する語

penis　▷解剖学用語。

dick　▷スラング。

cock　▷スラング。おそらく「雄鶏」からきています。生殖能力があり男性的であるからでしょう。

　　例 I had his cock up my arse, it fucking wrecked.

　　（彼にアナルセックスをされたんだけど，ものすごく痛かったわ）

　　I sucked his cock for ages.（彼のアレをずっと吸ってあげたわ）

todger　▷スラング。

wanger　▷スラング。

man-root　▷スラング。

　　例 She put his man-root right down the back of her throat.

　　（彼女は彼のペニスをのどの奥まで深くくわえた）

☺ **nob** ▷スラング。

例 His nob was hanging out of his pants.

（一物がパンツからはみだしていた）

👍 **old fella** ▷スラング。fellaはfellowの意の口語で，「男性」を意味します。

例 His old fella was in and out of her all fucking night, the man's a legend.（あいつのモノが一晩中彼女に出たり入ったりだったって，まったくすごい奴だよ）

☺ **chopper** ▷1970年代にはよく使われていた古くさい言い方。

例 Ha, men! Their chopper rules their lives!

（男なんてしょせん，人生ペニス次第なのね）

● **manhood** ▷「男であること」「男らしさ」という意味の単語です。

A boy grew into manhood.（男の子が大人になった）

というように使うことができますが，ペニスこそ男性自身の象徴ということから，スラングではmanhoodは「ペニス」を意味します。

例 Did you hear about that guy in America? His manhood was chopped off by that psycho wife of his.（アメリカのあの男の話聞いた？　頭のおかしい女房にモノを切り取られたんだって）

👍 **Johnson** ▷イギリスよりアメリカで多く使われる一般的な言い方。

☺ **man-gina** ▷最近できたスラング。『デュース・ビガロウ，激安ジゴロ !?』（*Deuce Bigalow: Male Gigolo*, 1999年公開）というアメリカ映画から生まれました。ginaはvagina（膣）の後ろの部分で，男性のvaginaの意。

☺ **he-muff** ▷これも映画からきた言い方。heは「男性」，muffはvaginaの意味。

☺ **blue veined Havana** ▷「青筋が立ったハバナ葉巻」の意味で，ペニスを葉巻に見立てた面白い言い方です。これは吸われること，つまりオーラルセックスも連想させます。

☺ **purple headed warrior** ▷「紫の頭をした戦士」の意味です。紫は亀頭の色を表しています。ペニスが性的な攻撃性をもった生き物の

ようであることからきている面白い表現です。

ペニス関連の語

🖕 **Prince Albert** 「ペニスにしたピアス」 ▷Prince Albert（アルバート公）はペニスにピアスをしていたと言われていることから，この言い方ができました。have a Prince Albert は「ペニスにピアスをしている」という意味です。

☺ **bell end** 「亀頭」

  例 His bell end was huge.（彼の亀頭はものすごく大きかった）

💣 **Jap's eye** 「尿道口」▷日本人の目の形に似て，吊り上がったように見えるため，こう呼ばれます。

🖕 **meat and two veg** ▷「肉と 2 種類の野菜」の意で，ペニスと睾丸を指す古いユーモラスな言い方です。イギリスではディナーに肉と 2 種類の野菜を食べるのが普通で，そのことからきています。

子供に対して使うペニスを意味する語

いずれも「おちんちん」といった意味です。

👍 **ding-a-ling**
👍 **winkle**
👍 **winkie**

睾丸を意味する語

🍼 **testicles** ▷解剖学用語。

☺ **balls** ▷スラング。

  例 My testicles are in agony, some fucker kicked me in the balls.
  （タマが痛い，どっかの馬鹿に蹴っ飛ばされた）

👍 **family jewels** ▷family jewels とはロイヤルファミリーの crown jewels のように一族に富と権力を与える宝石のことです。そこからこの言い方は睾丸を意味するようになりました。一族の繁栄を支える

二つの宝石です。

😊 **marbles**　▷古めかしい言い方。本来はビー玉のこと。

😊 **bollocks**　▷スラング。

陰嚢を意味する語

⚗ **scrotum**　▷解剖学用語。

例 My fucking scrot hurts like hell, some bastard caught me in my family jewels.（陰嚢が死ぬほど痛い，どっかの野郎がおれのまたぐらを摑みやがって）　▷scrot は scrotum を縮めた形。

😊 **sack**　▷「袋」から。

😊 **ball sack**

😊 **extra elbow skin**　▷まれですがまだ使われる表現です。陰嚢の感触がひじのあたりの皮膚と似ているため。

カルチャー
トーク

　男性の性器について話すことは上品とは言えませんが，現代社会にはことあるごとにそれをほのめかすような風潮が見られます。

　特にペニスの大きさは男性の間ではよく話題にされます。もしペニスのことを話しているのを耳にすることがあったら，次のような言い方を聞くかもしれません。

　　It's a shower not a grower.

または

　　It's a grower not a shower.

　このshowerはシャワーではなく，正式な英語ではありませんがshow（見せる）に-erを付けたものです。一つ目の文は「見せるものであって成長するものではない」，つまり「ペニスが柔らかいときでも大きいが勃起してもあまり大きくならない」ということです。二つ目の文はその逆で，「柔らかいときは小さいが勃起したらすごく膨張する」という意味です。

　また次のような言い方もあります。

　　Size does not matter.（大きさは関係ない）

　　Every inch counts.（1インチでも大きいほうがいい）

　私は前に全国放送されていたテレビコマーシャルで，とてもセクシーな女性が車の中の広さを測り，カメラを色っぽく見ながら

　　Every inch counts.

と言うのを見たことがあります。直接的に言わなくてもその意味は確実にあるのです。

女性の体
Female Body Parts

　この類の言葉は日本では教えられることはまずないでしょう。ここに挙げた語句は非常に下品なので決して口にすべきではありません。このような言葉は普通，社会の最下層の人々だけが使うと考えられています。とはいうものの，私はこれまでにここに挙げたすべての言葉を医者，紳士，軍隊の士官，教師，その他いろいろな知的職業の人々が使っているのを聞いたことがあります。つまり使う人が限られているというよりは，使う場面が非常に問題だということです。くれぐれも気をつけてお楽しみください。

女性器を表す表現のいろいろ

vagina　▷膣を表す上品かつ解剖学的用語。

twat　▷膣の非常に下品な言い方。

cunt　▷これは間違いなく英語で最も忌まわしい，絶対に使ってはいけない単語と考えられています。女性の性器のほか，嫌な人を表すのにも使われます。

minge　▷膣の非常に下品な言い方。

slash　▷膣の非常に下品な言い方で，「小便する」という意味もあります。

box　▷膣の下品な言い方。中に何かが入る空間があることから。

axe wound　▷女性の性器が斧（axe）でつけた傷（wound）に似ていることから。

hairy axe wound　▷上と同様ですが，毛深い膣のこと。

☺ **rusty axe wound** ▷上と同様ですが，女性が赤毛の場合，錆びた (rusty) ように見えるため。

☺ **flange** ▷膣の下品な言い方。flangeは二つのものを溶接でつなげるときに接合部の縁にできるわずかな出っ張りのことです。この場合，女性の大陰唇を意味します。

👍 **Telly Savalas** ▷テリー・サバラスはテレビ番組『刑事コジャック』(*Kojak*) で有名な禿頭の俳優。女性がTelly Savalasを持っているというと，局部に陰毛が全くないということです。

☺ **pussy** ▷女性の陰部を意味し，以前より受け入れられるようになってきた語ですが，上品な会話では使わない方がよいでしょう。

👍 **brazilian** ▷膣の両側の上から中ほどまで陰毛が垂直に細く垂れ下がったような部分を残して脱毛してあること。

☺ **muff** ▷膣の下品な言い方。

☺ **hairy muff** ▷特に陰毛の濃い女性の性器のこと。このhairy muffはfair enough（了解。結構です）と似た音に聞こえるため，fair enoughと言う代わりにふざけてhairy muffと言うことがあります。たとえば，

    A）I will pay for the cigarettes and you pay for the beer.
      （俺がたばこを買うから，お前がビールを買えよ）
    B）Hairy muff.（いいよ）

☺ **gash** ▷膣の下品な言い方。女性器が切傷（gash）のようだという侮蔑的な表現。

☺ **fanny** ▷膣のあまり下品ではない言い方。アメリカでは「尻」の意。

☺ **front bottom** ▷あまり下品ではない言い方。女性器が尻のように見えることから。

💣 **badly stuffed kebab** ▷女性の性器の形を描写している大変下品な言い方。kebab（カバブ，ケバブ）はピタというパンに肉を詰め込んだ中東の代表的な肉料理。

☺ **beef curtains** 「陰唇」 ▷どことなくビーフを思わせることから。また局部が二つに分かれていてカーテン（curtain）を連想するため。

☺ **flaps** ▷女性の陰部の下品な言い方。大陰唇が垂れぶた（flap）のように見えるという比喩。

☺ **beaver**「陰部」 ▷ビーバーは毛皮に包まれた動物で女性の局部を連想させることから。

👆 **bikini line**「ビキニライン」 ▷女性がビキニを着けるとき，横からはみ出さないように陰毛を剃るラインです。

☺ **spider's legs** ▷下着からはみ出した陰毛のこと。陰毛を剃っていないとビキニから spider's legs がはみ出していると言われてしまうかもしれません。

👆 **tulip** ▷女性の陰部の上品な言い方。ふつう母親が娘に教えるときなどに使う言い方。

👆 **money box** ▷tulip と同様に女性の陰部の上品な言い方。

👆 **tupence** ▷tulip と同様，母親が娘に教える女性器の呼び名。昔，イギリスでは 2 ペニーのことを twopence と言い，それが縮まってtupence と言っていました。tupence という言葉を聞いたら普通はお金の方を言っているので気をつけてください。

乳房（breasts）を表す表現

☺ **tits/rack/babylons/bristols/melons/jugs/knockers/bejongers/boobs**

　　上に挙げた語句はすべて「乳房」の意味ですが，卑語ですので上品な会話では使わないほうがいいでしょう。

❖ 小さな胸（small breasts）

💣 **bee stings** ▷蜂に刺されたくらいにしか膨らんでいない貧乳のこと。

💣 **mosquito bites** ▷蚊に刺されたくらいにしか膨らんでいない貧乳のこと。

💣 **fried eggs** ▷目玉焼きのように胸が小さく平たいという侮辱的な言い方。

肛門と尻 （anus and buttocks）

😊 **dirt box** 「肛門」 ▷排泄物の入れ物であることから。

😊 **chocolate starfish** 「肛門」 ▷チョコレートは排泄物と同じく茶色であり，肛門はヒトデ（starfish）のような形であることから。

😊 **brown eye** 「肛門」 ▷これも茶色で，形が目のようであることから。

😊 **arse** ▷尻を表す一般的な言い方。

表現のいろいろ

上に紹介した語句を用いるような文脈では，以下のような表現に出くわすことが多いでしょう。

● **I bet she has ...** 「彼女はきっと〜に違いない」 ▷この場合，胸や臀部は見えているわけですから，陰部のことを言っているわけです。女性器を表す前述のような語句を入れて使います。

> 例 I bet she has a hairy muff.（彼女は絶対毛深いぜ）
>
> I bet she has a rusty axe wound.（彼女はきっと下の毛も赤いよ）
>
> I bet she has spider legs.（彼女，毛が絶対はみ出してるぜ）

● **She has a big pair of ...** 「彼女のおっぱいは大きい」

これに上に紹介した乳房を表す語句をあてはめるだけです。

> 例 She has a big pair of boobs.
>
> She has a big pair of knockers.
>
> She has a big pair of bejongers.

● **Her tits** ［または他の語句］ **are like ...** 「彼女のおっぱいは小さい」

以下は胸の小さな女性を指す言い方ですが，大変侮辱的なので絶対に使わないことをおすすめします。ただ覚えておくのにとどめてください。

> 例 Her boobs are like bee stings.
>
> Her tits are like fried eggs.

カルチャートーク

　ここに挙げた言葉はすべてイギリスで使われていますし，これ以外にも数多くあります。しかし，99％男性同士が，女性や女性の体について話す場合に使う言葉です。使うとしてもごく親しい友人と話しているときに限った方が無難ですし，それもお互いに関係がない人について言うときだけにとどめておいた方がいいと思います。

　余談ですが，欧米人男性はたいてい女性が陰毛をごく短くしているか全く剃ってあるのが当たり前だと思っています。日本の女性は何もしないのが普通なので，外国人男性が日本人女性とのセックスについて話すとき，決まって話題になるのが日本の女性が毛深いということです。

　またイギリス文化には女性について頭に深く刻み込まれた固定観念があります。それは事実無根なのですが依然として存在しますし，みなさんも知っておいた方がいいと思います。イギリスでは，金髪の女性は頭は悪いけれど遊び相手としては最高で，一方ブルーネットの女性は知的だけれどおかたくて遊び向きではないと言われています。管理職はブルーネットの女性の方が知的だと無意識に感じているので，金髪の女性より多く採用すると思われています。しかしもちろんこの情報に裏づけはありません。

ホモセクシュアル

Homosexual

　イギリスは一大ゲイ社会であり，同性愛は完全にイギリスの文化に受け入れられています。私はマンチェスター在住なのですが，マンチェスターにはゲイの人たち向けの通りや一角があります。これはゲイ・ビレッジgay villageと呼ばれていて（本当の村ではありません），店やバー，クラブ，カフェなどが集まっています。性転換者や同性愛の人たちが一緒にいるのは非常によく見かける光景です。これは日本でいうと新宿2丁目のような地域と考えていいでしょう。

　イギリスでは一般的にホモセクシュアルの問題はよく話題になるので，皆さんもおそらくこの話題について会話をする機会があるでしょう。日本の人たちは，ほとんどQueen's Englishスタイルで話しますから，どんな場面でもまず問題ないと思いますが，くれぐれも丁寧な言葉や受け入れられている言い方だけを使うように気をつけてください。

同性愛の男性を表す表現

　ホモセクシュアルを表す言葉の中で問題なく使えるのはgayまたはhomosexualだけです。それ以外の言葉はほとんどが侮辱的で下品な言い方ですから，もし耳にしたら攻撃的な意味で使われていると思って間違いありません。

🧪**gay**　「ゲイ」「同性愛者」　▷同性愛者を指す比較的上品な言い方。かつては「陽気な」という意味だったので，50年以上前に書かれたものを読んでいたりお年寄りと話しているときは元の意味で使われて

いるかもしれません。

homosexual 「同性愛者」「ホモ」　▷同性愛者を指す標準的な言い方。

queer 「同性愛者」「ホモ」　▷同性愛者に対するやや失礼な言い方。

　例 Fuck off, queer.（あっちへ行け，オカマ）

homo 「ホモ」　▷homosexual を縮めた侮蔑的な言葉。

　例 Piss off, you homo.（あっちへ行け，ホモ野郎）

bum-boy 「おかま」「ホモ」　▷男性のゲイの関係で受け身になる側の男性を指す。

　例 Eh! Bum-boy, why don't you smoke the cock! Fucking queer!

　（何だって，オカマ野郎。ちんちんでもくわえてろ！　この変態野郎）

faggot 「同性愛者」「ホモ」「ゲイ」　▷ホモを指す非常に失礼な言い方。

　例 I hate faggots.（オカマは大嫌いだ）

uphill gardener 「ホモ」　▷間違ったやり方で地面を掘っている人の意。同性愛者が自然の摂理に反していることを暗示しています。

　例 This is a bar for uphill gardeners.（ここはホモ専用のバーだよ）

fudge packer 「ホモ」　▷チョコレートファッジを詰める仕事をする人にたとえたもの。肛門の中の排泄物にペニスを押し込む行為を指す。

　例 A）Do you think that guy is a fudge packer?（あいつホモだと思う？）

　　 B）Bent as a 9 bob note.（絶対ホモだね）

bent 「オカマの」　▷ゲイの男性を指す失礼な言い方。「不正な」という意味もあります。

bent as a 9 bob note 「不正な」「見るからに同性愛者である」　▷ bent は「不正な」の意で，bob は大英帝国時代の硬貨の単位。しかし 9 bob note（9 ボブ紙幣）は発行されたことがないので，このイディオムはもともと「間違っている」という意味でした。その後 bent が「同性愛の」という意味で使われるようになってきたので，このイディオムもゲイを表すようになりました。アメリカでは，a 9 bob note の代わりに a three-dollar bill と言うようです。

camp （男性が）「なよなよとした」 ▷男性が女っぽく振る舞うこと。campは「同志，仲間」という意味で，必ずしもゲイを指すわけではありませんが，すぐにゲイを連想させる言葉です。

fairy 「オカマ」 ▷女っぽいゲイの男性のこと。

例 You look like a fairy.（オカマみたいに見えるぞ）

queen 「オカマ」「ホモ」 ▷これはdrag queen（女装したホモ）からきています。派手な格好で女装している，非常にごつい男性を指します。

例 This place looks like it's a queen bar.（ここはホモのバーみたいだぜ）

cock smoker 「ホモ」 ▷これは男性がもう一人の男性のペニスを口にくわえ，葉巻のように吸うことからきています。cockはペニスの意の俗語。

sausage jockey 「ホモ」 ▷jockeyは競馬の騎手。男性が別の男性のペニスの上に騎手のように乗っかるという意。

例 Look at that little sausage jockey, I bet he takes it up the arse.（あのちびのオカマを見ろよ。絶対かまほられてるな） ▷arseは「尻」の意で，take it up the arseは「アナルセックスをやらせる」こと。

cock boy 「ホモ」 ▷同性愛者を指す無礼な表現。

queer as folk 「同性愛の」 ▷かつては「人は時として奇妙な行動をする」（There's nowt so queer as folk.）という意味でしたが，有名なゲイのテレビ番組（Queer as Folk，イギリスのチャンネル4が1999年に放映したゲイ・ドラマ）の名前として使われたために今ではゲイを表します。

bum burglar ▷bumは「お尻，けつ」，burglarは「強盗」の意なので，bum burglarは肛門を犯す人を意味します。

例 Don't touch me, you bum burglar.（俺に触るな，オカマ野郎）

同性愛の女性を表す表現

gay　「レズ」　▷同性愛者を表す丁寧な言い方。男性に対する gay と同様に，元来「陽気な」という意味を持っていました。

dyke　「同性愛の女」「レズ」　▷男性的なゲイの女性を表す失礼な言い方。

　例 I wouldn't like to fight that dyke over there, she looks well hard.
　　（あそこにいるレズとはけんかしたくないな，すごく強そうだから）

lesbian　「レズビアン」　▷同性愛の女性を指す標準的な用語。語源はギリシャ神話に登場するレスボス Lesbos という女だけの島の名前からです。

lesbo　「レズ」　▷lesbian を短くした言い方。非常に失礼な言い方。

minge eater　「レズ」　▷minge は女性器を表す俗語。「女性器を食べる」とはレズビアンの行為を表すので，minge eater は「同性愛の女」という意味です。また，言葉遊びの一種ですが，これを非常に速く言うとインド人やパキスタン人の女性の典型的な名前のように聞こえるので，インド系やパキスタン系のレズビアンを意味することもあります。

　例 I'd love to see those two minge eaters go at it.
　　（あの二人のレズがやっているところを見たいよ）

carpet muncher　「レズ」　▷上の minge eater と同様，女性同士のオーラルセックスからきています。この場合，carpet は陰毛を表し，munch は「むしゃむしゃ食べる」こと，つまりオーラルセックスのことを言っています。

muff diver　「レズ」　▷muff はヴァギナを表す語で，dive はここでは「入る」の意。

トランスセクシュアル（性転換願望者）に関する表現

● **trannie** ▷transsexual を短くした言い方。大変失礼な表現です。

☺ **she-male** 「シーメール」 ▷女装していて，性転換手術を受けた，または受けたいと思っている男性。

例 That's disgusting, a she-male.（むかつくぜ，オカマめ）

👍 **lady-boy** ▷she-male と同様。

カルチャー
トーク

　イギリスの同性愛者の人たちは表面的には受け入れられています。けれども労働者階級には平気で不快感をあらわにする人々もいます。これは中流階級や上流階級の人が同じ感情を持っていないということではなく，ただ中流や上流の人々の方が遠慮深く，社交性や礼儀を持ち合わせていることが多いというだけです。ここに挙げたような言葉を実際耳にすることがあるかもしれませんが，下品な言い方が使われていたら，まずそれは侮蔑するのが目的だと考えていいでしょう。同性愛についてどんな言葉遣いをするかで，その人の育ちも大体わかると言えます。

性 行 為

Sexual Acts

　セックスはおそらく人類が世界共通に語ることのできるたった一つの行為でしょう。イギリスでは同性同士ならセックスに関する会話はまったくオープンにしますが，この場なら大丈夫だと確信が持てない場合は，自分からセックスの話題を持ち出さない方が無難です。この種の会話はたいてい酒を酌み交わし口が軽くなってきて初めて出てくるというのは，日本でも同じだと思います。ここに挙げてある言葉には過激で，日常会話で社交上受け入れられていないものも含まれていますので，くれぐれも注意してください。

セックスに関する表現

🏺 **intercourse** 「性交」　▷医学用語で上品な言い方。

🏺 **sex** 「セックス」

☺ **shagging** 「セックス」　▷友人同士の会話なら使えます。ただし sex の方が無難です。

💣 **fucking** 「セックス」　▷どちらかと言うときつくて下品に聞こえます。

☺ **nobbing** 「セックス」　▷これはペニスを意味する nob からきている言葉遊び。動詞化して行為を表すために -ing をつけたもの。

☺ **hoof** 「セックスする」　▷牛や羊のひずめ hoof から。男性の性的攻撃性からきています。

　　例 I love hoofing my woman.（恋人とセックスするのが好きだ）

☺ **give one** 「セックスする」　▷男性が，セックスで快楽や受胎など何かしら与えているという発想から。

例 I'm going to give her one.（彼女とセックスするぞ）

😊 **pink wings** 「セックス」 ▷この節にはwingsのつく語句が三つ出てきます。wingsとは空軍の空挺部隊からきた表現です。空挺部隊は特殊部隊であり、これに入隊すると制服に翼（wings）の形のバッジをつけることができることから、wingsは強い願望を達成したということを表します。pink wingsには普通の性行為のほかに処女喪失という意味合いもあります。

😊 **ramming** 「セックス」 ▷ramには「詰め込む、激しくぶつかる」という意味があり、これもセックスの動物的な面からきている言い方。

😊 **humping** 「セックス」 ▷humpは「こぶ、盛り上がったところ」の意で、臀部が盛り上がっている人の体形からきています。

例 My girlfriend loves humping.（ガールフレンドはセックスが好きだ）

😊 **rafting** 「セックス」 ▷この語は川などでボートを漕ぐラフティングの意味もあるので注意してください。

体位 sex styles

😊 **doggy style** 「後背位」
👍 **from behind** 「後背位」
👍 **on top** 「騎乗位」
🍾 **missionary position** 「正常位」

男性に対するオーラルセックス

女性が男性に対してするオーラルセックスの言い方を挙げます。

🍾 **oral sex** 「オーラルセックス」「フェラチオ」
😊 **blow job** ▷フェラチオの一般的な言い方。
😊 **BJ** ▷blow jobを短縮したもの。
😊 **suck off** 「フェラチオをする」 ▷女性が吸う（suck）ことから。
😊 **go down** 「オーラルセックスをする」 ▷一般的な言い方。

例 Will you go down?（フェラチオしてくれる？）

💣 **fuck the mouth** 「オーラルセックスをする」 ▷男性が女性の口で

性交を行うこと。

女性に対するオーラルセックス

男性が女性に対して行うオーラルセックスの言い方です。

- 😊 **go down** 「オーラルセックスをする」 ▷一般的言い方。
- 😊 **licking the bean** 「クンニリングス」 ▷bean とはクリトリスの別名で，lick は「なめる」の意。

   例 I hate licking the bean.（クンニリングスは大嫌いだ）

- 💣 **sucking the clam** 「クンニリングス」 ▷clam（貝）は膣の別名で，suck は「吸う」の意。
- 😊 **muff diving** 「クンニリングス」 ▷muff は膣の別称で，dive は「飛び込む」の意。

アナルセックス

- 🍶 **anal sex** ▷アナルセックス，肛門性交を指す一般的な語。
- 😊 **brown wings** ▷前述のように wings は何かを「達成した」ことを表し，brown は排泄物の色を表します。
- 💣 **uphill gardening** ▷uphill は「上り坂の」，つまり「骨が折れる」という意味で，挿入するのに強く突かなければならないことと，間違った方法であることも暗示しています。ふつう同性愛者の人が使う言い方です。
- 💣 **fudge packing** ▷fudge（ファッジ。柔らかいチョコレート菓子）は排泄物の質感と色から連想した洒落で，ペニスが肛門の中の排泄物を押し込むことからきています。通常，同性愛者の人が使う言い方です。
- 😊 **up the arse** ▷アナルセックスを指す一般的な語。動詞（句）の後に続けて副詞的に使われます。

   例 She is a slag she takes it up the arse.（彼女は尻軽でアナルセックスをやらせる）

- 😊 **bumming** ▷アナルセックスを指す一般的な語。bum は「尻」の意

の俗語。転じて動詞としても使われます。

例 I saw a gay porno, two men were bumming.
　（ゲイポルノを見たら，男二人でかまをほってたよ）

＊

ふつう，人がセックスについて話すのは自分や他人の経験を話すか自分の願望を言うことが多いものです。男性の場合は自分がしたことを話し，女性はされたことを話すことが多いので，状況にあわせて文法も使い分ける必要があります。

たとえば，女性が「土曜の夜にアナルセックスをした」と言う場合，皆さんは次のように言うと思われるかもしれません。

On Saturday I had anal sex.

けれども，ネイティブはおそらくこう言います。

Dan did me up the arse on Saturday.

そしてDanの立場から言うとこうなります。

I got my brown wings on Saturday.

これは彼がアナルセックスしたのが初めてだという意味も含んでいます。

マスターベーションに関する表現

wank　「オナニー（をする）」　▷マスターベーションのふつうの言い方。

toss off　「マスをかく」　▷マスターベーションのふつうの言い方。

bash the bishop　「マスターベーションをする」　▷亀頭が司教（bishop）の帽子に似ていることと，bash（強く打ち付ける）とbishopが韻を踏んでいることからできた言葉遊び。

choke the monkey　「マスターベーションをする」　▷ふつうの言い方。

例 I'm horny I want to choke the monkey.
　（ムラムラしてオナりたい気分だ）

☺ **5 finger shuffle** 「マスターベーション」 ▷トランプのシャッフルに似ていることから。これは「盗む」という意味で使われることもあります。

☺ **say hello to Pam and her five daughters** ▷Pam（パム）は女性の名前で、Pamela（パメラ）の愛称です。Pam は palm（掌）と似た音なので、Pam とその 5 人の娘（自分の指）とセックスしていると見立てています。

　例 She was well fit, I'm going to visit Pam and her five daughters when I get home.（彼女最高だったな。家に帰ったらマスかくぞ）
　　▷say hello to ... の応用した言い方です。

☺ **throw one off** 「マスターベーションをする」 ▷自慰のふつうの言い方。

☺ **the stranger** ▷男性が自分の左手の上に座り、感覚がなくなってからマスタベーションをすると別の人が触って性交しているかのように感じること。

射精（ejaculation）に関する表現

👍 **come** 「いく」「射精する」 ▷射精することの一般的な語。
　例 I'm coming.（いきそうだ。いくぞ）
　例 I've just come.（いったところだ）

☺ **shoot** 「射精する」 ▷一般的な言葉。
　例 I shot in her mouth.（彼女の口に発射した）

☺ **come shot / cum shot** 「射精」
　例 I gave her the come shot.（彼女に射精した）

☺ **money shot** 「射精」 ▷ポルノ映画で「金が稼げる（客が喜ぶ）シーン」、すなわちセックスシーンの最後の射精のこと。特に、観客に行為が終わったことを見せるため、女性の体内ではなく、顔や胸などに射精すること。

☺ **vinegar stroke** ▷射精寸前のところ。そのときの顔が酢を飲み込んだように見えるため。

例 My girlfriend hates the vinegar stroke.
（俺の彼女はフィニッシュ寸前が嫌いなんだ）

その他の表現

- ☺ **tit wank** 「ぱいずり」 ▷ペニスを女性の胸の谷間に入れて性交を行うこと。

- ☺ **red wings** ▷生理中の女性にクンニリングスをすること。wingsは前述のように「達成」を表し，redは生理中の女性と性交することを表します。生理中の女性にクンニリングスをすると顔に血がついて「赤い翼」のように見えることから。

- ☺ **snowballing** ▷精液を口に含みパートナーに口移しすること。

- ● **felching** ▷肛門か膣から精液を吸いだすこと。

- ☺ **skiing** ▷女性が2人の男性の間に座り，同時に2人にマスターベーションすること。

- ☺ **threesome** ▷3人で一緒にセックスすること。数はfour, five, sixまで増えて，それ以上はorgy（乱交パーティー）と呼ばれます。

- ☺ **orgy** 「グループセックス，乱交パーティー」

カルチャー トーク

　日本では街頭の広告にも性が氾濫し，ポルノグラフィーも簡単に手に入りますが，イギリスではそれよりずっと一般から遠く隔離されています。イギリスでポルノグラフィーを販売するときは，茶色い紙で表紙を隠して子供の目に触れないように棚の最上段に置くのが普通です。ここからポルノグラフィーは top shelf magazines と言われています。

　さらに性に対する寛容度はイギリスでは格段に厳しく，獣姦（bestiality）や小児性愛（pedophilia）に関するものはすべて法的に禁止されています。小児性愛は過敏なほど嫌悪されていて，それに関するものはすべて受け入れられていませんので注意が必要です。私は東京にいたとき，友達と有名なアニメショップに行ったところ，同性愛と小児性愛に関するアニメ雑誌が低い棚に置いてあって，だれでも手に取れるようになっているのを見たことがあります。私たちは大の男ですからそれほど簡単にショックを受けるわけではありませんが，そのときはさすがに驚いて困惑してしまいました。もし私がそれを買ってイギリスに持ち帰ったら逮捕されていたかもしれません。

妊娠と出産

Pregnancy and Birth

　生命の誕生は毎日起きている世界の神秘の一つです。イギリスでは他のありとあらゆるものと同様に，この神秘にもちゃんと俗な言い方があります。どんな言葉を使うかで，その人の育ちやどの階級出身かが大体わかります。

妊娠に関する表現

pregnant 「妊娠している」 ▷基本的で上品な言い方。

　例 Reiko is pregnant, did you know?

　　（レイコが妊娠してるって，知ってた？）

preggers 「妊娠している」 ▷pregnantのスラング。非常に下層階級的な言い方に聞こえますが，よく使われます。

　例 Matthews's sister is preggers again!

　　（マシューの妹がまた妊娠したよ！）

have a bun in the oven 「おなかに赤ちゃんがいる」 ▷妊娠したことを「bun（ロールパン）がオーブンの中にある」とたとえたスラング。

　例 She has a bun in the oven.（彼女は妊娠している）

up the duff 「妊娠している」 ▷非常に下品な言い方。

　例 Are you up the duff?（できちゃったの？）

expecting 「おめでたである」 ▷expecting a child（身ごもっている，子供が生まれる）を縮めた上品な言い方です。

　例 She's expecting.（彼女は子供が生まれる）

with child 「おなかに赤ちゃんがいる」「妊娠している」 ▷正式で

はありませんが，丁寧な言い方です。

　　例 I am with child.（妊娠しています）

👍（**be**）**carrying**「妊娠している」▷女性が 9 か月赤ちゃんを身ごもる（carry）ことから。

　　例 I am carrying your baby.（あなたの子供がおなかにいるのよ）

👍（**have**）**got one on the way**「妊娠している」▷one は子供を意味します。子供がこの世界に生まれる途中である（on the way）ということ。

　　例 Kathie has got one on the way.（キャシーは妊娠している）

😊（**be**）**having a sprog**「がきんちょができる」▷sprog（がき）は子供を意味する下品な言い方です。これを使う人は育ちがあまり良くないと思われます。

　　例 She's having another sprog.（彼女，またできちゃったんだよ）

出産に関する表現

🍼（**be**）**giving birth**「出産する」▷基本的で上品な言い方。

　　例 She is giving birth right now.（彼女は今，分娩中です）

🍼 **waters have broken**「破水した」

　　例 Kevin's girlfriend, Maggie, her waters have broken.（ケビンの恋人のマギーが破水したってさ）

🍼 **go into labour**「陣痛が始まる」▷labour は「労働」という意味ですが，文脈によっては子供を生むという労働，つまり「陣痛」の意味になります。

　　例 She has gone into labour.（彼女は陣痛が始まったところだ）
　　　 She went into labour yesterday.（彼女は昨日陣痛が始まった）

😊（**be**）**spitting them out like greased pips**「子供をぽんぽん産む」
▷これはたくさん子供を産む女性に対する大変失礼な言い方です。greased pips（油を塗った種）は力をかけるとするりと飛び出すので，それくらい女性が子供を簡単に産むということです。spit out は「プッと吐き出す」という意味です。

例 That slag, she is spitting them out like greased pips.

（あのあばずれ，やたらぽろぽろよく産むなあ）

🖐（**She has**）**child bearing hips** 「安産体形だ」 ▷これは肉付きが
よくていかにも子供が産まれやすそうな腰をしている女性をいう言い
方です。文字通りの意味で使われるほか，太っているというほどでは
ないが，少し肉付きのいい女性をいうこともあります。

例 A）She is a bit fat.（彼女はちょっと太ってるね）

B）No, I don't think so, I think she has child bearing hips.

（いや，そうじゃない。安産型なんだよ）

😊 **drop one** 「子供を産む」「産み落とす」 ▷非常に下品な言い方です。

例 Did you know Crystal has dropped another one?

（クリスタルがまた子供産んだって知ってた？）

カルチャー
トーク

　日本でもイギリスでも出生率が低下しています。若い層の納税者が
少なくなっていくのでどちらの政府にとっても危機的状況です。けれ
どもイギリスではもっと深刻な問題があります。全体的な出生率は下
がっているのですが，下層階級の出生率は大幅に上がっているのです。
下層階級は労働者の階級だと思われているため，これは一見いいこと
のように見えますが，実は働かずに社会福祉の世話になっている人が
増加しているのです。

　さらに下層階級のシングルマザーも増加しています。シングルマザ
ーは無料で家が与えられ，子供が18歳になるまで毎週お金がもらえ
るため，税支出は大幅に増えています。

　また，医療費全額無料の健康保険制度NHS（National Health
Service）は財政悪化とサービス低下の狭間で，青息吐息という状
態です。

家 族

Family

　家族という単位の基本的な構成メンバーは日本の英語学習者ならよく
知っていますし，motherやbrotherなどの基本的単語は非常によく使わ
れます。しかしながら，家族の言い方には日本の人にはなかなか使いこ
なせない種類の語彙もあるのです。

兄弟・姉妹の言い方

❖兄弟を表す言い方

● **br-u-th** ▷これは英語で正式に認められている言葉ではありませんが，
人に自分の兄弟のことを話すときに使う言い方です。兄弟に向かって
呼びかけるときには普通使われません。発音はbrotherいう単語のう
ちerを取ってthまでで切ります。ただしbroth（スープ）という意味
の単語もあり，これは違う発音になるので，ここではbruthと表記し
ました。正式な綴りはありません。

● **our kid** ▷自分の兄弟姉妹を言うときに使う北部イングランドの言
い方。

　例 Is our kid in?（お兄ちゃん［弟］は家にいる？）

❖姉妹を表す言い方

● **sis** ▷brotherの短縮形と同じようにこれもsisterを縮めた言い方で，
書いてあるとおりに発音します。

　例 What you up to sis?（お姉ちゃん，何やってるの？）

● **our kid** ▷自分の兄弟姉妹を言うときに使う北部イングランドの言
い方。

例 Our kid is in a right foul mood.

（お姉ちゃん［妹］はすごく機嫌が悪いよ）

❖いとこ・はとこを表す言い方

● **couz** ▷cousin（いとこ）を短くした形。cus, cuz と書くこともあります。

例 All right couz, what's up?（やあ, 元気？）

● **second cousin** ▷「はとこ」は second cousin で, いとこの子供のことですが, これも cousin に入ります。

例 He's my second cousin.（彼は私のはとこです）

親を表す表現

❖母を表す言い方

● **mum** ▷mother を縮めた言い方で, イングランドで使います。

例 All right mum, what's for tea?（ねえ, お母さん, 夕飯は何？）

▷tea は二通りの意味があります。この節のカルチャートークを参照してください。

● **mom** ▷mother を意味するアメリカの言い方。現在ではイギリスでも使われているのを聞いたことがありますし, 徐々に広まっています。

例 Hey, mom.（ただいま, お母さん）　▷これはアメリカ用法です。

● **ma** ▷mother の略語です。

例 Where's me ma?（お母さんはどこにいるの？）　▷me はここでは my という意味です。

● **mummy** ▷この語は二通りに使われます。しゃべり始めたばかりのような小さい子供が言う場合と, 上流階級の若い娘が使う場合です。これは多少固定観念化されてはいますが, 実際, 地域によっては本当に使われています。

❖父を表す言い方

● **dad** ▷多くの人が使う father の意味の語。

例 Dad, can I lend a fiver?（お父さん, 5 ポンド貸してくれる？）

▷fiverは「5 ポンド」の意味です。また多くの人がborrowと
lendをよく混用します。

● **pa** ▷patriarchy（家父長制）という単語と関連があり，派生語は
さまざまなヨーロッパの言語にあります。

例 Where's my pa?（お父さんはどこにいるの？）

● **sir** ▷アメリカ用法で父親を意味する場合がありますが，時代がか
った言い方です。イギリスでは今のところ聞いたことはありません。

例 Thank you, sir.（ありがとう，お父さん）

例 Yes, sir.（はい，お父さん）

▷イギリス英語ではsirは軍隊で，あるいは顧客や騎士^{ナイト}に対して話
すときだけ使います。

● **daddy** ▷この語は二通りに使われます。しゃべり始めたばかりの
ような小さい子供が言う場合と，上流階級の若い娘が使う場合です。
また，いかにも上流階級の娘が言いそうなこととしてステレオタイプ
化された言葉でもあります。

❖義理の関係を表す言い方

● **step-**「継ー」▷両親が離婚して，また別の相手と結婚したときに，
再婚相手に子供がいればあなたの step-brother（継兄弟）や step-
sister（継姉妹）になり，再婚相手は step-mother（継母），または
step-father（継父）と言います。

例 This is my step-father John.（こちらは私の継父のジョンです）

● **in-law**「義理の」▷これは結婚相手の家族について使います。結
婚は法的なものなので，結婚によってできた人間関係はin-lawと言
います。けれどもin-lawsと複数形になると，ふつう配偶者の両親の
ことを指します。さらにイギリスでは義理の母親を嫌う男性はごく一
般的で，これをネタにしたジョークがたくさんあります。

例 My mother-in-law is Japanese.（私の義母は日本人です）

● **half-**「異母ー」「異父ー」▷half-brotherやhalf-sisterは片親だけ
同じ兄弟姉妹のことです。

例 She's my half-sister.（彼女は私の異母［異父］妹です）▷これはあ

まり使わない言い方です。ふつうはただ brother や sister と言いますが、特に言う必要があるときに使います。

カルチャートーク

前述のポイントを説明するためにイギリスの食事に触れたいと思います。イングランド南部では食事の基本的な順番はこうなります。

    breakfast → lunch → dinner

イングランド北部では以下の順になります。

    breakfast → dinner → tea

そのため Where is me tea? は「夕飯はできてる？」という意味になります。

イングランドでは家族の重要性は薄れてきています。家族の単位は両親と子供から成る小さな核家族であり、家族の結びつきは弱まっています。スコットランドやアイルランド、ウェールズの家族の結びつきはもっとずっと強いのですが、それは彼らがケルト的なライフスタイルを持っているためだと思われます。山岳地帯や行くのが大変な所ほどケルト的なものが残っていると言えます。私の祖母はアイルランド人でしたので、親戚がたくさん集まるときよく

    The family is getting together.（家族が集まる）

というところを

    We are having a gathering of the clans.

    （一族の集まりがある）

と言っていました。clan という言葉はふつうケルト族の家族という意味合いがあります。tribe はたくさんの家族の集まったものを意味しますが、今では歴史的または人類学的な意味で使われるだけです。

年齢の表現

Expressions of Age

　年齢というのはたとえ意識していないとしてもいつも私たちの頭にあるものです。時間というパラドックス，それは私たちが測ろうとしても測り知れない無限のものであり，まさに私たちの人生を支配している要素です。時間は人に年齢をもたらし，年齢は語彙や話し方に違いを作り出すのです。

老人を意味する言い方

- **old coot** 「じいさん」 ▷軽蔑したような口調で老人を言う言い方。
  例 Get out of the way, you old coot. （どきな，じいさん）

- **granddad** 「じいさん」 ▷自分の祖父以外に，一般に高齢の男性のことを言います。口調や状況によっては侮辱的な言葉になります。
  例 Alright granddad, I think you have had enough to drink.
  （さあじいさん，もう飲みすぎだよ）

- **grandpa** ▷granddad に同じです。
  例 Come on, grandpa, I think you have had enough to drink.
  （さあじいさん，もう飲みすぎだよ）

- **grandma** 「ばあさん」 ▷自分の祖母以外に，一般に高齢の女性を意味します。granddad と同じく口調や状況によって失礼な言い方になります。

- **one foot in the grave** 「墓に片足を突っ込んでいる」 ▷とても年をとっているのでほとんど墓に入っている，すぐにも死にそうだということ。

例 Doesn't Simon look old; I think he has one foot in the grave.

（サイモンて老けてるよね。墓に片足突っ込んでるな）

☺ **old dog** 「老人」 ▷新しいことが覚えられない老人を侮蔑的に呼ぶ言い方です。

例 Come on, you old dog.（さあ，じいさん）

☺ **old sea dog** 「老船乗り」 ▷昔，船乗りであったような老人。顔は風雨にさらされ革のように硬くなっているような人を形容する言い方です。

例 Look at that bearded man over there, he's a bit of an old sea dog.

（あそこのひげの男を見ろよ。老船乗りって感じ）

● **ancient** 「年老いた」「古くさい」 ▷もともとは「古代人，古代の」の意。

例 My mobile phone is ancient.（私の携帯は古めかしい）

● **prehistoric** 「時代遅れの」 ▷古くさいものを形容する言い方です。もともとは「先史時代の」の意。

例 Oh my god! Your computer is prehistoric.

（うわっ！ 君のコンピューターは年代ものだね）

若者・赤ん坊を意味する言い方

👆 **youngster** 「若者」 ▷十代の若者を言う言い方。または年をとった人が自分より若い人を言うときに使うこともあります。

例 He should not be doing this job, he's just a youngster.

（彼にはこの仕事は無理だ。まだ若造じゃないか）

👆 **just a baby** 「まだ若すぎる」 ▷ある人が何かをするには若すぎると言いたいときに使います。赤ちゃんや子供のことを言っているのではありません。

例 John is too young to join the army, he's just a baby.

（ジョンは軍隊に入るには若すぎる。ほんの赤ん坊じゃないか）

🍼 **newborn** 「生後まもない新生児」

例 Did you know Jackie has a newborn?

（ジャッキーに生まれたばかりの赤ちゃんがいるって知ってた？）

toddler 「よちよち歩きの赤ちゃん」

例 Look how nice that toddler's smile is.

（見て，あの赤ちゃんの笑顔，なんてかわいいんだろう）

cradle snatcher ▷自分よりずっと年下の若い女性と性的関係を持つ人のことで，「ゆりかごを盗む人」の意味です。

brand spanker 「新品」「出来立てのもの」

例 I have bought a car, it's a brand spanker.（車を買ったんだ。新車だよ）

カルチャートーク

　過去1世紀の間にイギリスでは，そしておそらく他の国でも高齢者に対する態度に変化が見られます。今では高齢者が敬意を払われたり尊敬されたりすることは少なくなり，足手まといだと考えられているようです。イギリスではこのような世代間の不和が深刻で，ほとんどの老人がテクノロジーの進歩についていけないためにますますひどくなっていると言えます。家族でもないかぎり老人と接触しようとしない人が多く，社会が分断されてしまっています。

　お年寄りと話すときは正しい文法で話し，新しいスラングはなるべく使わないようにした方がいいでしょう。老人は新しいイディオムはほとんど理解できないでしょうし，また若い人も老人が使う昔のイディオムを理解できないでしょう。

老人 VS 若者

Complaints between the Old and the Young

　年齢戦争。といっても老化するまいと必死に抵抗することを言っているのではなく，老人と若者の世代間にある戦いのことです。現代はいまだかつてないくらい激動の時代であることは確かです。私の祖父母の世代は，歴史上どの世代も経験したことがないほど大きな変化を経験してきました。ガス灯や馬や荷車の時代から，第二次世界大戦，車の普及，テレビ，ビデオなどがやってきて，そしてさらに今はDVDとインターネット，ジェット機，ロボット工学，宇宙開発競争の時代です。

　さあ，戦いの火ぶたは切って落とされました。かたや老人軍，かたや若者軍です。

老人が若者に文句を言うときの表現

● **the youth of today** 「近ごろの若者」　▷老人が文句を言うときに使う言い方。

　囲 Somebody has drawn graffiti on the wall outside my house, the youth of today!

　（だれかがうちの壁に落書きをした。まったく近ごろの若いやつは！）

● **in my day** 「私が若かったころは」

　囲 In my day nobody would draw on another's wall.（私が若かったころにはだれも他人の家の壁なんかに落書きしなかったものだ）

● **when I was a lad** 「私が若かったときは」　▷男性の高齢者が言う言葉です。lad は「男性の若者」。

　囲 When I was a lad everybody had to go in the military for two years.（私は若かったころはだれでも 2 年間軍隊へ行かなきゃならなかったもんだ）

● **when I was a lass**　「私が若かったときは」　▷高齢の女性が言う言葉です。lass は「若い娘」。

例 When I was a lass we used to go on bike rides for hours.
（私が若かったころはよく何時間もサイクリングしたものよ）

● **They don't know they've been born.**　「生まれたことも知らない」「苦労を知らない」　▷現代は生きていくのがあまりに簡単で，母親のお腹のなかにいたときと変わらないくらい安穏と暮らしているという意味で，よく使われる言い方です。

例 The youth of today complain about being bored, but when I was a lass we didn't have computers and game consoles, they don't know they've been born.（きょうびの若者はつまらないなどと文句を言うが，私が若かったころはコンピューターもゲーム機もなかった。連中ときたらまったくお気楽なものだ）

● **It's a different world.**　「世の中全く変わってしまった」　▷世の中の変化が激しくて，老人にとっては全く違う惑星のようだということ。

例 You have so much technology, it's a different world.
（なんともすごいテクノロジーだな。世の中，全く変わってしまったよ）

● **I remember when this was all fields.**　「ここが全部野原だったころを覚えている」　▷イギリスでは都市化が急速に進んでいるため，老人はほとんどの町に広々とした野原があったころを覚えています。今ではそのほとんどに建物が建ってしまっています。

例 Do you see all those houses over there; well I remember when that was all fields.（あそこにあるたくさんの家が見えるかな。あれが昔は全部野原だったもんだ）　▷例文では離れた場所のことを言っているので this が that になっています。

● **when I was wee**　「若かったとき」　▷wee はスコットランド語で「若い」という意味です。

例 When I was wee, we had to go to an outside toilet.

（若かったころは外にあるトイレに行かなければならなかった）

●**It was different in my day.** 「私が若かったころは違っていた」 ▷
老人は，昔はどんなに物事が違っていたかいつも言っています。たし
かに違っていたのでしょう。

　例 It was different in my day, we never spoke to adults in that way.
　　（昔はこうじゃなかった。私らは大人にそんな口は絶対きかなかったも
　　んだ）

若者が老人に文句を言うときの表現

　率直に言って，若者は老人のことをたいして問題だと感じていません。
彼らは楽しいことが多くて，そんなことは気にならないのです。老人は
後知恵があるので若者のやることにあれこれ文句を言いますが，若者が
老人のことを言うとしたら，せいぜい次の程度のことでしょう

●**They're out of touch.** 「ずれてる」 ▷out of touch とは現実の世
情やテクノロジーに全くついていけていないということです。

　例 The old, they're just simply out of touch.
　　（年寄りはまったくずれてるね）

●**They live in a different world.** 「住んでいる世界が違う」 ▷現代
では生活様式が全く違ってしまっているということ。

　例 My granddad lives in a different world.
　　（うちのおじいちゃんは全く住んでる世界が違う）

年寄りを指す言い方

☺ **old codger** 「老いぼれ」「偏屈な年寄り」 ▷侮蔑的な言い方です。

　例 Look at that old codger over there.
　　（あそこのもうろくじじいを見ろよ）

　例 That old codger over the road keeps shouting at me.
　　（通りの向こうの老いぼれが俺に向かって叫んでるぜ）

☺ **old fart** 「くそじじい」

例 There is always a group of old farts outside the post office, all they do is complain about the youth of today. (郵便局の外にくそじじいがいつも集まって，やることといったらいまどきの若者の悪口だけだ)

😊 **old wench** 「くそばばあ」

例 My grandmother is an old wench; she just keeps talking and talking, all day.

(うちのばあさんはくそばばあだ。一日中ずっとしゃべりっぱなしさ)

😊 **old hag** 「鬼ばばあ」 ▷醜くて意地悪な高齢の女性を言う言い方。hag には「魔女」という意味もあります。

例 My girlfriend's grandmother is an old hag.

(僕の恋人のおばあさんは鬼ばばあだ)

例 I tried to help this old woman across the road today; she got angry with me, stupid old hag. (今日ばあさんが道を渡るのを助けようとしたのに，かえって怒られた。くそばばあめ)

若者を指す言い方

👆 **yob** 「チンピラ」「与太者」 ▷反社会的行為をする若者をいう。boy を逆さに綴ったスラング。

例 These yobs just get worse. (こういう無法な若者は悪くなる一方だ)

👆 **yobbo** ▷yob に同じ。

例 There was a bunch of yobbos outside the pub, they were shouting and screaming.

(不良の一群がパブの外にいて，大声で叫んだり金切り声をあげていた)

👆 **hooligan** 「ごろつき」「ならず者」 ▷hooligan はサッカーファンについてだけ使うとよく思われますが，暴力的なならず者全般を意味します。

例 There was a group of youths skateboarding outside her house all night, what a load of hooligans! (彼女の家の外で若者たちが一晩中スケートボードをしていた。何ていうフーリガンだ！)

**カルチャー
トーク**

英語にはこう言うことわざがあります。

Youth is wasted on the young.（若さは若者には無駄だ）

おそらくこれは本当なのでしょう。私も年をとるにつれてこの言葉
の意味がわかってきました。老人には文句を言う権利があるというこ
とがはっきり言えるでしょう。

過去20年で青少年の反社会的行為は非常に増加しています。イギ
リスの若者はどんどん暴力的で危険になってきています。本当に深刻
な問題なのですが，私たちはその解決方法を見つけられずにいます。

死に関する表現

Death

　死は人類すべてが避けることのできない厄難ですが，イギリス人にとって死はロマンチックなものでもあります。死んだら，天国が待っていて，死は復活の時までの休息だと私たちは思っています。これは実にキリスト教的な考え方です。ほとんどの人はあまり熱心なキリスト教徒ではないのですが，文化の中にはいまだにこのような考え方が根強くあります。

　また，イギリス文化はバイキング，ギリシャ，ローマ，ゲルマンなどいろいろな文化の影響を受けているので，死にまつわる習慣や葬儀の中にもいろいろな文化が混ざり込んでいると言われています。

死に関するさまざまな言い方

- ☺ **(as) dead as a door nail** 「完全に死んでいる」　▽生きているかもしれないという疑問の余地がなく，完全に死んでいるということ。この言い方はシェークスピアの戯曲『ヘンリー六世』（*Henry VI*）ですでに使われているほど古くからある慣用句です。door nail とは昔，ドアの補強や装飾に使われた長い鋲釘のことです。この言い方の由来については諸説ありますが，有力なのは鋲釘をドアの外側から打ち付けて，ゆるんで抜けないように内側に飛び出した部分を叩いて曲げた（これを dead nail と言います）ことからきているという説です。

- ☺ **(as) dead as a dodo** 「死に絶えた」　▷dodo（ドードー）は人間が生息地に入り込んだために絶滅した鳥です。そこからこの表現は「（ドードーのように）死に絶えた」という意味になります。また，物事が

「廃れた」という意味でも用います。

☺ (have) gone the way of the dodo ▷上に同じ。

☺ (have) kicked the bucket 「死ぬ」「くたばる」 この由来について
も諸説あります。一説には首吊り自殺をするときに，首にロープをか
けてから乗っていたバケツを蹴ることからきていると言われています。
またカトリックでは亡くなった人の足元に聖水の入ったバケツを置い
て，親族，友人がそれを遺体に振り掛けるという習慣があったので，
そこからきているという説もあります。

☺ six feet under 「埋葬されている」「死んでいる」 ▷キリスト教の
教えでは，やがてイエスが再臨してすべてのキリスト教徒を復活させ
「神の国」に連れていく日が来るとされています。そこでは生前の肉
体に戻り，無上の幸福のなかで暮らします（ただし，キリスト教徒でな
い人はすべて地獄に行くとされているのですが）。これは the
Resurrection（キリストの復活）と呼ばれます。ですから遺体はすべ
て埋葬されていました。労働衛生安全法によると，病気の感染蔓延を
防ぐために遺体は深さ6フィート（約183センチ）のところに埋葬さ
れなければなりません。そのためだれかが「地面から6フィート下に
いる」というのは，「埋葬されている」という意味です。現在では墓
地の不足により90％の人が火葬されています。そのほうが安上がり
なのです。でもこの言い方はまだ残っています。

☺ (have) met their maker 「死ぬ」 ▷イギリス人の多くはキリスト
教徒なので，神が人類を創造し，死んだら神に会えると信じています。
そこから，「maker（創造主）に会う」とは，すなわち死ぬことを意味
します。

☺ (be) knocking on heaven's door 「今にも死にそうである」 ▷天
国へ入れてもらうために天国の扉をノックするということからきてい
ます。ボブ・ディランが1973年に発表した「天国への扉」（Knockin'
on Heaven's Door）がよく知られています。

「死」に関する上品な言い方

👍 **(have) passed away** 「亡くなった」「逝去した」

👍 **(have) lost** 「亡くなった」

👍 **the late ...** 「故～」

例 the late Mr. Baker（故ベーカー氏）

👍 **(have) gone to heaven** 「天国に行った」 ▷大人が子供に，家族やペットが死んだと教えるときに使ったりします。

カルチャートーク

　私が個人的に思っていることですが，イギリスでは日本よりも人々は死者に対してもっと遠慮がないと思います。イギリス人は日曜などの昼間によく墓地を散歩します。家族で小さい町にドライブするのはごく一般的な日曜日の過ごし方ですが，そんなとき決まってやるのが墓地の散歩です。墓地ではわざわざ一番古い墓を探したりします。これはふつう教会に一番近いところにあります。私が見つけた一番古い墓は12世紀の十字軍で戦った騎士のものでした。また，かなり珍しい趣味といえますが，墓の拓本をとる人もいます。紙を墓石の上に置いて炭でこすり墓碑銘を写し取ります。

　イギリスには死にまつわる次のような習慣や言い伝えがあります。
＊アイルランドでは Banshee（バンシー。または wailing Banshee）と呼ばれる不思議な妖精がいます（wail は「泣き叫ぶ」という意味）。これは白髪の老女で，聞いていられないくらいの大声で泣き叫びます。Banshee の声を聞いた人は家族のだれかが死ぬ，またその姿を見てしまったら自分が死ぬと言われています。
＊死んだ人の目の上にコインを 2 枚置きます。こうすると死んだ人の魂を川の向こう岸にある天国へと渡す渡し守にお金を渡して連れていってもらえるのです。この川は River Styx（ステュクス川。三途の川）と呼ばれています。もしお金を持っていなければ渡ることができません。ただしこの習慣は廃れつつあります。

＊家の中に鳥が入ってきたら家族のだれかが死ぬと言われています。

＊Ashes to ashes, dust to dust.「灰は灰へ，土は土へ」。これはだれかが埋葬されるとき，土をつかんで棺にかけながら牧師が言う言葉です。

＊Death または the Grim Reaper は「死神」を意味します。黒または白のマントをまとい，顔は骸骨，手には大きな鎌を持ち，ときには黒い翼があるという姿と考えられています。気をつけてほしいのは，死神はキリスト教の教えで神の使いだということです。このことを知らない人がほとんどですが，死神は邪悪なものではなく，死人の魂を集めるという彼に課せられた仕事をしているだけなのです。ここから the Grim Reaper という名前がきています。reap は作物などを刈り取ることです。だから大きな鎌を持っています。grim とは「気味の悪い，厳しい」などという意味ですから，つまりぞっとするような魂の収穫者というわけです。

第**4**章

生 活・社 会

天気
Weather

　イギリスは雨で有名な国です。たしかにたくさん雨が降りますが，決して毎日というわけではありません！　イギリスは大変じめじめしていますが，いつもそうとは限りません。日本と同じように四季があります。ただ，より変化が激しいのです。日本では年間を通じてどの時期でも平均気温が大体わかりますが，イギリスでは何日か暖かかったかと思うと零度近くまで急降下したり，10分雨が降ったあと午後にはバーベキューができるくらい暖かくなったりします。イギリスには基本的な天気のパターンはあるのですが，雨が降り始めたら10分続くのか3日続くのか予想がつきません。イギリスの天気について予報できることは，天気は変わる！　ということだけです。

暑さを表す表現

🫗 **(It's) hot.** 「暑い」

👐 **(It's) boiling.** 「うだるように暑い」

　　例 It was fucking boiling yesterday.（昨日はものすごく暑かった）　▷ fucking は強調です。

👐 **(It's) scorching.** 「じりじりと焼けつくように暑い」

👍 **You could fry an egg on the pavement.** 「（舗道で目玉焼きができるほど）ものすごく暑い」　▷非現実的なたとえを使って暑さを表した表現です。

寒さを表す表現

（**It's**）**cold.** 「寒い」

（**It's**）**Baltic.** 「（バルト海のように）すごく寒い」 ▷バルト海を航海する船乗りたちからきた言い方。北の果てであるバルト海と同じくらい寒いということです。軍関係者が使うことが多いでしょう。

例 It will be Baltic tomorrow. （明日はすごく冷えそうだ）

（**It's**）**freezing.** 「凍えそうに寒い」

（**It's**）**perishing.** 「（死にそうなほど）ひどく寒い」 ▷perish は「死ぬ，滅びる」という意味です。

風に関する言い方

the four winds 「あちこち」「四方八方」 ▷風は東西南北のどこからでも吹いてくるため，この慣用句ができました。

It's blowing a gale. 「風がとても強い」

例 Naomi said it was blowing a gale while she was in Yokohama.
（ナオミは横浜にいた間ずっと風が強かったと言っていた）

Billy wind 「風のビリー」 ▷風を擬人化した言い方で，子供に対して使います。

例 Billy wind is outside, put your scarf on.
（外は風があるからマフラーをしていきなさい）

雨に関連する言い方

「土砂降りである」を表すには次のような言い方があります。

It's raining cats and dogs. ▷とてもよく使う言い方です。

It's pissing down. ▷piss は「おしっこをする」の意味で下品な言い方なので，親しい友達同士でしか使えません。

It's lashing down.

It's throwing it down.

例 It's fucking throwing it down. （ひどい土砂降りだ）

▷この fucking も強調です。

👍 **It's throwing buckets down.**
👍 **It's pelting down.**

霜

👍 **Jack Frost** 「霜のジャック」　▷霜 (frost) を擬人化した言い方で, 子供に対して使います。

雪

　現在イギリスでは, 雪は山間部を除いてごくたまにしか降りません。温暖化のためとも言われていますが, 絵のようなイギリスのホワイトクリスマスはもう過去のものとなっています。けれども雪を使った言い方は残っています。

🍶 **a thick blanket of snow** 「一面に降り積もった雪」　▷ベッドにかけた毛布 (blanket) のように雪がすべてのものの上に降り積もっている様子を表します。

👍 **The snow is sticking.** 「雪が溶けずに残っている」　▷雪が地面に落ちてすぐ溶けていくかどうかを表す言い方です。もし雪が sticking なら溶けていないということで, 積もって a blanket of snow (一面の雪) になるかもしれないのです。積もらないで溶けていく場合は

　　The snow is not sticking.

と言います。

カルチャートーク

　イギリスではどんなに寒いかを表現するために, 天気があなたにどんなことをするかという言い方をすることがあります。子供のころ天気が悪いときにコートを着ないで外へ行こうとすると, 祖母によく叱られました。日本人ならこんなふうに言うでしょう。

　　Please put your coat on, it is windy outside.

　　(外は風が強いからコートを着ていきなさい)

けれども，祖母は次のように言ったものです。

Put your coat on, the wind is so strong today, it will cut you in two! (コートを着なさい。今日は風が強いから体を二つに切り裂いてしまうよ)

Don't go out without a coat, the wind will cut you to the bone. (コートを着ないで外へ行ったらだめ。風が骨までおまえを切ってしまうよ)

The wind will cut right through you!

(風がひどくておまえを切り裂いてしまうよ)

It will chill you to the bone out there, put a coat on!

(骨まで凍えてしまうからコートを着なさい！)

また，天気は擬人化されたり超自然的性質を与えられたりすることもあります。

There is a devil of a wind out there.

(外には風の悪魔がいる)［＝風がひどい］

There is an evil wind out there.

(外は邪悪な風が吹いている)［＝風がひどい］

イギリスの各地域には天気についての定評があります。一般的には次のように言われています。

スコットランド　　：とても寒くて湿度が非常に高い

イングランド北部：湿度が高くて寒い

イングランド南部：暖かくて天気がよい

ウェールズ　　　　：定評なし

アイルランド　　　：緑豊か。天気がよい

ロンドン　　　　　：湿度が高い

マンチェスター　　：ものすごく湿度が高い

このような一般化はいつも当てはまるわけではありませんが，一片の真実を含んでいます。いつもこのような天気ではありませんが，このパターンに当てはまることもあるということです。

アルコール

Alcohol

　イギリスの人々は遡ること新石器時代以降と言われるくらい古くから
アルコールを飲んできました。水が悪かったせいで水に代わる飲み物と
して必要だったのです。おかげでイギリス人は体ばかりか言葉まですっ
かり酒浸りです。

　酒を飲んで酔っ払った人を見かけるのは平日でもほとんど毎晩ですが，
特に多いのはもちろん週末です。酔っ払いを観察すると，大体 3 段階を
経るようです。まずガンガン飲むぞと宣言したがり，そして飲んで酔っ
払い，最後に月曜の朝，同僚と「週末どうだった」とおしゃべりして終
わりとなります。

　イギリスでは飲みすぎる人が多いためか，ほろ酔いの様子を表す言葉
はあまりありません。その一方で，大酒を飲んでぐでんぐでんになった
様子を表す言葉は数限りなくあります。たとえば典型的な言い方はこん
な感じです。

　　She was **totally fucking** hammered last Sunday.

　　（彼女はこの前の日曜日，べろべろに酔っ払ってた）

　太字のところは酔っ払った様子を強調しているだけです。入れれば程
度が強調できますし，入れなくてももちろん意味は通じます。fucking
をとって totally だけでも同じ意味になります。hammer は大いに飲む
ことで，この場合 hammered は「酔っ払った」状態を表します。

　また，同じように強調する言い方として以下のような表現もよく使わ
れます。

　　completely fucking

entirely fucking

fucking

「泥酔している」様子をいう表現には，たいてい "めちゃめちゃで使い物にならないひどい状態" を表す一般的な言葉が使われます。酒についての会話の中で使われると酔っ払った様子を表しますので，状況に合わせて理解することが大切です。もう一つ例文を挙げてみましょう。ここでは destroyed「壊れた」という言葉が「完全に酔っ払った」という意味で使われています。

I was **fucking** destroyed last night.（昨夜はひどく酔っ払ったよ）

アルコールに関してよく使われる表現

booze 「酒」 ▷アルコール全般を表す総称。

plonk ▷安いワイン，安酒の意。

例 I want a bottle of plonk.（お酒が 1 瓶欲しい） ▷日本の皆さんが，たとえば「酒を買いに行ってくる」と言いたいとき，

I am going to buy some alcohol.

と言うでしょうが，ネイティブならたぶんこう言います。

I am going to buy some plonk.

このように名詞を入れ替えれば文の形はそのままで大丈夫です。

pint ▷ビールなどパイント単位（ 1 パイント＝約0.57リットル）で計るアルコール。

例 I would kill for a pint.（ビールがどうしても飲みたい）

grog ▷アルコールを指す古風な言い方。

amber nectar ▷直訳すると「琥珀色の甘美な飲料」。アルコールの牧歌的な呼び方。

loopy juice ▷イギリスのリンゴ酒の別称。これは強精効果があることで知られています。loopy は「頭がおかしい，狂った」の意味で，juice は液体を表します。

例 I had some loopy juice the other night.

（この間の夜，リンゴ酒を飲んだよ）

👍 **tinny/tinnie**　▷缶に入ったアルコール。

👍 **6-pack/six-pack**　▷プラスチックでとめられたビールなどの 6 缶パックのこと。6-pack のもう一つの意味はすごく鍛えた筋肉自慢の男性の腹筋のことです。この二つの意味をかけて，酒好きの太った人が

I have a 6-pack.（6-pack 持ってるぜ）

と言ったりします。引き締まった腹筋のことかと思いきや，ビールの 6 缶パックを出してみせるわけです。

例 I will pick up a six-pack on my way home.

（帰りがけに 6 缶パックを買っていこう）

「ほろ酔い」の状態を表す表現

👍 **tipsy**　「ほろ酔いの」　▷「千鳥足」の意のくだけた言い方。

例 I will get a little tipsy tonight.（今夜ちょっと飲もうかな）

👍 **merry**　▷「陽気な」「浮かれた」ということから「ほろ酔いの」を表す口語。

例 I got a bit merry last night.（ゆうべはちょっと酔っ払った）

👍 **jolly**　▷merry と同様に「楽しい」「愉快な」の意から「ほろ酔いの」を表す口語。

例 She is a little jolly, isn't she?（彼女はちょっとご機嫌だね）

「すごく酔っ払った」状態を表す表現

😊 **blitzed**　「酔っ払った」　▷blitz には「酔わせる，電撃的攻撃をする」の意があります。

例 My mate was completely fucking blitzed last weekend.

（友達が週末ぐでんぐでんに酔っ払った）

😊 **sloshed**　「酔っ払って」　▷slosh はお酒をぐいぐい飲むこと。

例 I am going to get well and truly sloshed tonight.

（今夜は調子がよくなってほんとに酔っ払うぞ）

😊 **wasted**　「ベロベロに酔っ払った」

例 My mother was wasted last Christmas, she never usually gets that drunk.（母はクリスマスにべろべろに酔っ払った。普段は絶対そんなに飲まないのに）

☺ **destroyed** 「すっかり酔った」

☺ **annihilated** 「めちゃくちゃに酔っ払った」

　　例 I am well pissed off with work, I am going to get totally annihilated when we get to the pub.

　　（仕事のことで頭にきてるんだ。パブに行ったら徹底的に飲むぞ）

☺ **pissed** 「ひどく酔った」

　　例 Are you pissed?（酔っ払ってるの？）

☺ **wankered** 「酩酊した」

　　例 Stop doing that, your are wankered.

　　（そんなことするのはやめろ。おまえ，酔っ払ってるぞ）

☺ **blottoed**

　　例 His father gets blottoed every night.（あいつの親父は毎晩酔っ払う）

☺ **trashed** 「ぐでんぐでんに酔っ払った」

　　例 She was trashed when I saw her out.

　　（私が見送ったときには彼女はぐでんぐでんだった）

💣 **fucked** 「ひどく酔っ払った」

　　例 Nozomi is completely fucked.（のぞみはすっかり出来上がってる）

💣 **off**（**me/my/his/her/their**）**tits** ▷tits は「乳房」の意。

　　例 They are off their tits.（彼らはぐでんぐでんだ）

☺ **shedded** 「泥酔した」

　　例 Getting shedded before a date is not a good idea.

　　（デートの前に酔っ払うのはまずいよ）

👍 **screaming drunk** 「ひどく酔っ払った」

　　例 Antony is screaming drunk.（アントニーはものすごく酔っ払ってる）

👍 **plastered** 「酔っ払った」「酩酊した」

　　例 They are plastered, let's keep out of the way.

　　（やつら酔っ払ってるぞ。近寄らないようにしよう）

💣 **shit-faced** ▷get shit-faced で「酔っ払う」の意となる。

例 Only half an hour of work left, I'm going straight to the pub and I am going to get completely shit- faced.

（あと30分で仕事が終わるからパブに直行して酔いつぶれるまで飲むぞ）

☺ **hammered** 「酔っ払った」

例 I want to get hammered but I have to be up in the morning.

（飲みたいけどけど朝起きなきゃいけないんだ）

☺ **wrecked** 「ひどく酔っ払った」 ▷麻薬でふらふらの状態を表すことも多い。

例 We are off to get wrecked as quick as possible.

（もう行くよ，大いに飲みに行くんだ）

「二日酔い」を表す言い方

🍶 **hung over** 「二日酔いの」

例 I am hung over.（二日酔いだよ）

👍 **a banging headache** ▷bangingはガンガンと音をたてているような様子を表します。

例 I had a banging headache.（二日酔いで頭がガンガンした）

☺ **a screaming hangover** 「ひどい二日酔い」

例 Katsuko has a screaming hangover.（カツコはひどい二日酔いだ）

☺ **feel like shit** 「気持ちが悪い」

例 Ross feels like shit because he was out in Shinjuku all last night.

（ロスは昨夜一晩中新宿にいたから二日酔いでひどい気分だ）

👍 **feel like death warmed up** 「ひどく具合が悪い」「疲れきっている」

例 You look like death warmed up.（すごく気分悪そうだね）

☺ **cry out for huey** 「吐き気がする」 ▷cry outは「大声を出す」という意味ですから，口を大きく開けているイメージが浮かびます。Huey（ヒューイ）は古くからあるイギリス人の名前で，口から吐き戻す音に似ているために使われています。

例 I was crying out for huey.（二日酔いで吐いていた）

Did you cry out for huey?（二日酔いで吐いた？）

😊 **pray to the porcelain god** ▷飲みすぎで気分が悪くなってトイレで吐くこと。porcelainは「陶器」の意で，トイレの便器を表します。prayは「祈る」ことで，ひざまずいて祈る姿から酒に酔って便器で吐く意になります。

例 I was praying to the porcelain god.（トイレで吐いてたよ）

I'm going to the bathroom to pray to the porcelain god.

（トイレに行って吐いてくるよ）

カルチャートーク

イギリスには binge drinking（酒宴での飲みすぎ，飲んで騒ぐこと）という言葉があります。これは短時間に大量のアルコールを飲むという意味です。4時間でビールを10パイント（約5.7リットル）飲むなんていうイギリス人は珍しくありません（それほど大した量ではないと思われるかもしれませんが，イギリスのビールは日本やアメリカの"水みたいな"ビールと違ってずっと濃くて強いので，アメリカ人がイギリスに来てビールを飲むとたいてい酔い潰れると言われています）。

さて，一晩 binge drinking をやってしまったら翌朝は二日酔いと戦わなければなりません。イギリス人の二日酔い解消法といえば……

＊**水** 水をガブガブ飲んでアルコールを体から洗い流してしまおうというわけです。

＊**英国風朝食をしっかり食べる** 脂っこい英国式の伝統的な朝食を食べると二日酔いの症状がおさまるとイギリス人は信じています。この英国風の朝食は，greasy fry up とか a full breakfast，a full fucker と言われています。

I feel like shit, I need a full fucker.

（気分が悪いから，しっかり朝食を食べなくちゃ）

＊**hair of the dog（迎え酒）** 起きたら二日酔いの症状がおさま

るまでまた飲み続けます。

＊冷たいシャワーを浴びる

＊生卵を食べる

　結局二日酔いが起こらないようにするのが一番ということで，飲む前にミルクを 1 パイント飲んで胃に膜をはるという方法は一般的です。こうするとアルコールが消化されて血中に吸収されるのが遅くなります。最後に，いろいろな種類の酒を一緒に飲まないという昔ながらの方法も確実だと考えられています。

マンチェスターのパブ（Sinclairs Oyster Bar and the Old Wellington Pub, 写真：Mike Scott2）

パーティーのいたずら

Party Tricks

　人間がアルコールの蒸留を始めて以来，ずっとパーティーというものはありました。パーティーでは乱れて常軌を逸することもあります。イギリスのパーティーでよく見られる光景や悪ふざけをいくつか挙げようと思います。ここではあまり紹介できませんが，イギリスには数多くの飲み比べのゲームがあり，それについて書くだけで本一冊になってしまうくらいです。

Party Tricksのいろいろ

● the shotgun

　まず缶ビール（イギリスの缶ビールは日本のものより大きい）を上下逆さに持って上面，つまりプルトップがない底面に穴をあけます。その穴を指でふさぎ，缶を振ってから顔の上に持っていきます。次にプルトップの近くに口をもっていきプルトップを引っ張って同時に指を離します。空気が上から入るのでビールがプルトップから口へすごい勢いで入っていきます。1缶空っぽになるまでやらなければならないのですが，これはイギリスの大きい缶ではけっこう大変です。

● the yard of ale

　ビールやエール（ビールの一種）用のyard glass（ヤードグラス）という背の高い特別なグラスがあります。ほとんど1ヤード（約91.5cm）あるくらい細長いのでこの名前がついています。これは大変古いゲームで今はあまり見かけなくなりましたが，私は最近パーティーで見たことがあります。一気に1ヤードのエールを飲み干さなければなりません。

● **left handed drinking game**

これは全員が利き手と反対の手だけを使って飲むようにするというゲームです。酔っ払ってくるとこれがだんだん難しくなっていき，もし利き手で持ってしまったら飲み物を飲み干さなければなりません。

● **down a pint**

downは一気飲みすることです。１パイントはイギリスの飲み物を量る単位で約0.58リットル（アメリカでは0.55リットル）です。だれが一番速く飲み干せるか競争することもよくあります。

● **take a stupid picture of the sleeping man**

これは世界共通のいたずらではないでしょうか。酔いつぶれた人に変な格好をさせたり，食べ物を乗せたり飲み物をかけたりして写真を撮ります。

● **tea-bagging 「ティーバギング」**

これは見ている人にはかなり楽しいいたずらです。まず犠牲者を選びます。たいてい，眠り込んでしまった人か酔いつぶれてしまった人が選ばれます。その犠牲者の顔の上にだれかがパンツを下ろして（つまり下半身丸出しで）腰を下ろします。それから犠牲者を起こします。起きたら両目の上に睾丸があり，鼻と口のところには肛門がきているというわけです。

● **de-bagging**

男性のパンツを脱がすことです。皆の前で下半身丸出しにされてしまうのです。

● **testicular displacement game**

これはあまり見かけませんが，面白いゲームです。男同士でパイントグラスに水を入れておきます。順番にその中に睾丸とペニスを入れます。水があふれて陰部の体積分減るわけです。グラスに印をつけてはまた水を一杯にしてこれを繰り返します。全員がこれをやり終わって印が一番上にある人が負けです。印が一番上にあるということは一番小さい睾丸とペニスの持ち主ということになるからです。負けた人は罰として残った水を飲まなくてはなりません（私は親友がこの水を飲んでみんなが唾

然としているところを撮ったおかしい写真を持っています)。

●**human pyramid** 「人間ピラミッド」

　言葉から連想されるとおり，酔いつぶれた人をなるべくたくさん積み上げていきます。

●**the conga** 「コンガダンス」

　とても有名な踊りです。大勢の人が前の人の腰に手をあてて一列になって踊りながら家中を回ります。

カルチャートーク

　日本では，パーティーに来ませんかとよく誘われました。今は日本でいうパーティーの意味がわかるようになりましたが，イギリスとは同じではありません。イギリスではパーティーはだれかの家でやるのが普通ですが，日本では居酒屋でやります。イギリス人にとっては居酒屋に行くことはパブに行くのと同じです。だれかの家でやるパーティーの場合，たいてい乱れてものすごく飲んだりゲームをしたりします。人も大勢集まり，音楽を大きくかけたりするのが普通です。

　日本でいう「パーティー」は，英語ではgatheringに当たります。ですから

　　Do you want to come to a party?

ではなく

　　Do you want to come to a small gathering?

と言うほうが適当でしょう。

　パーティーの種類には，次のようなものもあります。

　　a dinner party（ディナーパーティー）

　　a children's party（子供のパーティー）

　　an engagement party（婚約パーティー）

盗み

Stealing

イギリスでは法律によると，

　　Possession is nine tenths of the law.

　　（占有は九分の勝ち目＝借り物は自分のもの）

という原則があります。これはもしあなたが何かをいったん占有すれば，他の人がそれが自分のものだと証明できないかぎり90％あなたのものだということです。また，

　　Finders keepers.（拾ったものは自分のもの）

という言葉もあります。その結果イギリスでは日本より人が不正直になっています。日本で財布を落としてもたぶん戻ってくるでしょうが，イギリスでは戻らないことが多く，たとえ財布は戻ったとしても中の金はまずなくなっていると思った方がよいでしょう。

「盗み」に関する言い方

🍶 **steal** 「盗む」

　　例 Don't steal; it's not right.（盗みはするな，不正なことだ）

👍 **on the rob** 「盗み」

　　例 He's been on the rob again.（彼はまた盗みをやった）

👍 **nick** 「盗む」「かっぱらう」

　　例 I have had my car nicked.（車を盗まれた）

🍶 **thieve** 「盗む」

　　例 Be careful; somebody might thieve that if you leave it there.

　　（そんなところに置きっぱなしにしたら盗まれるかもしれないから気を

つけなさい)

👍 **take** 「奪う」「取り上げる」

> 例 Don't take things that don't belong to you.
>
> (人のものを盗ってはいけない)

👍 **pinch** 「盗む」「くすねる」

> 例 She has had her purse pinched. (彼女は財布を盗まれた)

👍 **lift** 「盗む」「万引きする」

> 例 He had his wallet lifted. (彼は財布を盗まれた)

👍 **walk off with** 「持ち逃げする」

> 例 Somebody walked off with me necklace.
>
> (だれかにネックレスを持っていかれた) ▷このmeは「私の」という所有格です。第2章 (95ページ) を参照してください。

👍 **make off with** 「持ち逃げする」

> 例 If you make off with that money you will be nicked.
>
> (その金を盗んだら逮捕されるよ) ▷nickはこの場合「逮捕する」という意味です。

👍 **whip** 「(むち打つように) さっととる」

> 例 Whip that chocolate cake before my brother eats it all.
>
> (お兄ちゃんが全部食べる前にそのチョコレートケーキをとっちゃいな)

👍 **pilfer** 「くすねる」「ちょろまかす」

> 例 Antony, stop pilfering the ice cream, there will be none left for your brother. (アントニー, アイスクリームをつまみ食いするのをやめなさい, 弟の分がなくなるでしょ)

👍 **filch** 「くすねる」「盗む」

> 例 He's going to filch my stuff. (彼は私のものを盗もうとしている)

👎 **shoplift** 「万引きする」

> 例 Shoplifters will be prosecuted.
>
> (万引きは告訴します) ▷shoplifterは「万引きする人」の意味。イギリスのほとんどの店にある掲示です。

👍 **raid** 「襲う」「押し入る」

例 Somebody raided a shop in town.（だれかが町にある店に押し入った）

🔋 **robbery** 「強盗」「強奪」

例 There has been a robbery at my mate's house, he is well pissed off.（家が強盗に入られたんで，友達はすっかり頭にきてるんだ）

🔋 **burgle** 「～に泥棒に入る」

例 I have been burgled.（泥棒に入られた）

🔋 **loot** 「略奪する」

例 After the hurricane people were looting and scavenging.

（ハリケーンの後，人々は略奪やごみ漁りをした）

🔋 **relieve** 「失敬する」　▷relieve A of B で「A から B を取り除く」の意味。転じて，だれかから何かを失敬することをユーモラスに言いたいときにも使います。

例 I relieved him of his belongings.（彼の持ち物を失敬した）

🔋 **deprive** 「奪う」　▷deprive A of B で「A から B を奪う」の意味です。

例 She was deprived of her virginity.（彼女は処女を奪われた）

🔋 **acquire** 「手に入れる」「盗む」　▷本来はふつうに「入手する」を意味する語ですが，steal の意味で使うこともあります。

例 He acquired it through underhanded means.

（彼は汚い手をつかってそれを手に入れた）

🔋 **snatch** 「ひったくる」

例 He snatched the woman's purse on the bus.

（彼はバスに乗っていた女性のかばんをひったくった）

🔋 **ram-raid**　▷車で店に突っ込んで商品を奪うこと。

例 The jewellery shop on the high street was ram-raided at the weekend.（表通りの宝石店は週末に車で襲撃され盗みに入られた）

🔋 **joy-ride**　▷（若者などが）車を盗んでガソリンがなくなるまで乗り回すこと。

例 Four male youths were killed in a road traffic accident during a joy-ride.（4 人の若者が盗んだ車を乗り回していて交通事故で死んだ）

「詐欺」に関する言い方

👍 **daylight robbery** 「白昼強盗」 ▷請求があまりにも高いので強盗のようだという言い方です。

🚫 **have been jewed** 「ぼられる」 ▷人種差別的でとてもネガティブな言い方です。ユダヤ人（the Jewish）は金をためこんでいるという固定観念があるので，高く払わされたときにこう言います。

👍 **They saw you coming.** 「あなたはカモにされた」 ▷文字どおりには「彼ら（店員）はあなたが来るのを見ていた」ですが，着飾って買い物に来た金持ちを見て店員が値を吊り上げるということから，こうした言い方が生まれたのではないかと思います。

👍 **con** 「詐欺」「ペテン」「損な取引」

👍 **You've been had.** 「あなたはぼられた」 ▷be had は「ぼられる」，つまり相手があなたより得をするという意味です。

👍 **ripped off** 「ふんだくられる」 ▷これも jewed と同様に必ず完了形で使われます。

カルチャートーク

　イギリス人の買い物客が一番気にするのはぼられないで得な買い物をすることです。日本に住んでいたとき，私は日本の人たちがブランド品に高いお金を払うのに驚き，実用品でも簡単に高いお金を払うことによく驚いたものでした。ブランド品や高価なものを買うイギリス人もいますが，日本では低所得者でもお金をためて高価なブランド品を買うのに対して，イギリスではふつう高価なブランド品は富裕層が買うものです。ほとんどの人は安い買い物がしたいといつも考えているので，逆に安い買い物ができなかったときに「ぼったくられた」という言葉がたくさん生まれたのでしょう。

暴力

Violence

　イギリスの歴史上，かなり長い間，法律の体系は暴力を基盤としていました。有史以前から中世にかけて「決闘裁判」（trial by combat）として知られるものが存在していたのですが，その基本的な考え方は，もし二人の人がけんかをしてどちらも自分が正しいと言って譲らなければ，とことんまで戦ってどちらが正しいか決めるというものです。戦えば嘘をついている者は正しい者に勝つことはできないと当時は信じられていたので，それが正当化されていたのです。

　この"正当な戦い（fair fight）"という考え方は私たちの世代にまで綿々と引き継がれています。子供のころ私は柄の悪い地域で育ったのですが，私の母は子供のけんかが始まるとたとえ相手のほうが数が多くても私が勝たないかぎり家には入れてくれませんでした。

暴力に関連する表現のいろいろ

　この種の言葉が会話で話されるとしたら，暴力をふるうぞという脅しとか，過去のけんかや暴力沙汰で起こったことを話すという場合が考えられます。暴力的行為を表す語句を使うであろういろいろな状況を想定してみましょう。

punch　「パンチ」
　例 I will punch you if you don't shut up.（黙らないと殴るぞ）

knuckle sandwich　▷顔面へのパンチ。特に口元辺りに食らわせるパンチのこと。

例 If you don't eat your vegetables I will give you a knuckle sandwich.

（野菜を食べないとゲンコツだぞ）　▷父親が子供に言う軽い脅し。

👍 **square jaw**　▷顔面，特にあごにパンチすること。

例 He shouted at Mike and then Mike square jawed him.

（やつがマイクにどなったらマイクにあごをパンチされた）

👎 **jab**　「ジャブ」　▷相手に近い腕で素早く繰り出すパンチ。

例 His jab was so fast I didn't see it coming.

（彼のジャブは速くて目にも留まらなかった）

👎 **hook**　「フック」　▷顔面の横を引っ掛けるように打つパンチ。

例 The man on the left caught the man on the right with a hook.

（左の男が右の男にフックを食らわせた）

👍 **windmill**　「ウィンドミルパンチ」　▷攻撃する人が後方に手を伸ばしてから大きく振り回すパンチ。風車（windmill）の羽根の動きからの命名。

例 That guy cannot fight, he was just wind-milling.

（あいつにけんかはできない，ただ腕を振り回していただけだ）

👎 **one inch punch**　「ワンインチパンチ」　▷寸勁（すんけい）。ブルース・リー主演の映画『燃えよドラゴン』（*Enter the Dragon*）で有名になったパンチ。相手からほんの 1 インチ（約2.5センチ）の距離から打つのですが，ものすごいダメージを与えます。

例 He did the one inch punch.（彼はワンインチパンチを繰り出した）

👎 **uppercut**　「アッパーカット」　▷あごの下を狙って打つ上向きのパンチ。

例 I didn't see the uppercut coming, the next moment I was on the floor.（アッパーカットがくるのが見えなくて次の瞬間には床に倒れていた）

👍 **kidney dig**　「キドニーパンチ」　▷背面の腎臓のあたりを打つパンチ。dig は「打つ」の意。

例 I will give you a kidney dig if you don't shut up.

（黙らないとキドニーパンチをお見舞いするぞ）

👍 **donkey punch**　「ドンキーパンチ（をする）」　▷背面の腎臓あたりを打つパンチ。

　　例 He was donkey punching.（ドンキーパンチをしていた）

👍 **dead leg**　「足のしびれ」　▷感覚がなくなるまで足を打つこと。

　　例 I hit my leg on the corner of the table and now I have a dead leg.
　　（テーブルの角に足をぶつけて，痛くて足がしびれている）

👍 **dead arm**　▷感覚がなくなるまで腕を打つこと。

　　例 That hurt, I have a dead arm now!（痛かったよ。まだ腕がしびれてる）

🍶 **slap**　「平手打ち」「平手打ちする」

　　例 If you don't be quiet I will give you a slap.（黙らないと張り倒すぞ）

🍶 **headbutt**（または **butt**）　「頭突き」「～に頭突きを食らわす」

　　例 He butted me so hard that my nose broke.
　　（ひどい頭突きをされて，鼻が折れた）

👍 **nut**　「頭突き」「頭突きをする」　▷headbutt の別名。

　　例 I gave him a cracking nut.（あいつに強烈な頭突きをした）　▷この
　　cracking は「非常に優れている」の意。

😊 **Glasgow kiss**　▷headbutt の別名。スコットランドのグラスゴー出身の人はけんかと頭突きで有名であることから。

　　例 I went to Scotland, it was not good, I got the Glasgow kiss.
　　（スコットランドに行ったけどよくなかった。頭突きを食らったよ）

🍶 **kick**　「蹴り」「蹴る」

　　例 I kicked him in the balls.
　　（彼の睾丸を蹴った）　▷この balls は男性の睾丸のこと。

🍶 **round house**　「回し蹴り」

　　例 That guy must know karate, he did a round house to my head.
　　（あいつ頭に回し蹴りするなんてきっと空手をやってるぞ）

🍶 **back kick**　「後ろ蹴り」「後ろ蹴りをする」

　　例 He back kicked me in the fucking stomach.（彼に腹に後ろ蹴りをされた）　▷この fucking は驚き，信じられない気持ちを表してい

ます。

🍶 **front kick** 「前蹴り」「前蹴りをする」

例 I can front kick really high.（すごく高く前蹴りができる）

🍶 **eye gouge** 「目つぶし」「目つぶしをする」

例 If you don't get out of my face I will gouge out your eyes.

（そこをどかないと目玉に指をつっこむぞ）

🖐 **fish hook** ▷相手の口の中に指を入れて引っ掛け, 唇や頬を裂くこと。fish hook には「釣り針」の意がある。

例 Did you see that guy in the film, he fish hooked someone, I have not seen someone do that for years.

（あの映画の男を見たかい？ 口ん中に指を突っ込んでたけど, あんなことやるやつしばらく見たことがなかったよ）

🍶 **knee** 「ひざ蹴り」「ひざ蹴りをする」

例 He tried to rugby tackle me so I kneed him in the fucking head.

（彼が俺をタックルして倒そうとしたから俺のほうがやつの頭にひざ蹴りをした） ▷rugby tackle は体重を相手の腿にかけて引き倒すこと。またこの fucking はさらに攻撃的にするために付け加えています。

🍶 **elbow** 「ひじ打ち」「ひじ打ちをする」

例 I elbowed my mate in the head by accident.

（間違って友達にひじ打ちをしてしまった）

🍶 **choke** 「窒息させる」 ▷のど笛を締め付けること。

例 If he does not shut up I am going to choke him to death.

（あいつが黙らなければ首を締め上げてやる）

🍶 **strangle** 「のどを絞める」 ▷首を押さえて脳への血流を遮断すること。strangle と choke は混同されることが多く, 同じように使われています。

例 The man attacked me and he tried to strangle me.

（あの男が攻撃してきて俺の首を絞めようとした）

🍶 **stab** 「刺す」「突く」 ▷ナイフで刺すこと。

例 I have been stabbed three times in the leg.（足を 3 回刺された）

👍 **knife** ▷ナイフで刺すこと。

　例 My friend was knifed last week, he is in hospital.

　　（友達が先週刺されて入院中だ）

😊 **stick you** 「突き刺す」 ▷ナイフで刺すという脅し。発音はstick yaとなる。

　例 I'm going to stick ya, you fucking idiot.（刺すぞ，馬鹿野郎）

🍶 **slash** 「切り裂く」 ▷ナイフで切りつけられること。slashには「小便」の意もあるので注意してください。

　例 He slashed me across the face.（彼は私の顔を切りつけた） ▷このslashは「小便をする」意ではありません。もし誰かの顔に小便をひっかけるという場合は，He had a slash on my face. となります。

🍶 **pistol whip** ▷ピストル（の台尻）で顔や頭を殴ること。

　例 In the film the hero pistol whipped him on the back of the head.

　　（映画で主人公が彼の後頭部を銃尻で殴った）

👍 **box your ears** 「横っ面を殴る」 ▷悪いことをして叱るときに頭を打つこと。父親が小さい息子によく言う言い方です。

　例 If you don't go to bed I will box your ears in.

　　（寝ないとおしおきだぞ） ▷inは頭にめり込ませるというニュアンスで，よく上のように言います。

👍 **gut him/her** ▷腹を割いて腸を引きずり出すこと。

　例 I watched a film about the yakuza the other day and the gangster gutted the other guy with a knife.（この間見たやくざ映画でやくざが相手のはらわたをナイフでえぐり出してた）

🍶 **wind** ▷胸骨の下あたりを打つこと。息ができなくなる。

　例 I was playing football the other day and a guy winded me when we collided.（この間サッカーをやっていたら，誰かがぶつかってきて胸を打って息ができなくなった）

カルチャー トーク

　イギリスではけんかに対する考え方が，近年，ごく短い間にすっかり変わってしまいました。私の父が若かったころは，二人の男が同意の上でけんかするかぎりだれも止めに入らなかったそうです。しかし最近のイギリスでは，けんかは社会的に大きなタブーになっていて法律で厳しく罰せられます。それでも夜の都会の真ん中はまだかなり危険です。撃たれたり刺されたりということはまずないでしょうが，けんかには出くわすことはあるでしょうし，気をつけなければ巻き込まれかねません。

　私たちに馴染みのある古いイディオムからけんかにまつわるものを挙げてみましょう。

＊throw down the gauntlet

　　（戦いを挑む。挑戦状をたたきつける）

　これは昔の決闘の習慣からきています。侮辱を受けた男は（中世騎士の）籠手（gauntlet）をぬいで床にたたきつけました。相手の男がこれを拾ったら彼は挑戦をうけたことになり決闘になります。現代ではスポーツやビジネスなどで相手に挑戦をするとき比喩的にこのイディオムが使われます。

　　slap the man in the face with the glove

　　（手袋で相手の顔を打つ）

という言い方もあります。

＊pistols at dawn（夜明けの決闘［明朝ピストルで決闘だ］）

　手袋が投げつけられ挑戦が受けられたら，二人は決闘の時間と場所を決めます。決闘はたいてい夜明けに行われました。火器伝来以降はピストルが使われました。そこから今では二人が言い争いになった場合，

　　They are having pistols at dawn.（彼らは言い争いをしている）

のように言います。

ドラッグカルチャー

The Drug Culture

犯罪と暴力の巣窟と映画で描かれているような過酷な裏社会。たしかにこれもドラッグの一面ではありますが，ドラッグの世界にはもう一つの顔があります。イギリスではドラッグカルチャーが蔓延していて，一般家庭のほんの玄関先まできているのです。

暴力と犯罪はたいていドラッグの売人を連想させます。犯罪の多くが行き着くところはドラッグがらみのギャングの抗争ではないか，と思われることもあるでしょう。現実には，知り合いにドラッグの売人がいなくても，ドラッグをやる友達から自然に情報が入るでしょう。ドラッグの世界もカルチャーの面では犯罪性も限られており，ほとんどただの気晴らしとしてのドラッグに関する用語がたくさんあるだけです。

イギリスであなたの知人が非常に高い割合でドラッグをやるからといってショックを受けないでください。ドラッグはA，B，Cという三つのクラスに分類されます。クラスAは最も危険で，クラスCは毒性が最も低いと言われています。みなさんはドラッグカルチャーから生まれた言葉など知りたくないかもしれませんが，現実に英語を使う限り映画やニュースや会話の中できっと耳にすることがあるでしょう。悲しいことですが，ドラッグがらみの犯罪と闘う人やそれに警鐘を鳴らす人がいる一方で，そうした状況を利用する人もいます。蔓延するドラッグに対して人々はさまざまなかかわりをもっていますが，だれもそれを食い止めることができない状態です。ドラッグはイギリスの現実であり，なかば公然となっているのです。

麻薬全般に関する表現

🏺 **narcotics** ▷ドラッグ類全般を指す科学的用語。

例 Today the police seized a shipment of narcotics bound for the streets of London.（今日警察はロンドン市街に出荷された麻薬を押収した） ▷よくあるニュース記事です。

🏺 **drugs** ▷麻薬を意味する一般的用語。

● **shit** ▷ドラッグに関する文脈では麻薬の意味になります。「くそ」という意味もありますので注意してください。

● **gear** ▷麻薬を表す俗語。

● **substance** ▷麻薬, 薬物を表す一般的な語。

例 The suspect has been involved in substance abuse.（容疑者は麻薬乱用にかかわっていた） ▷警察のコメントなどでよく聞きます。

麻薬のいろいろ

❖コカイン

コカインはアメリカ映画の影響で, いかにも犯罪者が使いそうなイメージがありますが, イギリスではプレッシャーを強く受けるエリートビジネスマンによく使われています。コカインは高価なので高収入の人しか買えません。また, このようなストレスの強い職業の人々は, 集中力やエネルギーを持続させるために使うことが多いのです。

ちなみに, コカコーラは内容物にコカインが含まれていたためその名前がつきましたが, コカインが欧米で違法化されてからは使われていません。

🏺 **cocaine** ▷コカインを表す一般的な語。

● **coke** ▷cocaine を略した俗語。

例 I had a gram of coke.（コカインを1g持っていた）

● **snow** ▷コカインを表す俗語。コカインは白い粉であるため。

例 He was snorting snow the other day.
（彼はこの間コカインを鼻から吸い込んでいた）

● **Charlie**　▷コカインを表す俗語。

● **blow**　▷コカインを表す俗語。

● **pink champagne**　▷スピードとコカインを混ぜたもので，ピンク
色をしています。

❖マリファナ（🏺marijuana）

　マリファナはイギリス文化ではかなり容認されています。まだ違法で
はあるのですが，麻薬のなかでも非常に程度の軽いものであると考えら
れています。警察はマリファナに対し強い態度をとっていますが，マリ
ファナを吸ったからといって刑務所に行くことはありませんし，一度は
使ったことがある人も多いでしょう。通りで人々がマリファナを吸って
いても驚かないでください。まさか警察官の目の前ではやらないですが，
道を歩いていてマリファナのにおいがしてくることはしょっちゅうあり
ます。

＊マリファナを表す語

● **hash**

● **dooby**

● **dope**　▷アメリカ用法ですがイギリスでも使われます。

● **ganja**　▷marijuanaが転訛したもの。

● **shit**　▷ドラッグ全般に使う語ですが，マリファナの意味にも使われ
ます。

● **leaf**　▷マリファナには葉が使われるため。sweet leafとも言います。

● **weed**　▷マリファナが雑草のように見えて，植物の形で使われてい
るため。

● **grass**　▷草であることから。

● **green**　▷緑色であるため。アメリカではgreenというと「お金」の
意味もあるので注意してください。

● **bud**　▷マリファナの花穂（bud）から。

● **smoke**　▷白い煙が出るため。

＊加工したマリファナ

● **solid**　▷茶色い小さなブロック状に加工したもの。

● **space cakes** ▷材料にマリファナを混ぜて焼いたケーキ。

＊紙巻きマリファナたばこを表す語

● **dooby snack**

● **spliff**

● **joint**

＊マリファナ吸引用具

● **bong** ▷マリファナ吸引用水パイプ。

● **bucket** ▷マリファナを吸う器具。またはそれを使ってマリファナ
を吸うこと。水を入れたバケツを使うためこう呼ばれます。

　例 Do you want to do a bucket?（マリファナ吸う？）

❖エクスタシー（🏺 ecstasy）

● **E** ▷ecstasyの頭文字から。エクスタシーの人気が最高潮だった
1980年代，1990年代にエクスタシーを表す言葉として最も一般的で
した。

● **pills** ▷今ではEよりもこちらの方がよく使われます。happy pills
とも言います。

● **smiley faces** ▷スマイルマークがついているエクスタシー錠がある
ため。

● **disco biscuits** ▷ディスコやレイブ（大がかりなディスコパーティー）
でエクスタシーがよく使われていたため。

❖アンフェタミン（🏺 amphetamine，覚せい剤）

● **speed** ▷即効性があることから。

● **wiz**

● **billy**

● **fet** ▷amphetamineを縮めた言い方。

● **go** ▷他の語ほど使われません。

❖LSD 🏺 を表す語

● **acid** ▷アシッドハウス音楽（アナログシンセサイザーの変調効果
を多用した電子音楽）を連想させる語で，よく使われます。

● **trips**

● **tabs**　▷LSDを染み込ませた紙状のもの。

❖アヘン（🏺 opium）

　アヘンはかつて20世紀初頭に世界的に広まりましたが，今では精製してモルヒネやコカインとして使われることがほとんどです。

● **poppy**　▷アヘンはpoppy（ケシ）の種からとるためこう呼ばれます。ヘロインの入ったマリファナたばこのことを指すこともあります。

❖ヘロイン（🏺 heroin）

● **smack**　▷ヘロイン注射をするときに，腕の静脈を浮き出させるため腕を強くたたく（smack）ことから。

● **brown**　▷精製過程で燃焼させて茶色になることから。

❖デートレイプ薬（🏺 date rape drug）

　GHB（ガンマヒドロキシ酪酸）のことです。女性を酩酊させてレイプするのに使われることが多かったためこのように呼ばれています。

　　例 A girl was sexually abused after her drink had been 'spiked' with the date rape drug.

　　（デートレイプ薬を飲み物にたらされて女の子が性的暴行を受けた）

❖マジックマッシュルーム（magic mushroom）

　幻覚を引き起こす作用のある自生しているきのこ類です。縮めてshroomとも言います。

重さに関する表現

　ドラッグの売買は重さで行われます。

● **gram**　「グラム」

　　例 I want a gram of Charlie.（コカインを 1 グラム欲しい）

● **ounce**　「オンス」　▷ 1 オンス＝約28グラム。

　　例 She bought an ounce of weed.（彼女はマリファナを 1 オンス買った）

● **kilogram**　「キログラム」

● **kilo**　「キログラム」　▷kilogramを短縮した語です。

　　例 They had a kilo stolen on Monday night.

（彼らは月曜の夜 1 キロ盗まれた）

● **keys** 「キログラム」　▷kilo と音が似ているため使われる隠語。正式な綴りはなく，ただ口で言われるだけです。ここでは発音が正しく伝わるようにこの綴りを選んであります。

● **bar**　▷棒状に成形されたドラッグの切片。

値段に関する言い方

　少量のドラッグは決まった値段の分だけ袋詰めして売られています。単位はイギリス通貨のポンドです。

● **10 bag**　▷10 ポンド分のマリファナ袋詰め。
　　例 Can I just have a ten bag this time?
　　　（今日は 10 ポンド袋を 1 袋だけくれ）
● **20 bag**　▷20 ポンド分のマリファナ袋詰め。
　　例 I found a twenty bag the other day hidden in my drawers.
　　　（この間引き出しに隠してあった 20 ポンド袋を見つけた）

表現のいろいろ

● **Are you holding ...?**（～を持ってる？）
● **I've just had some top ...**（すごくいい～が手に入ったんだ）
● **Have you got any ...**（～を持ってる？）
上のような文の後に，以下のドラッグを表す単語が続きます。
＋ shit/gear/drugs/cocaine/coke/snow/Charlie/blow/marijuana/weed/grass/green/smoke/shit/hash/dope/solid/ganja/bud/leaf/sweet leaf/dooby/dooby snack(s)/ecstasy/E/pills/happy pills/smiley faces/disco biscuits/speed/wiz/Billy/fet/go
● **I fancy a ...**（～が欲しい）
● **Shall we have a ...?**（～をやろうか？）
● **He's having a ...**（彼は～をやっている）
　　＋ bong/joint/bucket/spliff

●**I'm tripping on ...**（〜をやってトリップしている）
　+ acid/tabs

**カルチャー
トーク**

　　イギリスの人々は仲間うちではよく自分のドラッグ乱用についてオープンに話します。ドラッグの使用方法についてよく使われる言葉に次のようなものがあります。映画やパーティーなどの人の集まりなどで耳にすることがあるかもしれません。

　snort（コカインを鼻で吸い込む）

　line（吸い込むために筋状に置いたコカイン）

　drop（[錠剤を] 摂取する）　▷多くはLSDについて使われます。

　high（ハイになって）　▷ドラッグに酔って気分が高揚した状態を表します。

　downer（ドラッグが切れたときにおちいるうつ状態）

　whitey（ドラッグの乱用のため気分が悪くなっている人の症状）　▷顔が青白いことからきています。たいていマリファナについて使う言葉です。

　toke（タバコの煙やドラッグの煙を吸うこと）

人 種 差 別 語

Racist Words

　イギリスは紛れもなく多文化（multicultural）国家です。第二次世界大戦以降，大量の移民や外国人が入ってきた結果，人種間の緊張関係は非常に高まってきており，最近ではEU諸国からの移民が波のように押し寄せてきています。そのためもしイギリス文化をよく知ろうとするなら，いやでも人種差別的な言葉を耳にすることになります。この章に出てくる語句は決して自分から口にしないことを強くお勧めしますが，理解しておくことは非常に大切です。

　もしあなたが人種差別的な会話に入ってしまったら，山ほどこの種の言葉を聞くでしょうが，おそらくそのすべてが言葉の暴力であり，他の文化を貶めるものです。以下の例文を見れば，英語がいかに攻撃的な言葉と文法を持っているかおわかりになるでしょう。例文の中でfuckという言葉が繰り返し出てきますが，fuckにはたくさんの意味があり，それぞれ違った意味で使われています。

黒人black peopleを表す表現

🚫 **nigger**　▷黒人の蔑称。おそらく最悪の侮蔑語ですが，他のcoon，boonなどの蔑称も同じく非常に侮蔑的ですから絶対に使わないでください。

　　例 You stupid fucking nigger.（馬鹿な黒人野郎だな！）

🚫 **nigga**　▷niggerの別の言い方で，黒人同士で用いられ，特にラップ音楽などでよく使われます。黒人以外は決して使いません。

　　例 What's up, my nigga?（元気？）　▷これは黒人同士で使われる言

い方です。黒人が使うかぎり問題ないのです。

🚫 **coon**　▷黒人の蔑称。

例 This pub is full of fucking coons.（このパブは黒人でいっぱいだ）

🚫 **boon**　▷黒人の蔑称。

例 Look at all those fucking boons.（あの黒人のやつらを見ろよ）

🚫 **spade**　▷黒人の蔑称。トランプのスペードが黒いことからきています。黒人を侮蔑した as black as the ace of spades（真っ黒で汚い）というよく知られたイディオムがあります。

例 I am not racist. I call a spade a spade and a spick a spick.（私は人種差別はしない。黒人を黒人、ヒスパニックをヒスパニックと呼ぶだけだ［ありのままにものを言っているんだ］）　▷これはよく知られている言い方で、自分は人種差別していないと言いながらまわりの人を見下しているような人が使います。これはあるイギリス海軍の下士官がかつて私に言った言葉です。

🚫 **chalky**　▷チョーク（chalk）は白いので逆説的に黒人に対して使うようになりました。イギリスの軍隊でよく使われていましたが、今はあまり使われないようになってきました。

例 Come on chalky, keep up with the white guys.
（おい、黒人、白人に負けるなよ）

🚫 **spear chucker**　▷chuck は「投げる」意なので、「槍（spear）を投げる人」。槍と盾を持ったよくあるアフリカ人のイメージからきています。

例 Hey, spear chucker, fuck off.（おい、黒人、あっちへ行け）

🚫 **shake spear**　▷「槍を振る」という意味で上記と同様に黒人を指します。これはシェークスピアにかけた駄洒落です。

例 Hey we have a playwright in the house, look it's shake spear.
（おい、この家に黒人の劇作家先生がいるぞ、見ろよ）

🚫 **shade**　▷影が黒いことからきている黒人の蔑称。

例 Hey it just got dark in here, look at all the shades.
（おい、なんか暗くなったぞ。見ろよ、あんなに黒人がいるぞ）

💣 **big mamma** ▷太った黒人女性のこと。

例 Look at the arse of that big mamma.（あのビッグママの尻を見ろよ）

🚫 **blacky** ▷黒人の蔑称。

例 Hey, blacky, why don't you and your mates fuck off?

（おい，黒人，仲間と一緒に出て行け）

💣 **golly wog** ▷ゴリウォグ。golliwog とも。黒人を指す古風な言い方。ゴリウォグ（ゴーリーとも）は真っ黒な顔をした人形ですが，1895年にフローレンス・アプトン（Florence Upton）が挿絵を描き，母親のバーサ・アプトン（Bertha Upton）が物語を書いた絵本で登場し，人気を博しました。イギリスの食品メーカー，ロバートソン社は1900年代の初め，商標として Golly をイメージキャラクターに使用しました。かつてイギリスのある有名なジャムメーカーの名前でしたが，名前とマークを変えざるをえなくなりました。

🚫 **wog** ▷黒人の蔑称。

例 Fuck off back to the jungle, you fucking wog.

（この黒人野郎，ジャングルへ帰れ！）

🚫 **golly** ▷黒人の蔑称。

🚫 **tree swingers** ▷黒人はいまだに原始的なサルのように木の上で暮らしていると馬鹿にしている言い方。

例 Climb the trees, tree swinger.（木に登れよ，黒人のサル）

☺ **wigger** ▷ウィッガー。white と nigger をくっつけた語。黒人のラッパーやギャングを気取ってアクセントやスタイルをまねしている白人のこと。

例 Look at that tosser, he thinks he's a wigger.

（あの馬鹿を見ろよ，黒人のつもりだぜ）

🚫 **coconut** ▷自分の祖先と縁を切りたいと思っている黒人を言う言い方です。本人の努力で英国の上の階級にのし上がっているため，外側は黒く，中は白いココナッツのようだという意味です。

例 Look at that shade in the suit, he wants to be a coconut.

（あのスーツを着た黒人を見ろよ。白人になりたがってるぜ）

🚫 **spick** ▷黒人やラテン系の人を指す蔑称。

外国人に対する表現

❖日本人 Japanese

🚫 **Nip** ▷日本人の蔑称。Nipponからきている。

例 Look at that fit nip.（あのまぶい日本人女を見ろよ） ▷fitはここでは「美しい」という意味です。日本女性は多くのイギリス人男性の憧れです。

🚫 **Jap** ▷日本人の蔑称。

例 I remember fighting the fucking Japs in the war, they were fucking psycho.（戦争では日本人のやつらと戦ったもんだ。あいつらは完全に頭がいかれてた）

🚫 **Japs** ▷Japの複数形。

🚫 **slant eyed/slanty eye** ▷slant（またはslanty）は「吊り上った」の意。アジア人の目の形を表します。

例 Hey, slanty eye, fuck off before I nut you.

　（おい，吊り目，出て行かないと殺すぞ）

😊 **kamikaze** ▷第二次世界大戦のときの神風特攻隊から英語になった言葉で「死を省みないほど無謀な（ことをする人）」という意味で使われますが，場合によっては日本人を指すこともあります。

例 Hey, look out, the fucking kamikazes are here.

　（おい気をつけろ。カミカゼ野郎がここにいるぞ）

❖中国人 Chinese

🚫 **Chinks** ▷中国人の蔑称。

例 I'm going to the Chinky for dinner.（これから夕飯を食べに中国人の店に行くんだ） ▷イギリスのフィッシュアンドチップスの店の大半は中国人が経営していて，このような店はChinkyと言われます。

🚫 **slant eyed/slanty eye** 「吊り目」 ▷「日本人」と同じ。

❖イラク人 Iraqi

◉ jam-raqi ▷イラク人の蔑称。

例 Look out for jam-raqis, those terrorist bastards.

（イラク野郎に気をつけろ。テロリスト野郎だぞ）

◉ rag head ▷rag は「ぼろ布」の意。ターバンからきた呼び名。

例 Be careful of any suicide bombers. There are loads of rag heads around here.

（自爆テロに気をつけろ。このへんはターバン野郎がいっぱいだぞ）

❖フランス人　French

☺ Frog ▷フランス人が蛙の足を食べるので。

例 The Frogs are fucking queers.（フランス人はほんとに変なやつらだ）

☺ Froggie ▷上に同じ。

☺ Frenchie ▷フランス人の一般的言い方。

例 Hey, Frenchie, sell me some onions.（おい，フランス野郎，玉ねぎを売ってくれよ）　▷よくあるフランス人のイメージは青と白の洋服にベレー帽をかぶり，自転車にのって玉ねぎを売っているというもの。

❖ドイツ人　German

☺ Gerry ▷ドイツ人の一般的言い方。

例 In the war we had to watch out for Gerry all the time.

（戦争中はずっとドイツ人に気をつけなきゃならなかった）

◉ Nazi ▷ナチスは現在では存在しませんが，いまだにドイツ人はナチスと呼ばれることがあります。また，ドイツ人に対して使うと侮蔑的になりますが，それ以外の人に「やたらとうるさく指図したがる人」という意味で冗談ぽく使うこともあります。

例 Hail Hitler, the Nazis are here.（ハイルヒットラー，ナチスがいるぞ）

❖パキスタン人　Pakistani

◉ Paki ▷Pakistani（パキスタン人）を縮めたもの。

例 I'm off to the paki shop for some cigs.（パキスタン人の店までタバコを買いにいってくるよ）　▷イギリスのコンビニエンスストアはパキスタン人かその周辺のアジア人がオーナーであることがよくあ

ります。

🚫 **a bud, bud ding, ding**　▷パキスタン周辺の言葉がイギリス人には
こう聞こえるというふざけた言い方です。

🚫 **rag head**　▷ターバンからきた呼び名。

❖オーストラリア人　Australian

🥄 **Aussie**　▷会話で普通に使われているごく一般的でなじみのある言
い方。たいていの場合使えますが，もし確信が持てないようでしたら
Australian と言った方が無難です。

　　㋹ Aussie women are well fit.（オーストラリアの女はいけてるぞ）　▷
　　これは差別的な言い方ではありません。

❖イタリア人　Italian

😊 **I-tai**　▷Italian という音を使った洒落。

　　㋹ I love I-tai food.（イタリア料理が好きだ）

　　　＊

　この節をお読みになって黒人に関する差別語が他の人種に比べて多い
と感じられたのではないでしょうか。イギリスは第２次大戦後，労働力
としてたくさんの黒人を受け入れました。その結果仕事を奪われた白人
の間に反感が生まれ，それに伴い差別語もまた数々生まれたのです。ま
た，当時は差別が比較的平然と見過ごされていたという社会状況もあり
ました。

　現在では黒人よりもパキスタン人やポーランド人などの増加が目覚ま
しく，これも新たな摩擦を生んでいます。けれども今ではずっと人種差
別に関して社会が敏感になっており，よほどのことがなければ大っぴら
に差別語を言う人はいなくなりました。そのためにかつての黒人に比べ
差別語が生まれにくい状況にあると言えます。

　　　＊

　このような人種差別語はどんな場面でも絶対に使わないでください。2,
30年前には許容されていた言葉でも現在では重大なタブーとなってい

ます。もしだれかが口にすればその人はかなり顰蹙を買うでしょうし，説明を求められて苦しい立場に追い込まれるでしょう。

　2008年のアメリカ大統領選の際，イギリスの閣僚がオバマ大統領当選のニュースを聞いて，次のようなジョークを言ったことが報じられました。

　　"U.K. could put golliwog back on jam jars now Obama's been erected."（オバマが当選したんだからイギリスもゴリウォグをジャムの瓶に復活させてもいいんじゃないか）

　この発言は世界中のメディアに取り上げられ，彼は失職することは免れたものの重大な苦境に立たされました。

　またごく最近にも，元イギリス首相のマーガレット・サッチャーの娘がテニスの黒人選手のことを"golliwog"と冗談で呼んだことが報道されてしまい，彼女は番組のキャスターを降板させられました。

　このように，人種差別語は表向きには使われないようになっていますが，死語になっているわけではなく人々の頭の中にはいまだに根強く残っています。もし何かの折にそれが口をついて出た場合，重大な問題と見なされます。その人が有名人または公職にある場合などはなおさらなのです。

**カルチャー
トーク**

　　イギリス社会の顔はこの50年で劇的に変化しました。非白人の割合は増加の一途をたどり，それに伴い英語そのものやアクセント（訛り）も大きく変化しています。外国語訛りが大量に流入したため英語がさまざまな色合いを帯びるようになり，その結果イギリスの国内にいてさえコミュニケーションが難しい状況が生まれています。特にここ10年ほどでEU諸国に労働市場をいちはやく開放する政策をとり移民労働者の数は飛躍的に増加しました。いまやイギリスは確実に多文化社会であり，プラスとマイナス両面でさまざまな変化が起こっています。プラス面としてはイギリスの文化の多様性は従来と比べて格段に豊かになりました。その反面では外国人労働者に対する反発も見られるようになっています。必然的に人種差別的な発言はどんなものでも厳しく糾弾され，イギリスのナショナリズム（愛国主義）は抑圧される傾向にあります。イギリスは間違いなく過渡期にあり，今はその大きな変化の真っ只中と言っていいでしょう。イギリスに流れ込んでくる実際の不法移民の数は全く把握されていません。これに関しては floodgate「水門」（不法移民の流入を堰き止める対策）を開けるべきか閉じるべきかという形でよく議論されています。イギリス文化の行く手になにが待っているのか誰にもわかりません。それは時が経ってから今を振り返ったときに初めてわかることでしょう。

　　ただ，確かなことはイギリスにいて英語を使う限りどんな言葉を使うか気をつけなければいけないということです。PC（political correctness＝政治的公正さ）はだれも傷つけないようにしようとする社会の流れであり，これは止まることはないのです。

サッカーの応援歌

Football Chants

　ひいきのチームカラーを身にまといマフラーを振り回しているサッカーファンの群衆はイギリスではよく見かける光景ですが，英語を学んでいる日本の皆さんには，彼らがおなじみの掛け声で応援している英語を聞き取るのはおそらく難しいかもしれません。その歌詞は，相手チームまたは自分のチームのだれかやレフリーを侮辱するものがほとんどです。

　よく歌われる歌の歌詞をいくつか挙げてみました。同じ歌詞の繰り返しが多いのですが，イントネーションや音程は一行ごとに変わるので誰にでもわかりやすくなっています。

応援歌のいろいろ　Songs and Chants

❖ 1　侮辱

Who ate all the pies?（だれがパイを全部食べた？）

Who ate all the pies?

You fat bastard（この太っちょ野郎）

You fat bastard

You ate all the pies（おまえがパイを全部食べた）

❖ 2　称賛

We love you England we do（俺たちはイングランドが大好き）

We love you England we do

We love you England we do

Oh England we love you

▷Englandのところをひいきのチーム名に入れ替えてもかまいません。

❖ 3　侮辱

You fat bastard
You fat bastard
You fat bastard
　▷飽きるまで続けます。

❖ 4　侮辱

Who's the bastard in the black（黒い服を着たやつはだれだ？）
Who's the bastard in the black
Who's the bastard in the black
　▷１行ごとにアクセントが違う特徴のある旋律を持つ３行詞。
　bastard in the black とはレフリーのことです。

❖ 5　称賛

There's only one（応援しているチームの選手名を入れる）
　▷飽きるまで続けます。

❖ 6　称賛

（監督の名前＋チームカラー）army
　▷たとえば,
　　Fergie's red and white army
　　（Fergie は Manchester United の監督で，赤と白がチームカラー）
　拍手を入れながらずっと続けます。

❖ 7　侮辱

Your shit and you know you are
（おまえらなんかくそ野郎だ。自分でわかっているだろう）
Your shit and you know you are

Your shit and you know you are
　　▷飽きるまで続けます。

❖ 8　　侮辱

You're not singing anymore（おまえたちはもう歌っていない）

You're not singing anymore

You're not singing anymore
　　▷自分の方のチームが得点したときに相手チームに向けて 3 回繰り返
　　します。相手のチームが失敗したから大人しくなっているという意味
　　です。

カルチャートーク

　　サッカーはすべてのイギリス男性の主食のようなものであり，この
ことは世界中でよく知られています。けれども大変人気のあるスポー
ツであるにもかかわらず，イギリスでは依然として下層階級のスポー
ツと考えられています。上流階級や上層中流階級の人はラグビーやク
リケットを好みます。そしてとびきりの金持ちはポロをやるのを好み
ます。ですからあなたの社交範囲によっては，サッカーファンが肩身
の狭い思いをしていることに気づくでしょう。

英語表現索引◉Index of English Expressions

◉見出し語の英語表現のアルファベット順に配列してあります。
◉英語表現の冒頭にあるthe，aはアルファベット順に含めず，〈 〉で示しました。
◉本文中，太字で示した日本語訳を（ ）に示しました。

●著者紹介

アントニー・ジョン・カミンズ
（Antony John Cummins）

1978年イングランドのオールダムに生まれる。マンチェスター大学修士課程修了，考古学で修士号取得。英語教師として2年間日本に滞在した後帰国し，現在もイギリス在住。ガーナの遺跡発掘に参加するなど考古学の研究を続けるかたわら，武道関係の著述家，DVDプロデューサー，児童書のイラストレーターとして活躍中。帆船航海，武道など趣味多数。著書に，*To Stand on a Stone: Fundamental Principles for the Martial Arts*（Wordclay社，同DVD（How2DVD社），*Conversations with an Assassin: Reflections on Modern Society* ほか。

●訳者紹介

三澤快枝（みさわ・よしえ）

国際基督教大学教養学部卒業（言語学専攻）。塾予備校英語講師などを経て現在英会話学校勤務。長年にわたり本書 “まえがき” にあるとおり標準的英語学習者として不毛な努力を続けていたところ，在日中だった著者から素顔の英語の面白さを学び翻訳者として本書に協力。

イギリス英語の悪口雑言辞典
True English

2009 年 7 月 20 日　初版印刷
2009 年 8 月　1 日　初版発行

著　者	アントニー・ジョン・カミンズ （Antony John Cummins）
訳　者	三澤快枝（みさわ・よしえ）
発行者	松林孝至
発行所	**株式会社 東京堂出版** 〒 101-0051 東京都千代田区神田神保町 1-17 電話 03-3233-3741　振替 00130-7-270
編集協力	日本アイアール株式会社
ブックデザイン	松倉　浩
DTP	株式会社明昌堂
印刷製本	図書印刷株式会社

ISBN978-4-490-10756-2 C0582

クイズで覚える英語イディオム520

牧野高吉著❖四六判256頁❖本体1,800円

◉日常よく使われる英語イディオムを厳選して収録。直訳では理解不可能な慣用句の由来や言い伝えをクイズ形式で楽しく紹介する英語イディオム小事典。

テーマ別 英語ことわざ辞典

安藤邦男著❖四六判312頁❖本体2,200円

◉950例の日常よく使う英語ことわざを75カテゴリー・238テーマに体系的に分類して紹介。使いたい場面に応じて適切なことわざを選ぶことができる。

はじめて書く英文手紙・Eメール

上地安貞・谷澤泰史編著❖A5判304頁❖本体2,200円

◉書きたい内容，場面に応じてすぐに使える英文手紙・Eメール・カードのモデル例文とサンプルレターを掲載。英語力が身につく様々な例文を豊富に収録。

コレって英語で？

デイリー・ヨミウリ編❖四六判224頁❖本体1,500円

◉読売新聞に好評連載中のコラムを収録。「イケメン」「癒し系」など世相を映す言葉から日本語独特の表現まで英語でどういえばいいのかわかりやすく解説。

Q＆A英語の疑問相談室

押上洋人・清水順・中山千佐子・楠浩恵著❖A5判272頁❖本体1,900円

◉デイリー・ヨミウリに好評連載中のコラムから厳選した80項目を収録。文法・表現から文化・勉強法まで豊富な例文とともにさまざまな疑問に答える。

最新ニュース英語辞典

デイリー・ヨミウリ編❖四六判504頁❖本体2,600円

◉政治，経済，社会・文化，国際，軍事・安全保障，科学技術・環境，スポーツなど分野別に主要な時事用語約7000語を収録。現代用語の和英表現辞典。

英語の感覚感情表現辞典

上地安貞・谷澤泰史編著❖四六判400頁❖本体2,200円

◉視覚・聴覚・味覚など五感を表す感覚表現から喜怒哀楽・性格・態度など気持ちを伝える感情表現まで英語でどういうのか発想分類別に約2200項目収録。

ロータス21　最新法律英語辞典

長谷川俊明著❖四六変型判804頁❖本体5,500円

◉海外取引・契約・交渉など国際ビジネスの場で実務に役立つ英語の法律用語約3700語収録。和英辞典の機能を果たす和英索引付。実務に生かせる英和辞典。

日本語の決まり文句英語表現辞典

竹村日出夫編❖四六判240頁❖本体2,000円

◉日本語の決まり文句を英語で表現！　「足が地につかない」「胃に穴が開く」「泣き寝入りする」「負けるが勝ち」など英語の表現で置き換えた文例を収録。

（定価は本体＋税となります）

Graphic Events: A Realist Account of Graphic Design

Onomatopee 223

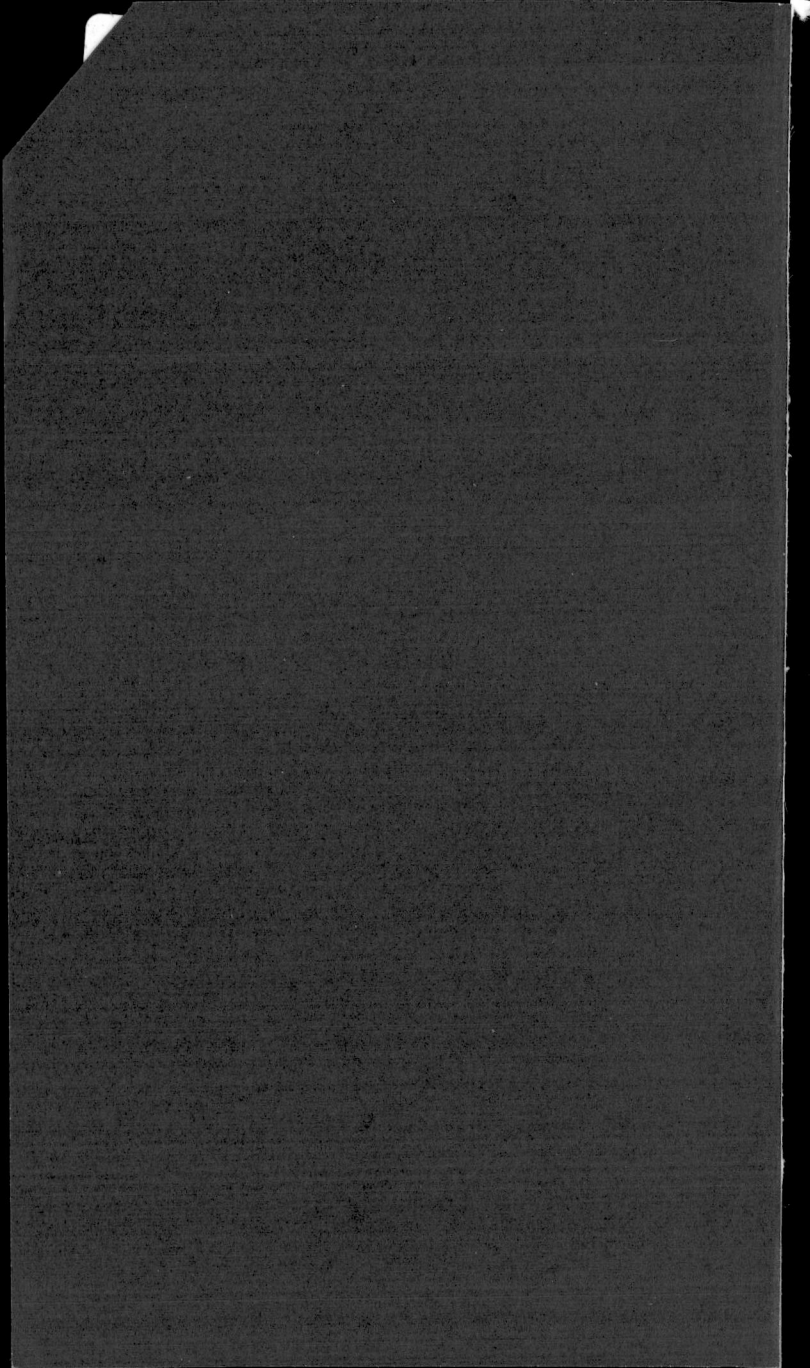

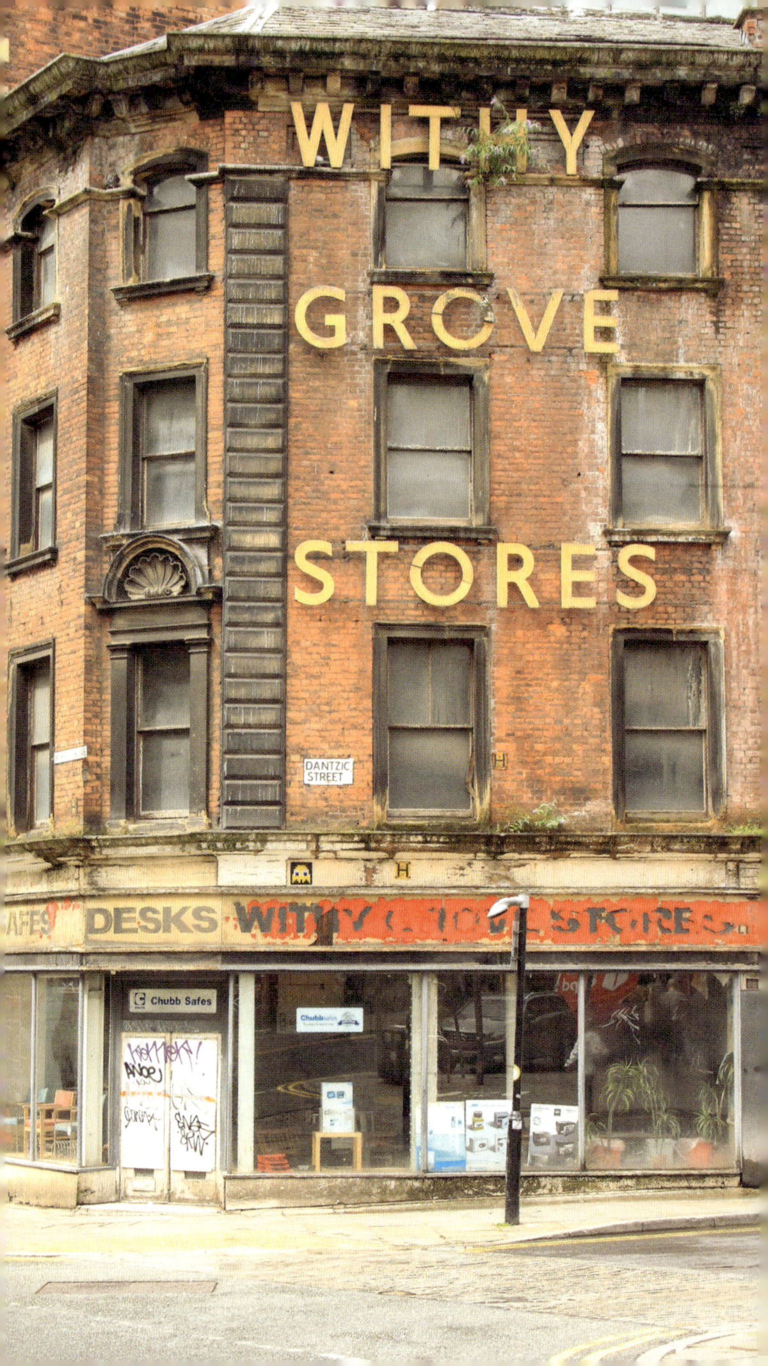
WITHY
GROVE
STORES
DANTZIC
STREET
DESKS
Chubb Safes

Foreword

by Alex Coles

Foreword

The traces a graphic leaves in the everyday, beyond its overly-simplified trajectory from designer to receiver, remain unconsidered in design discourses. "Where the graphic design is, and how it exists in that place, and the way we encounter it there", outline the editors of *Graphic Events*, are "problematic qualities that are overlooked". Graphics are live, living things but their agency is often passed over. Instead, centre focus is given to "design", as the first, and purest, state of a graphic's being.

The graphic event is fundamental to the very life of the medium. But even the most open-ended practitioners who have dynamized the space around graphic design by adding a performative dimension to a design's "release" into the world, seldom consider its enduring life or, for that matter, its afterlife. This is the underacknowledged, extended nature of the graphic event. The reason for this underacknowledgement must turn on the impossibility of being able to assert control, which is of course to say "design", over the graphic event.

Examining these overlooked events more closely, together the eclectic chapters in *Graphic Events* chart the life of a graphic design itself, as well as the lives of the professionals involved with commissioning, designing, distributing and archiving it. Graphic events, the editors succinctly declare, "evade design". The agency the graphic accrues from this evasion has significant potential. Felicitously, the editors use the term "deep milieu" to refer to this evading of design by the graphic event (where "milieu" denotes the vernacular field a graphic event takes place in, "deep" refers to its degree of immersion in that field). In this use, the parallel for the deep milieu is the notion of "deep hanging out" developed by ethnographer Clifford Geertz to indicate both the nature and the depth of a type of sustained field work. Notions of "deep design" tend more to infer a form of strategic market research rather than new methods and critical attitudes towards production and interpretation, as presented in *Graphic Events*. This deep milieu is what the graphic event is getting at, undoubtedly both the "deep milieu" and the "graphic event" will assume a place next to the other leading terms driving the discourse of design in the past decade or so, including relational design, designart, and speculative design.

Editorially, the way *Graphic Events* addresses the discursive poverty it identifies is by using a cluttered montage of realist graphic signs. The book perpetually traffics between image and text. There are moments when the reader is forced to move and manipulate the book in the situation they are reading it in according to the orientation of the text on the page. In this way, *Graphic Events* accumulates rather than designs the affective discourses the event turns on. Relying on contingency to this degree, the editorial approach calls to mind the aesthetic of practitioners associated with Fluxus, with their certain surrender of control.

The editors know that the very existence of the book *Graphic Events*, as a well styled and carefully edited entity, is of course itself problematic: by spotlighting and then naming this area, the "graphic event", the editors recoup it as a well-packaged part of the discourse of graphic design. Weighed against this is the fact that *Graphic Events* will itself have (and in reality already has) its own extended life beyond the one intended by the editors. While the nature of the book's own deep milieu is yet to be determined, it promises to provoke new, unforseen encounters with design.

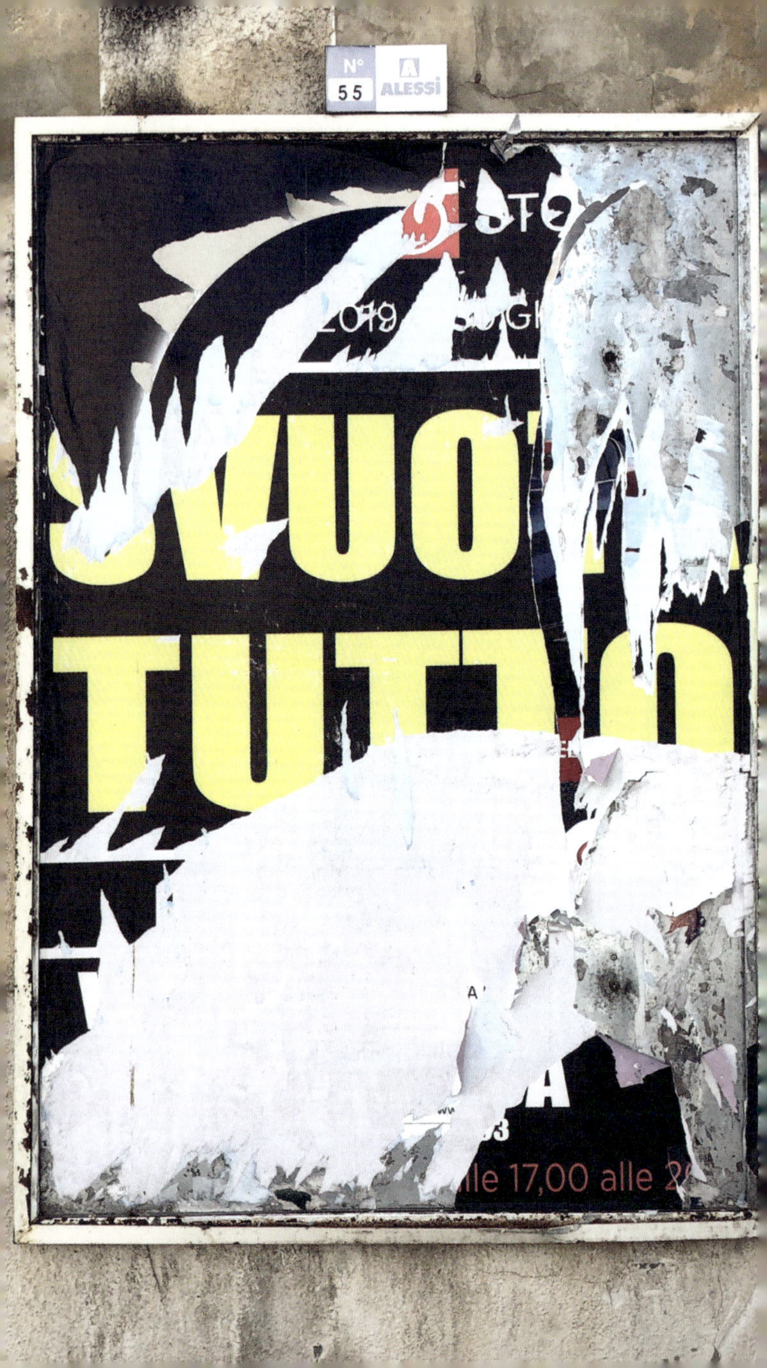

N°
55
ALESSI
2019
lle 17,00 alle 2

Introduction

Introduction

Graphic designs live ordinary lives. They are littered in ginnels, dog-eared in waiting rooms, hastily pasted on billboards, and stuck askew on old beer pumps. When these hardly remarkable things attract comments and when they are taken seriously – more often than not by designers – they are dislocated from these mundane ways of living. The dailiness of a graphic design's existence, as such, drops back to an irrelevant, deep milieu. What's being lost in this process of abstraction is the natural place of the graphic design, which is being treated as an incidental detail, only secondary, in discourses and representations of graphic designs. In this way, where the graphic design is, and how it exists in that place, and the way we encounter it there, are all problematic qualities that are overlooked for the sake of preserving the image of designs as things that are whole and reliably stable. The problem is not that this is a false or improper expression of graphics, it is just that it is the most dominant Consequently, there is little opportunity for other perspectives and alternative expressions to be taken seriously. Countering that, this book draws graphics back into the banal and exposes their intrinsic excesses. We do this to intensify our daily experiences with graphics and to show how graphics are disruptively living beyond their designs. We go about this, firstly, by showing that graphics are not just toeing the line of design, but that they have their own ways of being too.

There is a difference between the graphics that we imminently experience as pedestrians and the way that graphics are represented in design discourses. This is not a difference that needs to be resolved – we cannot all share the same perspective of the world – but in discourses of graphic design, this difference doesn't have much tension or confusion, or curiosity. From the beginning, we dramatise this tension by amplifying the difference between designs and graphics. We consider the former to be made up of deliberate intentions, plans, plots and ploys. In this way, it is the rationale and justification for the latter. Graphics, on the other hand, have a way of living that is often awkward, unplanned, and contingent. You see it everywhere you look. Think of the flakes and blisters of old painted signs, metal sheet signs with brittle layers of browning iron, cheap black vinyl signs flayed in the middle and curled at the edges. In this situation of "the everyday", we are coining the term "graphic events" as a way to play out this difference between graphics and their designs in a more critical discourse. We define a graphic event as the dynamic condition of a graphic that, by its nature, evades design.

It is important in establishing the condition of the graphic event that traditional design discourse is not rehearsed. As such, in order to give place to the graphic event, this book is littered with essays, interviews and irregular examples and illustrations in an attempt to generate a cluttered montage of new graphical thinking. It's a way for graphics to take unexpected shape. This way of opening graphics into a necessary incoherency provokes the type of curiosity felt when seeing something for the first time, it is unknown, not simple, straightforward, or self-contained. That being said, what follows are some salient points.

The graphic event relies on the priority of process over "thing", becoming over being, and dynamism over stasis. If we take this seriously – that everything is more or less contingent – then we need to earnestly reconsider what we automatically think to be fixed, to have a definite structure, or a reliable identity in graphic design. What makes things so contingent is that they are ongoing, they are, in a sense, enduring stuff with varying intensities of change. From this point of view, all things have emerged historically and their existence is ongoing with shifting amplitudes of difference – but we are getting ahead of ourselves. In the approaching essays and interviews this will all be explained specifically in context to graphic design, but it may be more intuitively graspable, firstly, in relation to nature.

For instance, relative to the life of a hill-walker's lungs, or the blossom of the shrubs they walk through, or a nimbus cloud overhead, the hills and valleys of the Peak District in Derbyshire, England appear as if they were timeless ground. However, they are formed by geological detritus settling and eroding over thousands of years. As such, this process of denudation means the Peak District can be said to have no absolute, fixed permanence because it has emerged and continues to physically change even if that change is almost imperceptible and irrelevant to us. Stability is relative after all. At the human scale of experience, the Peaks have a relatively low intensity of change when compared to the sun-faded and crumpled map they are charted on, but they have nonetheless fluidly come into being and continue becoming. It is this contingent *becoming* that makes designs (as fixed plans and determinate goals) so problematic and it is why we must coin the term "graphic events". It is in our interview with graphic artist Patrick Thomas (*Constantly There, Constantly Changing*) that this constructive contradiction of necessity and contingency is made apparent in his creative practice and teaching. It's made clear that with everything being in such a radical state of flux, the ways we come to constructively make sense of these dynamic goings-on is an important matter.

For instance, in Patti Smith's recent book *Year of The Monkey* she imagines local voyages that weave with graphics. In the introductory chapter, Smith describes a complex exchange with a graphic that ripples across the book's narrative. We think she is acting out new lyrical ways of being with graphics. There are many other traces of these kinds of encounters throughout *Year of The Monkey*. Alternatively, instead of being caught in the swells of Smith's dreamlike vignettes, poet Philip Larkin has a different standpoint, he is grounded by the pavement. From there, he describes the discomforting graphic lives of designs through repetitious pedestrian experiences of a single billboard in his poem *Sunny Prestatyn*, reprinted here in full.

The difference between the sober dispassion of Larkin and the deft speculations of Smith, when thinking about street graphics, is fundamental to the undercurrent discourse of realism in *Graphic Events*. The tone of our realist account of graphic designs is inherited from a literary point of view. Our early bar-corner conversations about this project would often return to twentieth century dirty realism in one way or another. Even though they are not directly referred to in this book, it was by reading McCullers, Carver, Bukowski, Fante, that we were drawn into a modest dirty realist frame of mind, whereby the main concern is the way a confounding world can be made sense of at a particular moment and from a certain, uncomfortable condition. The way those experiences are represented (de-scribed) gives them a sense of matter-of-factness, even if those representations are contradictory, overtly subjective, or quite obvious fantasies. Further to the point, those differences matter at a deeply intimate level. This is why *Graphic Events* is not dismissing the traditions of graphic design discourses but is instead imploring differences with them by validating underimagined tarmac-trodding perspectives of graphics in the everyday. As such, our realism is a pluralism.

Further obscuring the traditions of design discourses, in the two-part interview with philosopher James Williams (*A Splash and a Stain*), Williams explains his recent process philosophical alternative to structuralist semiotics and, amongst other things, provokes new ways of thinking about graphics by questioning how we formally analyse signs. With similar taste, but in an informal tone, the collaged interviews of DR.ME and Vicky Carr of Textbook Studio (*Beautiful, Obliterated*) considers the often wordless ways that the broken, torn, and lacerated appeal to designers despite their lack of order, structure, or reliability.

We primarily construct our definition of the "event" from process philosopher Alfred North Whitehead. His work is laced throughout our essays, most notably his concepts of the discerned and discernible and the transformative method of extensive abstraction. What's alluring in this definition is that the event is not something that can be conceived in advance, or held up to the light and scrutinised in exhaustive analytical detail, instead, to appreciate the richness of the event it must be experienced in the moment and creatively expressed. In *Signs of the Everyday, Every Day*, design historian Teal Triggs reflects on her routine of documenting street graphics, which she treats as things that are happening in fluid situations, rather than signs that are just simple, contained objects. This sensitive witnessing of street graphics in flux encourages Triggs to draw them into personal stories with extended social contexts.

In a similar way, we don't think that designers should be treating the radical contingency of the graphic event like a design problem that needs to be ironed out. And we don't think that designers should somehow be creatively applying graphic event-like qualities as if they were some sort of stylistic resource for design. Instead, designers should be prepared to live with these events as a never-entirely-graspable ontological condition. Finally, in a transcript of graphic designer Fraser Muggeridge's talk *A Knowing Wrongness*, he demonstrates the serious contemporary cultural currency of playful mistake making in type design. It punctuates our last essay, in which we show that the graphic event puts certainty at risk.

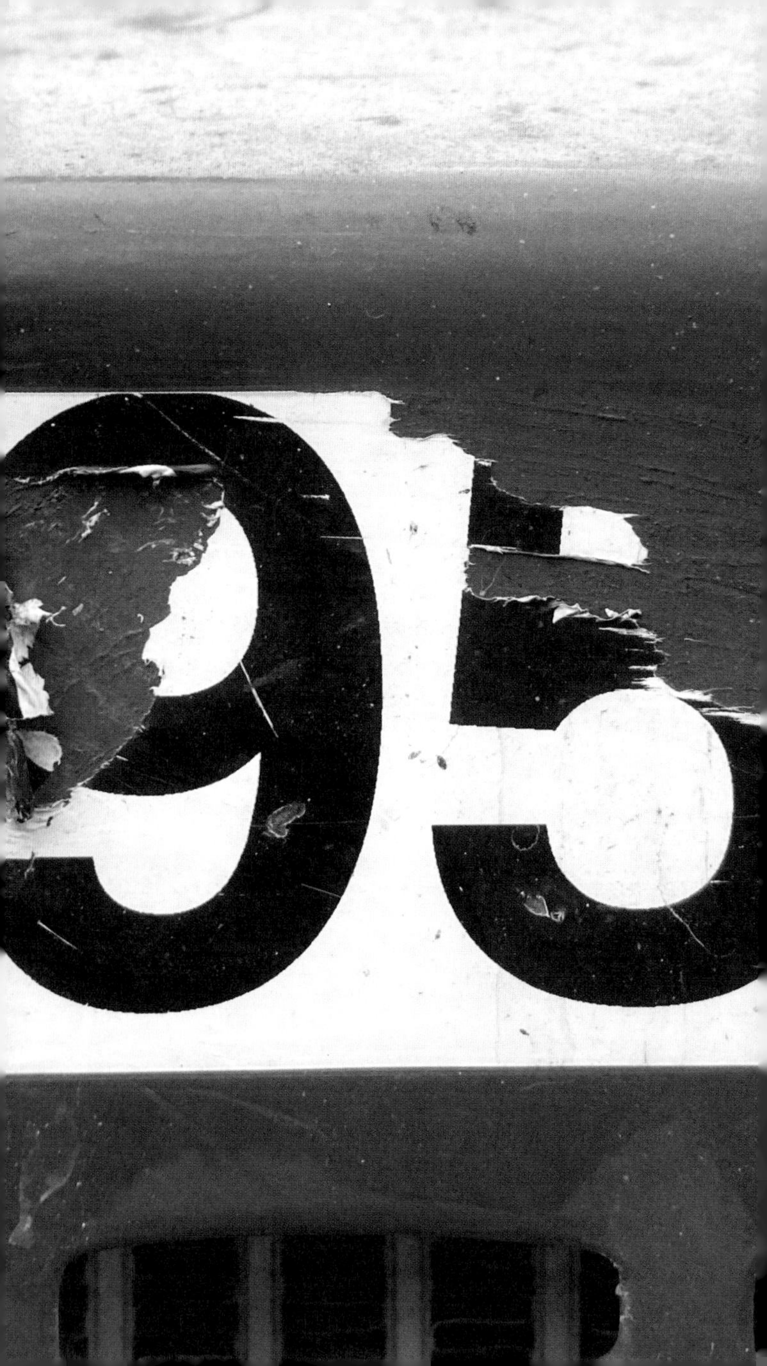
95

Grounded Encounters with the Unplanned

Grounded Encounters with the Unplanned

In illustrator Dugald Stermer's *Art of Revolution: Ninety Six Posters from Cuba* – a large, unwieldy book that compiles an array of outstanding Cuban poster designs – street graphics are, to some degree, cut out from their greater social and political contexts.[1] Susan Sontag critically describes the book as "prefaced, typographically packaged, printed, distributed, and sold [...] several steps away from its original use [...] a tacit betrayal".[2] As Sontag recognises, posters pre-suppose "the modern concept of public space", but there is no way to experience them in that public space in *Art of Revolution* because the way the posters are presented (as privately consumable commodities) excludes any sense of the graphic's ordinary lived condition in 1960s Cuba.[3]

It is as if anything that exists beyond the edge of the poster, past the boundary of the graphic as an abstract whole, is treated as insignificant because it surpasses the ideal, orderly limitations of the poster's design. Yuriko Saito, a professor of philosophy and keen advocate of everyday aesthetics, makes a similar point in reference to "paradigmatic art". She writes that the "smell of fresh paint and relationship to the surrounding wall paper or to the back of the canvas, no matter how intriguing, are intentionally bracketed".[4] In the same way, these are the unworded experiences of the day-to-day that are "bracketed" in representations of graphics in discourses of design, we will get to some specific examples of this bracketing later.

Now imagining a more capitalist setting (most likely in America) Sontag attempts to weave the lives of graphics back into their mundane origins by setting our experiences of them on littered streets. She suggests that "connoisseurs of new forms of beauty may find visual gratification in the unplanned collage of posters (and neon signs) that decorate the cities".[5] It is that grounded encounter with the "unplanned" that we are elaborating on in this book. We know there is a relatively long-standing practice of designers at street-level acting as urban "connoisseurs" – Sister Corita Kent, Nicolete Gray, David Carson, Ed Fella, Robert Brownjohn, to name a few[6] – but even when these designers pull back and change focus to see a broader, more concrete context of graphic designs in situ, there is still a sense that the life of the graphic is being compressed and somehow stabilized.

A tawdry illustration of this are the thousands of mockup life-like scenarios that are used as a way to embed graphics into everyday settings. As a designer, you can choose from: living room portrait, city downtown billboard, photo frame and potted cactus. Each template comes with its own quirk of facsimile too. Such as, a poster's corner peeling away from the wall, creased tape across curling edges, and mottled brick textures (the quintessential urban substrate in this uncanny valley). But they do not feel like graphics in lived life. Instead, they are there to repeat what has been prescribed (read: designed), that is why they appear like badly staged performances playing a bit too close to the script.[7] Seen from an anonymous point of view and void of any real-life situation, they are graphics showcased in the unreal (or: more real than real) reality of a placeless design-world.[8] However, just like stuffed animals in glass showcases – milky-eyed badgers on wooden stumps, and awkwardly poised lions on veneered plinths – there is a pitiful morbidity to counterfeit life.

These mockup scenarios are not inherently wrong but they are symptomatic of the dominant way we come to know graphics. That is to say, we are looking at graphics through the optic of design. But if we pause on a high street, and get close to a poster, it is full of life, more so than a framed rectangle propped on a clutter-free desk next to a high resolution cafetiere and potted plant. What we need is a perspective of graphics that is more affected and embodied. That would perhaps offer a point of view able to account for experiences that are true to life, rather than straightforwardly faithful to discipline. By doing this, we would notice the momentum of graphics as a surging undercurrent with an impulsive, obsessive, drawing attraction. We are not ready, just yet, to explain how this makes a graphic an "event".

Notes:

1.
Dugald Stermer, *Art of Revolution: Ninety-Six Posters from Cuba*. London: Pall Mall Press, 1970.

2.
Susan Sontag, *Posters: Advertisement, Art, Political Artifact, Commodity,* in Dugald Stermer, Art of Revolution: Ninety-Six Posters from Cuba. London: Pall Mall Press, 1970: xxii.

3.
Ibid, ii. A similar argument is made in Carlo Arturo Quintavalle, *The Development of Poster Art*, in Max Gallo, Posters in History. Bracken Books, 1989 (originally published 1972): 252-254.

4.
Yuriko Saito, *Everyday Aesthetics*. Oxford University Press, 2007: 18.

5.
Posters, xiii.

6.
Not to mention artists such as Raymond Hains, Mimmo Rotella, and Jacques Villeglé.

7.
In episode #193 of Jarrett Fuller's excellent *Scratching the Surface* podcast he is speaking with Tereza Ruller, a performative designer, Fuller says "every designer is using the same computer generated mockups […] which I think you could argue is a type of performance […] they are just performing the act of printing without actually printing". Jarret also recently commissioned for Eye on Design George Kafka's article *Are Mockup Designers the Most Influential Designers of Our Era?*

8.
Parallels to these issues can be seen when considering the "White Cube" of exhibitions and gallery spaces. See Brian O'Doherty, *Inside the White Cube: The Ideology of the Gallery Space*. The Lapis Press, 1976.

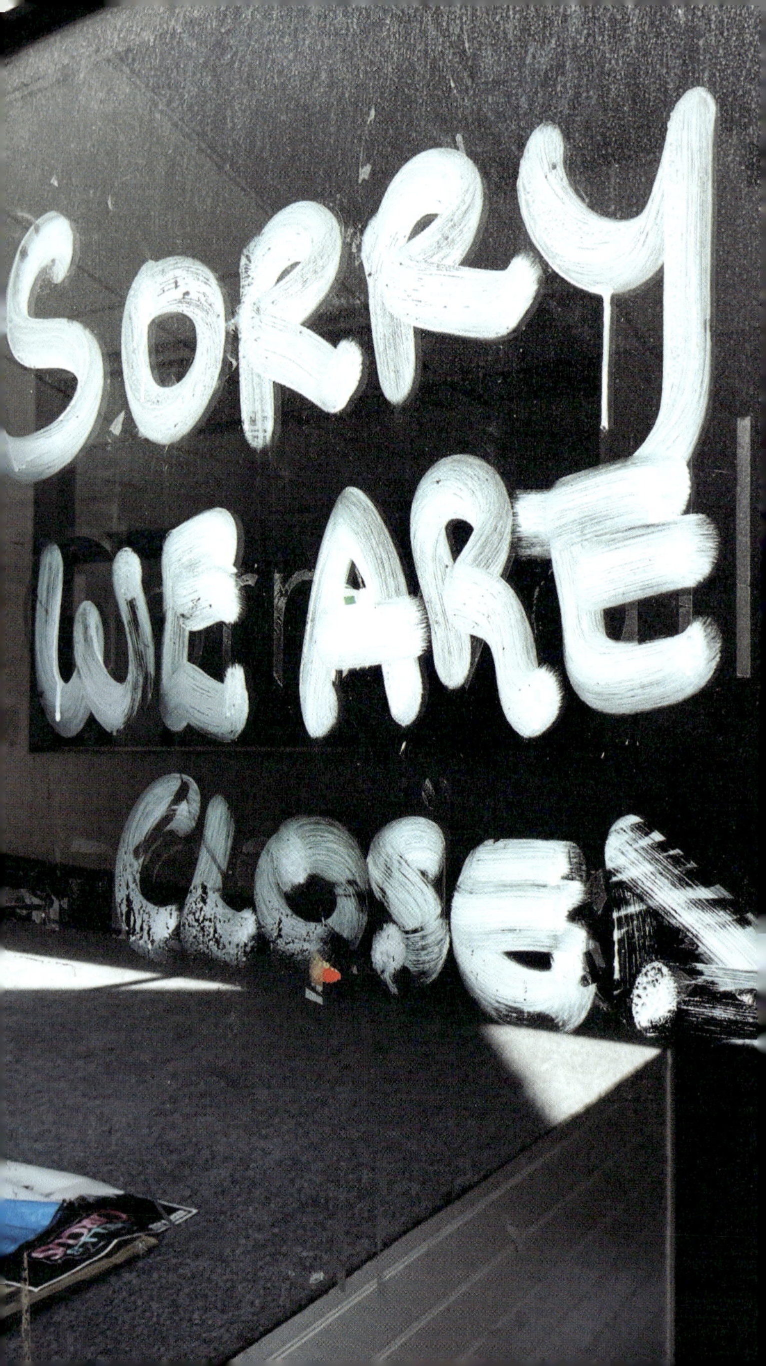
SORRY
WE ARE
CLOSED

The Lived Experience of Graphics in **Daily** Life

The Lived Experience of Graphics in Daily Life

Despite graphics being such a familiar part of everyday life, it appears that because they are designed, which is another way of saying that they come about by way of particular, deliberate intentions, we lose sight of their graphic nature, which is often awkward, unplanned, and contingent. In other words, what we see and hear in established discourse is the priority of the designed image of graphics and the dismissal of the lived experience of graphics in daily life.[1] The former concerns the preservation of ideal intention (design's necessity) the latter amplifies concrete experience (graphic's contingency). It seems, to some degree, that crystallizing the actuality of a design relies on virtualizing the graphic. At a cultural scale, isn't this what is happening in *Art of Revolution*? The way the graphic lives in excess beyond its design is not worth noticing, it is disregarded and therefore has no sensible appearance in the grander narrative of the graphic-as-design.[2] This is, as Sontag points out, what makes the collection and consumption of the political Cuban posters possible without "risk of cultural indigestion".[3]

We can see this loss of detail for the sake of coherent structure happening at a material level too. For example, with few exceptions, in John Barnicoat's *Posters: A Concise History*, there is no mention of striated textures from irregular substrates pushing through the paper, no air bubble blisters, or welts from nails sticking out of chipboard, there is little mention of neighbouring graphics or the possibility of their being graffitied, torn, or even pasted over with other posters.[4] But those material qualities are still noticeable, even if they are not being treated as sensible. We can see it in the photographs of posters on display in Margate and in the creases of the poster *Five Celebrated Clowns*, but it's a seamy part of a graphic's life, and it remains unsaid; not part of the concise history.[5] Instead, the graphics are shown to be designs that exist in a matter-of-fact way, simply and reliably just the way they were intended to be.

When thinking about "everyday surface aesthetic qualities" Thomas Leddy, a philosopher of art and aesthetics,

describes them as often appearing "polluted" and "fouled".[6]
He wants us to take these seemingly "lewd" and "pornographic"
appearances seriously; junkyards and roadside clutter, he
claims, also have sincere, aesthetic qualities.[7] In a similar vein,
theorist Michael Thompson claims that:

> "[T]he charm of rubbish theory is that it seems always
> to lead straight into illogicality, anomaly, and paradox.
> Regrettably, there are many who find these qualities not
> so much charming as monstrous, and there are some
> who would go so far as to maintain that the proper aim
> and object of serious thought should be the systematic
> exclusion of such monsters".[8]

This is what is at risk when we acknowledge graphics to
be more event-like than design-like. We are attending to a
"monstrous" kind of play for a discipline that is typically settled
in systematic, rational ways of working. At a sociological level,
the graphic event – as we will soon define it – is open to what
anthropologist Mary Douglas would think of as the polluted
and the taboo.[9]

In a way, designer Bruno Munari describes these
unanticipated "everyday surface aesthetic qualities" in his
short essay *Poster without End*.[10] He proposes that "every
figurative element of the poster that is cut by the right-or
left-hand edge will inevitably combine in some unforeseen
way, with the poster next door". Munari confesses that this
is happening "far from the mind of the designer". If we stood
in the London Underground at some platform edge, for
example, and we saw these strange Janus-faced posters
on the wall across from us, we would not say that the
posters were that way by design. But they are, nonetheless,
graphic designs that have *written* themselves into new
graphical forms. In this way, we can see that graphics are
not dependent on design. As such, we can say the posters
are more graphic than design because a graphic is not
only its design but also what it lives to become. If, from the

perspective of a pedestrian, rather than a designer, we think of the graphics that are close to us, and we think of them as being "without ends", as Munari finds them, then we can recognise their graphic ability to impulsively write themselves into their environment, becoming things unfixed from under the yoke of design.

Ultimately, the way graphics exist beyond design in the everyday, such as in the way that Munari writes about them, lacks critical address because of the dominance of the designerly framing of graphics. We have lost the living condition of graphics, in fact, we may never have had a clear sense of it.[11] How do we think about the incidental, unintended, dynamic, entropic qualities; the ordinary but unofficial cultures of graphic designs? Generally, in graphic design discourses, there is an overemphasis on what could be called the "plot" of a graphic's design, more on that later. It is worth keeping in mind that design is synonymous with planning, rationality, strategy, intention, revisionist progress, and so on. Therefore, the problem with thinking of graphics in exclusively design-disciplinary and design-discursive terms is that in those terms everything is underwritten and calibrated by design. That is to say, when we think of what a graphic is, we think of it in design historical terms – which are themselves not unproblematic[12] – and further to the point, what a graphic does is considered to be symptomatic of (traditionally) structuralist semiotics.[13] But if we think of graphics in less designerly ways, we literally see them living on and extending well beyond the plan, we could even say they are losing the plot.[14]

As such, if you believe us when we say that there are as many ways for a graphic to exist as there are ways to perceive it, then the sort of experiences we can have of graphics are dependent on the kinds of perspectives we bring to them. These perspectives are not metaphors for disciplines – the points of view of poets, architects or photographers, etc. – but are literal, situated points of view from a concrete place in the actual world. Imagine if we were to take seriously the idiosyncratic, personal, punctuating experiences we have with graphics and subversively enrol them in the discursive format (*formation discursive*) of graphic design.[15] The emergent lives of graphics, unintended by design, would make new ways of thinking about design necessary. For instance, in a scene from *No Direction Home,* through a playful smile, Bob Dylan muddles the words of two neighbouring street signs.[16] Pacing, he says: "I want a dog that's gonna collect and clean my bath, return my cigarette and give tobacco to my animals and give my birds a commission … I am looking for somebody to sell my dog, collect my clip, buy my animal and straighten out my bird … I am looking for a place to bathe my bird, buy my dog, collect my clip, sell me cigarettes and collect my bath …" where does this nonsense play sit in traditional graphic design discourse? Dylan is not so much re-examining city signs to uncover hidden messages, but he is playing them out in other (less useful) ways. In doing this he is rethinking (re-cognising) the graphics as something other than their designs. Perhaps Dylan is a bit of a lively example to start off with, we are just trying to show that there is a conflict between the ideal of a graphic – in other words: its design – and the concreteness of a graphic as a thing in the world.

It must be clear at this point that we are, to some extent, exaggerating graphic's discontinuity with design and experimenting with a (non-fatal) rift between them. Doing this makes it possible for us to consider how a graphic exists in the everyday, at the asphalt-level, in the "peculiar possession of the public".[17] By focusing on crude experiences, we are thinking of graphics without depending on an underlying system of rational, foundational design principles. Returning to the rawness of everyday graphic designs is a way to disrupt what we normally expect to be acceptable and proper when we think about graphic designs.

Notes:

1.
For the philosophical context of this in the sciences see Wilfrid Sellars, *Philosophy and The Scientific Image of Man,* in Science, Perception and Reality 2, 1963.

2.
By "sensible" we mean what are considered to be the permissible limits of what is proper to see and say in the contexts of particular discursive orders and social structures. See Jacques Rancière, *The Politics of Aesthetics*. Translated by G. Rockhill. Continuum, 2004 (originally published 2000).

3.
Posters, xxi.

4.
John Barnicoat, *Posters: A Concise History*. Thames & Hudson, 1972.

5.
Ibid, 231, 206.

6.
Thomas Leddy, *Everyday Surface Aesthetic Qualities: "Neat," "Messy," "Clean," "Dirty"*, in The Journal of Aesthetics and Art Criticism, 53.3, 1995.

7.
Thomas Leddy, *The Aesthetics of Junkyards and Roadside Clutter*, in Contemporary Aesthetics, 6.1, 2008.

8.
Michael Thompson, *Rubbish Theory: The Creation and Destruction of Value.* Oxford University Press, 1979. Thinking of rubbish in context to design criticism see Alice Twemlow, *Sifting the Trash: A History of Design Criticism*, MIT Press, 2017.

9.
Mary Douglas, *Purity and Danger: An Analysis of Concepts of Pollution and Taboo.* Routledge & Kegan Paul, 1966.

10.
Bruno Munari, *Design as Art*. Penguin, 2008 (originally published 1966): 88-89.

11.
See Johanna Drucker & Emily McVarish, *Graphic Design History: A Critical Guide*. Pearson Prentice Hall, Upper Saddle River, 2008. See also Alexandra Midal, *Design by Accident: For a New History of Design*, Sternberg Press, 2019. And also Grace Lees-Maffei and Nicolas P. Maffei, *Reading Graphic Design in Cultural Context*. Bloomsbury Publishing, 2019.

12.
Clive Dilnot, *The State of Design History, Part II: Problems and*

Possibilities, in Design Issues, 1984.

13.
See James Williams, *A Splash and A Stain*.

14.
"Losing the plot" is an informal British term, it means to be confused and to act without a sense of rational purpose.

15.
See Michel Foucault, *The Archaeology of Knowledge & The Discourse on Language*. Translated by A. M. Sheridan Smith. Pantheon Books, 1972 (originally published 1969).

16.
Martin Scorsese, *No Direction Home:* Bob Dylan. Paramount Pictures, 2005. Dylan has also sustained this interest in street signs and the vernacular in his recent paintings.

17.
William K. Wimsatt and Monroe C. Beardsley, *The Intentional Fallacy*, in The Sewanee Review, 54(3), 1946.

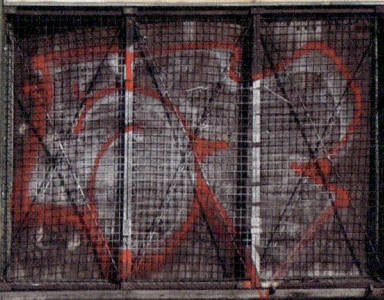

A Splash and a **Stain**

(Part One)

James Williams
Interviewed by James Dyer

A Splash and a Stain (Part One)

What was your motivation to write A Process Philosophy of Signs?

It has always struck me that the high point of structuralism, coming from Ferdinand de Saussure and then right up to Roland Barthes, had something very important to say about communication and the way in which we can think of what seem to be simple gestures and everyday things; they turn out to be positively analysable and very important in terms of that analysis. All of Roland Barthes' detailed observations that seem to be quite whimsical, looking at a motor car or something like that, can give you deep insight into society.[1] So I wondered why that had started to fade, I wanted to work out what the relation was to thinkers that came later – Jean-François Lyotard, Gilles Deleuze, Michel Foucault – and why they hadn't written a bit more about signs. Their philosophies were much more about becoming and movement, so the way you explain what a sign is within structures becomes extremely difficult because you lose the structure, or structure means something completely different. And yet, these process philosophers, you mention Whitehead in this *Graphic Events* book for instance, are very good at looking at signs. Whitehead, in a lovely book called *Adventures of Ideas*,[2] looks at moments and signs and history as process. So I thought, is it possible to think about that in a very formal way, can we reinvent structure (structuralism) to look at signs as process? I started playing around with different signs, often very simple signs, gestures for instance, types of fashion, but also signs in their political role. It is from there that I then moved on to a process philosophy of signs.

I did have graphic design signs in mind when I was writing the book, partly because of my previous work on Lyotard. Throughout his whole career he was interested in graphic design and signs of that kind.[3] The whole point of design as process is that it is never fixed and innocent. Any gesture, any sign that you make, is going to burst out in these multiple ways. I wanted to show how a very simple sign and gesture has this infinite, mobile and highly politicised context.

You mentioned "process philosophy", could you introduce this to an audience that may not be familiar with philosophy?

Process philosophy is a philosophy that prioritises events as things that are always changing and becoming different – and this is the important bit – in multiple ways. Such that, whenever you fix the event in a structure, a definition, an identity, a picture or a representation, you lose something, that's the key. So process philosophy is asking: how can we try as hard as we can to not lose that dynamic, how do we keep things in motion?

Why is it so important to keep things in motion? Is it just about having a more accurate representation of how things exist, or is there something else going on?

There are two reasons. The first is that by missing or denying change you are committing a violent act, you are not only denying the thing that is changing you are also denying all the values and lives around it. Process philosophy is a political philosophy, Whitehead doesn't always appear political, but he was, he was a progressive philosopher. The second reason is that you are making an error with respect to understanding how things are. If you select certain fixed grids, certain fixed relations and structures and it turns out that what you are trying to think about is in motion, you have missed the point. There is an error committed.

Why does that error matter?

The error matters because it makes you clumsy, restricted and incapable of grasping the potential and new development of something, a bit like someone who goes into an art gallery or looks at a new set of signs and goes: "that's rubbish" or "that makes no sense". The person is not saying something accurate about what's happening. They have just put themselves in a way of thinking that is not able to grasp what is happening.

You describe the process sign as: "the selection of a set against a background accompanied by intensive changes in relations".[4] I understand that this is not a strictly ordered process – from background to selection to intensive changes – but could you break down each of these aspects and describe how they work (if you would call them aspects)?

The problem for process philosophy is that if everything is a multiplicity of many changes and it is somehow wrong to fix them, how do you start to describe a sign? Well, you have to "fix" them but as little as possible. With signs this is even more difficult because a sign is something that, very often, has to be easily grasped. The selection explains the way in which you understand a sign at all; but, if it is to avoid giving the sign as fixed and permanent the selection must be temporary and open to change. Imagine working on any desktop publishing software, to begin you open a blank document and start making your sign. You have to select the font, its weight and colour and then you make your mark. So there is a "selection" that takes place for the thing to get off the ground. The next aspect is how you explain that this selection is still in motion, how it is still multiple and, importantly, how everything connects across many ongoing changes. That explanation depends upon the set of "diagrams". The diagrams map ongoing changes around the selection. It is very important that it is not one diagram but many, because the effects of a selected sign are multiple and controversial, leading to many different interpretations and consequences. Imagine, when you choose the colour of font, I say you can choose a hot or cold colour. In choosing a hot colour you restrict your options in terms of cold colours, so there is a motion going on, from cold to hot. If the graffiti that you put on the beautiful white walls of a pretty little village is a blood red colour, you are setting off a certain kind of movement, making certain things more likely, making certain things less likely and that is the diagram. There could be a diagram that says "this is the point where a revolution started" and another one that says "this is the most disgraceful piece of graffiti, the perpetrators must be punished". So we have the fixing selection and then the diagrams. These can be seen as many different interpretations of a selected sign, but they are in motion. The reason they are in motion is because they matter, they set the world around them in motion. It is easy to think of a meaning as a dictionary entry, as if it is something flat and unimportant, but a dictionary entry is very high stakes, people go to extreme lengths over them. So if you say the dictionary entry "Graphic Design" is "the art of logo making and typography" you will immediately get a lot of pushback. So there is always an emotional intensity. Although the word "emotion" is not quite right, I'd rather say an intensity, as in things getting stronger and weaker, changing in how they are valued, in order to avoid too strong focus on human emotions.

Can the "selection of a set" only happen in a deliberate, intentional way? You say that a selection is not reliant on a selecting subject, so how does this selection process work?

The selection process has two aspects to it. The first one is very pure. By that I mean that it allows a sign to appear in the first place. An example of that would be signs of fate. Let's say you are walking around and all of a sudden a tree falls *crash!* and that starts you reacting in a certain set of ways. That reaction is the second aspect of the selection, it is already towards a diagram – you could call diagrams interpretations – but the tree falling didn't have a subject. The selection happened, it was not made by anyone. That is very important, because otherwise you start to think that signs can only have human makers but think of the effect that dogs barking can have on us. A dog barking is definitely a sign, it can be a very important one, for all sorts of reasons: there is no intention, or it is an intention that does not resemble many forms of human intention. A dog barks, the moon appears, and a door creaks; there is your sign. Then, the diagrams start, you go: intruder? or you may go: my lover's back, and so on and so forth. So the selection has those two sides to it and you are completely right, one of them must not be thought of as having a subject. Now, some people might say that some signs definitely have subjects, but that's wrong, though there can be an intention to make a sign that doesn't account for the selection.

Can you elaborate more on that?

It's because the selecting subject can't control the way in which the selection then happens in relation to diagrams. A good example of this would be a graphic designer or an artist at the opening of an exhibition when the designer listens to what everyone is chattering about as they hold their glass of water or champagne or whatever and it is a huge disappointment and shock. The selections that have been made by the designer are not at all being picked up on in terms of the diagrams set up by the room. Everyone is talking about the frames! People are calling my work "gentle" and so on and so forth. It is not because people are making a mistake. It is because the selection is very open in terms of the sign and its diagrams – dependent upon them and inseparable from them. The designer cannot control them, the selection always has this double aspect. So when you think you are simply selecting Gill Sans typeface in bold and red, you are not simply and determinately selecting. In terms of a sign, it is always going to go beyond you as a designer and that's why the sign is always a process going beyond the selecting subject, if there is one.

What does this definition of a process sign mean for my day to day life when I am experiencing signs that just seem to straightforwardly signify, an exit sign for example? How does a process sign work in that context?

It works by saying it is perfectly OK to see that sign as an "exit" and so on, but it is also saying that you have to remain alert. Let's imagine that the "exit" sign is always written in a particular language, so now, instead of having "exit" in many different languages, you start to have around the world always "exit" not "sortie" or "wyjście" or "çıkış" or any other language but "exit" so what you think is simply a sign that says "exit" is also a way in which, for instance English, is a colonising language that is spreading. A process sign means that you have to retain that alertness to understand what the sign might be doing to you. Unless you retain that alertness and understanding of signs you cannot analyse the way in which they are having an underlying effect on you. The simplicity of the sign is always an illusion. For instance, if you think that the tube map is just a map of the London Underground then you are missing everything that the graphic designer (Harry Beck) has done; the shape of London has changed – geographers will tell you that – relationships within London have changed, London's economy has changed, and so forth. A sign is never innocent; it is never simple; it only appears to be innocent and direct.

Do you intentionally avoid the word "design" in your book? Because when you define a sign as a "selection" that seems to be a basic description of the design process – like an adroit selection process, designers reduce to sign, they are de-signing. Do you see process signs as being in some way antithetical or oppositional to graphic design?

No not at all. All designs have two moments in their lives. There is the creative moment – that is what I am trying to come closer to – but the other moment is retrospective and interpretative, it can be by the designer or by society or an academic, and many others. What I was trying to resist were those moments when architects, for example, look back to their work and say: "this is what I meant to do, this is what the building means, this is how it works". Those moments are always in some way denials of design, if design is understood as highly open; as a splash and a stain, rather than a meaningful mark. It is that openness that I insist upon.

It has often been a criticism of the Graphic Events project that for a design to work – "buy this pasta", for example – it relies on clarity of communication, it should not be "open". In these terms, a design is "good" when its intention is understood, when it is loud and clear. On the other hand, a design is thought to be "bad" when it is possible to be misused and misunderstood.

It is a social and political error to think that design is closed. For instance, if the design for your pasta package shows a certain type of imagined, romanticised view of what Italy was in the 1930s, you are reinforcing a false view of Italian history, strengthening false and sometimes racist views of contemporary Italian society, and you are also restricting what can be thought of as the "right" design of an Italian pasta package. So your clients might be happy, they might pay you, the design might work for a while but that in no way accounts for the value and life of the design. So that would be what's at stake in the wider diagrams and processes in the sign, irrespective of any perceived or claimed clarity.

Notes:

1.
Roland Barthes, *Mythologies*.
Translated by A. Lavers, Hill &
Wang, 1972 (originally published
in 1957).

2.
Alfred North Whitehead,
Adventures of Ideas. Macmillan,
1933.

3.
Jean-François Lyotard,
Discourse, Figure. Translated by
A. Hudek & M. Lydon, University
of Minnesota Press, 2011
(originally published 1971).

4.
A Process Philosophy of Signs,
148.

A Spontaneous Breathing World

A Spontaneous Breathing World

In a spry poem written by William Wordsworth, he begs the reader "Up! up!" away from the desk, from the book, from the specialism and into a world that he sees as spontaneous, impulsive and most vitally breathing.[1] He warns, "Our meddling intellect / Mis-shapes the beauteous forms of things:– / We murder to dissect". Isn't this recognisable in popular books about graphic design? We have already mentioned *Art of Revolution* but we can also notice it in Anthony Burrill's *Look & See*, David Carson's *nu collage.001*, and Andy Altmann's *tat**.[2] The graphics are cut away from the spontaneous, breathing world, and are embalmed for the sake of distilling their design, curiously, morticians call this "setting the features". When a graphic's features are "set" they are anesthetised and deathly rigid. To oppose this, Wordsworth asks us to step out into nature, he tells us to bring "[…] a heart / That watches and receives". If we are attending to graphics as they appear to be rather than representing them as they ideally "ought to be",[3] then there is vital aesthetic importance in this embodied, self-conscious, active passivity; watching and receiving, being affected.[4]

Buddhist philosopher D. T. Suzuki's essay *East and West* demonstrates two different ways of attending to the world[5] by contrasting a poem by Alfred Tennyson and one by Matsuo Bashō.[6] Both poems are about an encounter with a flower. Tennyson "plucks" the flower from a wall to analyse it objectively; it has to become something else (dead) for him to understand it. He wants to exhaust the thing "root and all". Suzuki says Tennyson moves from the "domain of feeling into that of intellect". When poet Matsuo Bashō, on the other hand, sees a wild plant blooming by a hedge, he admires it right where it is, "Bashō sees the nazuna and the nazuna sees Bashō".[7] Suzuki goes on to point out that Bashō does not even say anything about the wildflower in the poem. The encounter is expressed only at the end of the poem in an exclamation mark. Following Suzuki and Wordsworth, we might come to think of graphics as living, spontaneous things, and the ways that we attend to them and the ways that we describe them matter. For instance, the way Jacques Villeglé exhibits lacerated posters in art galleries, and how Sister Corita Kent decontextualises street graphics through "finders", and how Robert Brownjohn captures the fullness of a mundane street sign's character, they are all unique ways of "feeling" and "knowing" graphics, and they all matter distinctly.

It is worth passing deeper into this embodied experience of nature, as Wordsworth had it, and "absolute subjectivity", as Suzuki describes it. There is a modern urban equivalent to Bashō's encounter with the wildflower in Philip Larkin's poem *Sunny Prestatyn*.[8] Larkin wrote poems about common things in ordinary ways. His style of writing is restrained to common sense but compelled by personal experience, as if written from an analytic distance whilst still being grounded at some particular moment and place. Larkin's biographer describes his distance not as removed from the world but as "alert on its margin".[9] From Larkin's line of sight, breakfasts, billboards, shops, and trains lose their obvious, assumed qualities. They are still the same regular stuff, but their often-unregarded characteristics are drawn out into plain sight. In the poem *Sunny Prestatyn*, Larkin describes a poster. It advertises a holiday to the Welsh seaside town Prestatyn. There is a girl on the poster. She is glamorous, hyper-real, glowing against Larkin's routine background of Hull, a port city he once described as a dreary dump, fish smelling, a hole.[10] Offset from that grey urban place, in a tight white satin bathing suit, she kneels in sand.

Larkin must have seen the poster often to notice it "slapped up one day in March" to then being graffitied, stabbed and torn. Eventually, the image of the too-real-to-be-real woman deforms into waste "a great transverse tear / Left only a hand and some blue". Defaced, the poster is more clearly imbricated in the city's mundane palimpsest of image-and-text, it was soon replaced, Larkin says: "Now Fight Cancer is there." His poem shows the poster is complex, that it exists at each encounter in different ways and how that difference affectively matters, even if it is seemingly irrelevant in regular (prosaic) life. Larkin shows responsibility; literally, an individual ability to respond – he brings "[…] a heart / That watches and receives". He is a vigilant and sceptical passer-by that pauses, less deceived, with a distrust for the ideal and a pragmatic eagerness to notice what is actually, complexly just there.

Sunny Prestatyn shows an unsureness of the growing commercialism and idealism of daily post-war life. From glamour to graffiti, laceration to replacement, Larkin describes the life of a poster as a unique material thing, matted in its place, not just as an irrelevant part of the common public decor. He demonstrates how a graphic design is "always an object of circumstances, and consequently ephemeral".[11] His encounters with the supposedly low, trivial material of the poster – the "traverse tear", the crude graffiti – falls outside the syntax of design because they are details unjustified by the "point" of the poster, in other words: its design.

This friction between the unreal ideal of a design and the otherness of daily life is the theme of other Larkin poems too, most notably *Essential Beauty*.[12] Larkin describes large billboard advertisements as intrusive images of ideal things that are blocking, screening and covering the less-than-ideal places they are set in: "High above the gutter / A silver knife sinks into golden butter". As such, describing the way the posters live by drawing it out into episodes of decay (*Sunny Prestatyn*) and by tracking back to broaden the frame and see the billboards set surreally in place (*Essential Beauty*) shows the precariousness of structures and it undermines the intended "narrative", that is to say, how the design "ought to be". Larkin is recognising graphic details that strain the ideal of a design's intent. He is savouring the idiosyncratic material-semiotic tensions of the poster. In this way, what Larkin describes are *graphic events*.

Notes:

1.
William Wordsworth, *Tables Turned*, in William Wordsworth and Samuel Taylor Coleridge, Lyrical Ballads, with a Few Other Poems. Longman, 1798. Wordsworth would now probably say "Up! up!" away from Pinterest, Instagram, and Google Images.

2.
Anthony Burril, *Look & See*. Thames and Hudson, 2018. David Carson, *nu collage.001*. SYL, 2019. Andy Altmann, *tat*: Inspirational Graphic Ephemera*. Circa, 2021.

3.
Herbert A. Simon, *The Sciences of the Artificial*. MIT Press, 1996 (originally published 1968).

4.
See Reinhold Görling, Barbara Gronau, Ludger Schwarte (Eds.), *Aesthetics of Standstill*. Sternberg Press, 2019.

5.
Iain McGilchrist, *Ways of Attending: How Our Divided Brain Constructs the World*. Routledge, 2018.

6.
Daisetz Teitaro Suzuki, *Lectures in Zen Buddhism*, in Zen Buddhism and Psychoanalysis. Novello & Co., 1960.

7.
Ibid, 5, 4.

8.
Philip Larkin, *Sunny Prestatyn*, in The Whitsun Weddings. Faber & Faber, 1964.

9.
Andrew Motion, *Philip Larkin: A Writer's Life*. Faber & Faber, 1993: 327.

10.
We can imagine the poster is somewhere in Hull, but it's more likely a fictional encounter. James Underwood has recently described Larkin's early development of an "eye for the details of contemporary urban life". Underwood describes a scene in an unfinished and untitled story by a teenaged Larkin in which the protagonist "notices a number of advertisements, including one imploring him to 'Come to Sunny Jersey'". See: James Underwood, *Early Larkin*. Bloomsbury Publishing, 2021: 35-36.

11.
Jean-François Lyotard, *Paradox on the Graphic Artist*, in Michael Rock (Ed.), Multiple Signatures: On Designers, Authors, Readers and Users. New York: Rizzoli, 2013.

12.
Philip Larkin, *Essential Beauty*, in The Whitsun Weddings. Faber & Faber, 1964.

Sunny Prestatyn

by Philip Larkin

Come To Sunny Prestatyn
Laughed the girl on the poster,
Kneeling up on the sand
In tautened white satin.
Behind her, a hunk of coast, a
Hotel with palms
Seemed to expand from her thighs and
Spread breast-lifting arms.

She was slapped up one day in March.
A couple of weeks, and her face
Was snaggle-toothed and boss-eyed;
Huge tits and a fissured crotch
Were scored well in, and the space
Between her legs held scrawls
That set her fairly astride
A tuberous cock and balls

Autographed *Titch Thomas*, while
Someone had used a knife
Or something to stab right through
The moustached lips of her smile.
She was too good for this life.
Very soon, a great transverse tear
Left only a hand and some blue.
Now *Fight Cancer* is there.

...li...
ho di...
ged 2 Year
...food M.r Jo
ho died 2...
Aged

Living
with What's
Going On

Living with What's Going On

We commonly think of events to be a *coup d'etat*, a natural disaster, winning the lottery, or something like that, but for philosopher Alfred North Whitehead events do not have to be so melodramatic.[1] Instead, they are seemingly arbitrary things; the endurance of something's existence, for example, is enough for Whitehead to call it an event. He uses the concept to demonstrate how the things we think of as reliable, firm, fixed substances – any sort of stuff from atoms and solar systems to an A-Frame outside a café – are essentially in a state of flux. Simply put, "[w]herever and whenever something is going on, there is an event".[2]

For example, a billboard seems to be substance-like because it is solid, stiff and durable. However, Whitehead would argue that it is actually a dynamic entity. It is kinetic not only at a subatomic level, where it is a confusion of quantum activity, but also at a more familiar day-to-day level too. For instance, imagine that the billboard was being constructed opposite a school. The site of the billboard may have been fiercely contested by parents in the town, when it was being constructed there may have been arguments between builders and teachers shouting from their classrooms, there may be flecks of red paint hardened on the blue frame, left over from when it was first vandalised and repaired, and so on. These happenings are the dynamic qualities that are part of what makes the billboard an event. We admit that this is slightly pedantic and it requires an unusual scale of interest in the details of the taken-for-granted, but these are the ways in which graphics appear to be actual events and not just obedient broadcasters of content or bits of inanimate dead stuff. More to the point, it also means that when we treat a graphic as if it were a fixed, exhaustible substance-like thing we are to some extent denying its life and dismissing its vitality. James Williams thinks of that dismissal as a "violence", architect Friedensreich Hundertwasser would call it criminal sterilization.[3]

We have already seen this, to some extent, in Tennyson's poem, and *Art of Revolution*, and Barnicoat's concise history, and so on. Alternatively, to think of graphics in terms of events is to think about them as things that endure, occur, exist. Imagine them as day-to-day graphics that are just *happening*.[4] As such, a graphic event is not intangibly metaphysical, there is an immediacy and a concreteness to the event. It's the stuff you can point at, like a logo on an iron-rusted shipping container in some outlying field off a Northern canal network; that's a graphic event too.

Arguably, it has been for the sake of the certainty of knowledge and reliability of discipline that design discourses have overlooked these banal, everyday experiences. But if we focus on our lived experience of graphics in the everyday, we more often encounter graphics as "events" than as "designs". For instance, a company's name etched into the metal trim of a staircase in a ubiquitous block capital sans serif font, rusting and muddied. Evaporating in the sun, the patterned trail of a logo printed on the pavement from soles of shoes stepped in puddles. New white vinyl stickers stuck wonky on old black wheelie bins scuffed by mid-morning waste collectors. These are graphics as they exist in the reality of the "twilight world" – as an ancient philosopher once called it – and they are events. A notice pasted knee-high on a wall, weather worn and battered is a graphic event. The yellowed adhesive of security seal tape on a grey electrical box is a graphic event. The vinyl banner "WE BUY SCRAP" hooked high on a wall and pushed out of shape by a wild plant sprouting out of the bricks is also a graphic event.[5]

Whitehead specifically chooses the term "event" rather than "occurrence" or "happening" because it is the shortest word but it is our preference because etymologically it means to "come out".[6] We see the graphic event as something extending out from a banal background of other things and drawing us out, as pedestrians, too. It is similar to how graphic designer Robert Brownjohn describes this "bit of detail" down Fifth Avenue that catches a pedestrian's eye: "a big, fat, curly letter F".[7] The graphic *comes out* from the side of the building and with it draws the pedestrian out of their pavement-tromping banality too. It is how the graphic appears at the encounter and lives on that is the event. A graphic is an event when it is appearing, drawing, playing out. In short, a graphic is an event when it is *going on*.

Whitehead uses Cleopatra's Needle as an example of an event. It is a three and a half thousand year old Egyptian obelisk on Victoria Embankment, London. It came to London from Alexandria in 1878. Six members of the ship's crew died whilst transporting it during a storm at the Bay of Biscay. The base of the monument, along with the sphinxes that lie next to it, are scarred from the shrapnel of a bomb dropped in 1917. Of course, we can think of these as aspects of the eventful existence of Cleopatra's Needle, but we could also say the loss and gain of molecules, the dirt, moss, chewing gum, graffiti, and erosion all amount to a complex and almost trivial transitoriness of Cleopatra's Needle too. In an over-exacting way, the obelisk is not the same today as when it arrived in London, and it is not the same as it was five minutes ago, either.

If you look at an ordinary graphic in this way, and think about its transitoriness, the vitality of its existence-as-event is more vivid. Come back to the same graphic the next day and it has moved on, it is recognisable but different. You are still looking at the same discarded "To Let" sign as yesterday, for instance, but now you are late for work, the sun is not as low and glowing as it was the day before, there are too many people on the pavement for you to crouch down to get a good look at the way the old corrugated card has collapsed from water damage and left a ridged texture to the estate agent's phone number. Thinking of graphics in terms of events means that we are intensifying the newness of experiences with the familiar. Each time we see a graphic, we are seeing it anew. It is in this way that we can say graphic designs in lived life become more graphic and less designed in their eventful, enduring existence. Therefore, the event is a concept that allows us to distance ourselves from the incessant readymade bare facts of a graphic's design, such as the "message", the stock biography of the designer, the formal style, or what aesthetically Thomas Leddy would critically think of as the orderly, the clean, and the structured.[8] Instead, we are embellishing the "feelings of actual experience".[9] These are embodied feelings, in a place, at a time; there is an essential "withness of the body", as Whitehead calls it, when we think about graphic events.[10]

Ultimately, the graphic event asks: what do we feel to be happening? This sort of question is more in tune with the open conditions of possibilities of a graphic's existence than it is concerned with a graphic's design. If we suspend the expectation that graphics exist "as designed", as such, then we have a new attitude towards, and experience of, graphics in the real world; one that insists on the primacies of the agencies of both the pedestrian and the graphic. We are not wanting to undervalue the more established, traditional aspects of the graphic's design – of course they exist and play an important part – but it should not be the essential limit where graphics bottom out in critical discourse. Instead, when thought of as an event, a graphic's conditions of possibilities extend towards complexity and difference.

It is difference, not design, as such, that is essential to the graphic event.[11] Difference is felt when we are encountering the limits of a design. It is where the spontaneity of graphics – rather than the bounded certainties of design – are most prominent. Perhaps, this is what Rick Poynor was calling for in his "oppositional design criticism"?[12] The aim of the graphic event is not to disqualify design, but instead to show the reality of a graphic's life beyond design as a way to bring new perspectives into and upon graphic design discourses. To reiterate, we are not against design, we are wanting to bring design back to experience, situated in the real and caught up in the world. In this way, designers should not be working *out* contingency, or somehow using contingency, but *living with it*.

Living with What's Going On

Notes:

1.
We take our interpretation of the "event" from Whitehead, although the graphic event is not particularly philosophical and it is not properly Whiteheadian either. See Roland Faber, Jeffrey A. Bell, Joseph Petek (Eds.), *Rethinking Whitehead's Symbolism: Thought, Language, Culture.* Edinburgh University Press, 2017.

2.
Alfred North Whitehead, *The Concept of Nature.* Cambridge University Press, 1964 (originally published 1920): 78.

3.
See *Mouldiness Manifesto against Rationalism in Architecture*, www.hundertwasser.at, 1958.

4.
We mean "happening" with all the vim that Allen Kaprow would give it. See Allan Kaprow, *Essays on the Blurring of Art and Life.* University of California Press, 1993.

5.
Our primary focus is on the material, physical qualities of graphics. We look to James Williams' "process signs" to get at a more rigorously philosophical and semiotic understanding of graphic events.

6.
The Concept of Nature, 165.

7.
Robert Brownjohn, *Street Level*, in Typographica no. 4, December 1961.

8.
Thomas Leddy, *Everyday Surface Aesthetic Qualities: "Neat," "Messy," "Clean," "Dirty"*, in The Journal of Aesthetics and Art Criticism, 53.3, 1995.

9.
Alfred North Whitehead, *The Organisation of Thought.* Williams & Norgate, 1917.

10.
Alfred North Whitehead, *Process and Reality: An Essay in Cosmology.* Macmillan, 1929: 475-508.

11.
From a more systematic perspective, Anthropologist Arturo Escobar is also interested in how differences (from a biological, epistemic, and design-ontological contexts) can be "normalized" and "nourished". See Arturo Escobar, *Designs for the Pluriverse: Radical Interdependence, Autonomy, and the Making of Worlds.* Duke University Press, 2017.

12.
Rick Poynor, *Where Are the Design Critics?* in Design Observer, September 2005.

Constantly There, Constantly Changing

Patrick Thomas
Interviewed by Nick Deakin and James Dyer

Constantly There, Constantly Changing

You started Berlin Street Graphics early in 2017, had you photographed street graphics before then?

I started photographing details of everyday graphics in the 1980s. I would document my commute from home to the technical college where I was studying. Travel is important to me, new places keep my eyes open, when I see things – like variations of universal symbols and different cultures' take on everyday stuff – I catalogue it. Similarly, when I was on a foundation course at Central Saint Martins in the 1980s I would scan the streets along Tottenham Court Road, around Chinatown and in the underground, I just raked through stuff, you know? When I later enrolled at the Royal College of Art, my tutor Andrzej Klimowski would encourage me to do more of it too.

I think *Berlin Street Graphics* happened because I stopped cycling. I used to be a dispatch rider in London, I have always had a bike and when I first moved to Berlin my bike went missing, so I started walking everywhere. Walking brings you in much closer contact with the details of your environment. I started zooming in on things a little bit, getting quite close in there. I think I am probably stating the obvious here: when you are walking you are connecting more with the environment, more immediately than on a bike, in a car you are just bombing around in a tin box but walking you can really get close to stuff. So *Berlin Street Graphics* started in a very organic way, I was just photographing bits and pieces, I didn't really plan it or anything. It was only when I started to see these individual letter forms collected together in a grid that I saw this chopped-up nonsensical vernacular that evolves through doing; it was fortuitous, it wasn't planned.

So did photographing street graphics change from being spontaneous to something more deliberate?

I think so yeah. In the past it was graphics that randomly popped up and just caught my eye, but I get slightly obsessive, so I would find myself deliberately taking detours and looking for new graphics, I suppose this is what you and James would call a "graphic event"? I love that: graphic event. They are everywhere, and they are constant and constantly changing. So yeah I guess I became more focused on them somehow and started to search more carefully for them. So my commute, my day to day life, changed because of these graphics, it sounds a bit sad doesn't it? But it is true.

You also collect business cards from auto repair shops and offcuts from print room floors – Baudelaire may have called you a poète-chiffonnier – what is your attraction to these discarded and amateur graphics?

Stuff that is designed by non-designers fascinates me, we are back to the vernacular again. When I first moved to Berlin I was intrigued by these rogue cards, like tiny pixels littering the streets, and then I heard people talking about them in a derogatory way saying: "these people with their stupid advertising!" I enjoyed that reaction, so I started to collect a few of them. I wondered if they were all coming out of the same small print shop, if it was the same guy or lots of different people producing them. One thing led to another and now I have hundreds of the bloody things. They are all made with your standard crappy PC fonts and a bit of clip art, you will see the same picture of a van but it will be flipped and in various colours on different cards. Something very interesting happened the other day, someone started using a slightly slanted type. This is exciting, this is really exciting, this is like a big development somehow! I think I can trace this guy back, he seems to favour printing on pink cards. This is going to sound like I am joking, but I am not, they are absolutely perfect, you know, they completely fulfil their function, a graphic designer couldn't do it any better than that, they are just bang on, there is nothing you can add or take away from them.

Constantly There, Constantly Changing

With a certain self consciousness, you call yourself a graphic artist rather than a graphic designer, what motivated you to change from design to art?

Yeah, I am not even convinced by the term "graphic artist". Ideally I wouldn't have to label myself. I guess the graphic art thing came from my passion for traditional processes: painting and using silkscreen and stuff like that. It made sense at that moment in time, but these days I am not doing so much of it anymore, I delegate most of that work. I don't do commercial design, I haven't for a long time actually, I do bits and pieces if I like the sound of the project.

It is interesting that you mentioned Baudelaire before, Nick, because I did a project recently called the *Virtual Flâneur*. I had this idea to walk around Berlin in a white suit covered in dynamic QR codes, reading extracts from *The Painter of Modern Life* by Baudelaire, in which he famously refers to "flâneurs" and "passionate spectators". The QR codes pointed at random links that evolved throughout the day, always with some kind of socio-political content. I intended it to be deliberately pretentious.

In reality, half of the codes didn't work properly because of the movement of the material when I was walking but that didn't matter, it was about taking my practice into the streets and connecting with everyday people. I am doing a lot of stuff in public spaces these days. In 2018 I did a project supported by Arts Council England, it took place in Liverpool on St John's market. I gathered information from local people and I made this large projection on the side of a disused shop – somehow hacking people's shopping experience – but I don't know, is that graphic art? I don't think it is graphic design but it does feel like the language of graphic design. I know you have both heard this before, but I have always been perceived by designers as being an artist, and artists always think I am a designer. Whatever I do, even if I walk around Berlin in a white suit covered in QR codes, an artist will call me a designer and a designer will call me an artist.

I have heard you say before that you are interested in things that construct themselves, things that don't need too much intervention. Does this relate to your Multiples exhibition?

It is an idea that I started to physically put together around 2010 when I moved to Berlin. Similarly to the *Berlin Street Graphics* work, I was walking the streets of a new city, taking snapshots, finding bits of stuff in the gutter Baudelaire-style, bringing them back to the studio and then burning them onto silk screens and then, without planning too much, layering prints. I wanted to make interesting juxtapositions between things that don't normally belong together, and I called that series *Multiples*. It was exhibited in Düsseldorf, in the west of Germany. They had an interesting effect because you would walk into the gallery space, look up at the wall and you would start to instantly recognise icons, or some symbols or letter forms and then they would repeat in the space but they would never be repeated exactly the same way, or have the same context, there would always be a different combination. In a way, it was slightly disconcerting because the familiar also looked unfamiliar at the same time just by the play of contexts and relations. I suppose this is what everyday graphics are always doing, but we gloss over these awkward juxtapositions in day to day life.

Yes exactly, this is what we mean by the eventfulness of everyday graphics, they have their own impulsive liveliness. We think that noticing these things relies on a realist account of everyday graphic designs, would you say that your work is "realist" in terms of thinking of a world that is not ideal but one that is multiple, contradictory and complex?

I think very interesting things happen when things go wrong. Such as when Burger King puts their new logo on the side of a building and someone adds to it – like graffiti or a sticker or something – that's when graphics get interesting; when someone or something tweaks it a bit. I suppose that is a kind of realism. Similarly, with *Berlin Street Graphics*, a lot of them appear deformed, or manipulated or somehow something has happened to them or they have been cropped or pasted over or deconstructed somehow. Even if it appears to be a perfect letter form, look at the detail, there might be something interesting about the physicality of it, it might have been badly applied to a wall so there is a slight wrinkle or something like that.

In terms of everyday graphics, some of my favourite ones are on those telephone junction boxes. I think about when the engineer will come along and open it, like he is moving into this strange collage. Or where some kind of temporary cladding on a building is reused on another building and they get the order wrong when they put the boards on and you get this sort of deconstructed graphic, or even on sheet billboards, that lovely moment when it is late on a Friday and the guy pasting them up has got it slightly wrong and it is bloody freezing and he goes, aw fuck it!

Are you rearticulating these everyday experiences in your graphic works?

I am not always doing this hybrid of printing on old bits of crap, although I do like the contradiction and the strangeness of generating something on *Processing*, for example, and outputting it on a old bit of paper, I like that inconsistency, if that is realism or not I am unsure, it is an aspect, I suppose. I think just doing stuff in public that is accessible to the public is a realism, in terms of it being able to go wrong and break and have accidental encounters and unforeseen "events" happen, as you call them, like walking around streets standing in front of traffic in a white John Lennon suit covered in QR codes, and having people ask you "what the hell are you doing?" That is a certain sort of realism. Perhaps when I am doing this and taking my studio onto the streets and allowing the day to day to impact the way the work plays out is more real than taking the streets into my studio.

Does this connect with the generative process you are using in designing your latest publication Chroma?

Around 2015 I became aware of *Processing*, I think it was initiated in 2001-ish, so I guess I am quite late, it is software designed specifically for coding in the visual arts. I have been collecting colour swatches from print rip software, isolating the graphic elements and then chucking them into *Processing*, which then outputs these automated designs. All I then have to do is edit it, select stuff, curate. Essentially, it is a book that designs itself. It has to fulfil three functions, one is investigative of automation, the second is to celebrate traditional print – it is important that it is output as a traditionally printed ink-on-paper-object, not just something shared on a website – and the third is that it has a function, in that the viewer will be able to understand how colours interact. So there is no rigid structure, on the contrary, it is controlled chaos, it is an experiment. That randomness, it has always been there in my work somehow. I remember in the late-1980s, I was at the Royal College of Art and a guy called Gary Panter, who was an underground comic artist from the Raw collective in New York, came to give a talk. There was a moment when he showed us this really interesting process of combining images. He was taking unrelated pictures and layering them. I think he was painting on acetate or something and then overlaying it on different backgrounds. So there are three pictures; the two separate layers and the combination. I knew it needed to be investigated, and it stuck with me. I guess that is what I am still doing now.

Staying a bit longer with that contrast between design and accident, the aesthetic you are describing is similar to Karel Martens' prints on discarded cards and forms. What is the desire to bring the "real world" into your work?

I discovered Karel Martens quite late, early 1990s maybe, I was in Amsterdam and I went to a local newsagent to buy a prepaid phone card and it was designed by Martens for PTT Telecom, it is one of the CMYK numeric ones he set in Futura, really incredible work. But before Martens I was very interested in the work of abstract expressionism, especially Robert Rauschenberg, through to Pop Art, particularly Eduardo Paolozzi. Rauschenberg's work is very important to me. That is probably why I got into screen printing, more than Andy Warhol anyway. Rauschenberg said, "I think a picture is more like the real world when it's made out of the real world", he used lots of everyday graphics, like road signs, and discarded packaging and stuff like that. That's why I have this behind me now, I found it today on the road [Patrick shows us a flattened, grey cardboard box] – I will be printing on that this weekend.

Eduardo Paolozzi, one of the pioneers of British Pop Art, had a seminal show in London at the Museum of Mankind in the mid-1980s called *Lost Magic Kingdoms And Six Paper Moons*. In the catalogue for the exhibition there is a handwritten letter by Paolozzi, all in block capitals. He is calling for young artists to rethink the arbitrary distinctions between the sophisticated and the primitive. So he encourages them to use found, everyday objects as raw materials in their work; jump into skips, look on streets, etc. He calls these everyday materials an "unremitting and inescapable flood", it is a really beautiful letter.

You mentioned young artists, what are contemporary graphic designers and students of design in need of now?

I work intuitively and this informs my approach to teaching. I am honest with my students, I tell them I don't know exactly what the future holds in store, none of us do. What we have to do is remain sharp-eyed and adaptive. I certainly haven't got all the answers, I haven't got the rules (if there are any) I can't just hand down some kind of sacred knowledge that I was imparted by my teachers, and if you behave well and you get a big dose of it you'll be fine. It doesn't work like that.

Our tools have become so smart and we use them so intuitively that it is now relatively easy for non-formally trained designers to make work that undiscerning clients and members of the public might well find convincing. It might be shoddy, it might be derivative, it might not pick up any awards, but there will be a market for it. Throw machine-generated design – which is exploding right now – into the mix, and it will make for a precarious future for the traditional graphic designer sitting by their Mac waiting for the next job to come in via email.

I believe that the future will belong to those who make things happen, creatives who take more initiatives and who are disruptive, and I don't think that this fits the role of a traditional graphic designer as we understand it right now. Of course I'm not saying that the industry will disappear but I would advise students to keep a firm eye on emerging technologies, whether or not they choose to embrace them, and try to be aware of how this will impact their lives. Remaining vigilant is crucial for designers, if you feel that you are somehow becoming less observant, it should be an uncomfortable feeling.

Entrails
and All

Entrails and All

Considering the ordinary lived environment of a city, particularly symbols in cities, the iconic *Learning from Las Vegas* is an early critical review of architectural symbolism.[1] Robert Venturi, Denise Scott Brown, Steven Izenour and thirteen students from Yale University – two of which were graphic designers – visited Las Vegas in an attempt to analyse and make sense of this new city's peculiar novelties.[2] They were drawn to the way the idiosyncrasies of Las Vegas exist independent of the ordinary; the glut of competing YESCO signs for casinos, petrol stations, and hotels, and the ambiguity of car park wayfinding systems, and so on. But they are not quite the connoisseurs Sontag imagines, walking around the city enjoying unplanned collages. Instead, they never really seemed to be in Las Vegas, in terms of actually having their feet on the ground. Nobody writes about being sunburnt, nobody feels homesick, or excited to sneak off to the slot machines, or hungover. They call this deadpan disconnect a "pragmatic approach" to symbolism. With flat composure, they emphasise using concrete examples as opposed to thinking "abstractly through the sciences of semiology or through *a priori* theorizing".[3] However, just like all experiences, their pragmatic insights are still reliant on and informed by particular kinds of embodied, situated optics. Even if we ignore the power dynamics of students, staff and peers working together, and we brush aside the press's coverage of their study, and discount their investments in scientific materialism, the way they attend to Las Vegas with cameras, diagrams, data visualisations, helicopters, and cars, all matter because perspectives are positional and they are ingredient in what makes up Las Vegas as they come to know it. They cannot simply be indifferent, transparent observers.

The researchers claim to be "culling" information from Las Vegas but in that process of selective reduction they seem to also have excluded themselves from the study by attempting to erase their own unique marked positions.[4] As a result, we are left with sixteen people that have a unified, monocular perspective.[5] *Learning From Las Vegas*, as such, feels more like people describing what their sensory instruments have recorded – in a metaphorical and literal way – rather than any sort of report from the field. They call this objective, neutral, and truthful. You can imagine them like enormous mythical cyclopean creatures, straddling the Strip and pulling YESCO signs out of the ground (cables and all) to get a better look at them.[6]

For instance, by way of rental cars they analyse "enormous signs in vast spaces at high speeds". They are self-admittedly a "captive, somewhat fearful, but partially inattentive audience, whose vision is filtered and directed forward"[8] – they film approaching signs out of their windshield as they drive down the Strip from this "inattentive" position. They also make topographic maps of the roads and buildings from the "conquering gaze" of a helicopter.[9] In one instance, they collect all of this information into a seven by sixteen grid of stills.[10] These frozen moments manage to make Las Vegas feel weightless and lifeless; it makes us wonder what Étienne-Jules Marey could have made of Las Vegas, filming it from a moving car.[11] Rather than finding Las Vegas to be an actual place with real stuff happening in it, their representations of Las Vegas, which they have made by flying over it and driving through it, show something that looks more like an architectural model, or high-concept illustration; people look like cutouts and buildings jut out of the desert like prop facades. The researchers of *Learning from Las Vegas* show no immediacy or concreteness to their reality, nor any emotional involvement. When are they in the deep milieu, rendering what Tom Wolfe called a "detailed and 'everyday' realism"?[12]

What we are lacking from their deadpan descriptions is the bigness of lived experience. In *The Principles of Psychology*, William James describes a new born baby "assailed by eyes, ears, nose, skin, and entrails" experiencing the world as "one great blooming, buzzing confusion".[13] This embodied (entrails and all) impression of a world shining forth is illustrated by Tom Wolfe in his infamous reportage of Vegas' signs, as a "bubbling, spiraling, rocketing, and exploding in sunbursts ten stories high out in the middle of the desert".[14] From this New Journalistic perspective – a kind of journalism that historically foregrounded the reporter's limited, subjective experience – we are shown a unique, probably fabulated, and most importantly *partial* experience of graphics in the real world. In Martino Stierli's enthralling book *Las Vegas in the Rear View Mirror*, he brilliantly exposes the more human, personal moments of Venturi, Brown and Izenour's expedition.[15] He presents photographs of the students and of the architects that look more like private holiday snaps. They reveal a more tender subjectivity at play that has been screened off from the final study of *Learning From Las Vegas*, such as the above photograph by Steven Izenour.[16] The point is not that those snapshots are a truer, somehow more really real version of things, but instead that there is a meaningful, multivalent difference in how we can attend to the world and what that attention means. In contrast to this, in *Learning from Las Vegas*, they have managed to coalesce not only their different lived experiences but also to abstract the concrete reality of Las Vegas into something more comprehensively singular and unit-like; there is no "confusion" and there is no "bubbling", only bits of thingyfied stuff to be analysed and explained.

Notes:

1.
Robert Venturi, Denise Scott Brown, and Steven Izenour, *Learning from Las Vegas*. MIT Press, 1972.

2.
Their study was also translated into an exhibition, see *Signs of Life: Symbols in The American City*, 1976.

3.
Learning from Las Vegas, 131.

4.
Ibid, ix.

5.
See Lorraine Daston and Peter Galison, *Objectivity*. Zone Books, 2007.

6.
Just like Alfred Tennyson, pulling up the wildflower "root and all".

7.
Learning from Las Vegas, 4.

8.
Donald Appleyard, Kevin Lynch, and John Myer, *The View from the Road*. MIT Press, 1964: 5.

9.
Donna Haraway, *Situated Knowledges: The Science Question in Feminism and the Privilege of Partial Perspective*, in Feminist studies, 14.3, 1988.

10.
Learning from Las Vegas, 39.

11.
See Erin Manning, *Grace Taking Form: Marey's Movement Machines*, in Relationscapes: Movement, Art, Philosophy. MIT Press, 2009.

12.
Tom Wolfe, *The New Journalism*. Harper & Row, 1990 (originally published 1973): 57.

13.
William James, *The Principles of Psychology*. Henry Holt & co., 1890: 488.

14.
Tom Wolfe, *Las Vegas (What?) Las Vegas (Can't Hear You! Too Noisy) Las Vegas !!!!* in Esquire, February 1964: 98.

15.
Martino Stierli, *Las Vegas in the Rearview Mirror: The City in Theory, Photography, and Film*. Getty Research Institute, 2010.

16.
This subjective detailing, specifically from Denise Scott Brown's historical perspective, was recently presented in her published lecture *From Soane to the Strip,* 2019.

GROCERIES
VEG FRUIT

A Splash and a Stain

(Part Two)

James Williams
Interviewed by James Dyer

A Splash and a Stain (Part Two)

You say at one point in A Process Philosophy of Signs that a sign is a "selected set and its substratum" I couldn't agree more. Traditionally, in design, we tend to think of a sign as only the "selected set". The "substratum", as you term it, has rarely been taken seriously in graphic design discourse because it is extraneous to the design; it is the undesigned and undesirable. What difference are you defining between "substratum" and "context"?

Substratum is a much stronger term than context because substratum is all the things that are affected in terms of intensities and changes by the sign. There's an easy way of understanding this and that's to think of signs that appear innocent but that have strong intensity causing and affect causing on their substratum. You could design the perfect road for a certain throughput of traffic, for example, but if you put that road through somewhere where people live – that is the substratum, everything else around the road – you immediately change the way humans and animals can move through the place, you change the pollution, you change what's at either end of the road, and so on. This is true of any sign. If you change the shape of a pen (selection), you are also changing the body around the pen (substratum). Think of a well-designed gate, the substratum of the gate is not limited to the hinges and the entrance, it is who can go through the gate and who can't, the way in which a gate makes a noise, the way it allows light through it or not, and so on. And that substratum extends and extends and extends. The one thing that is really important to retain is that it is impossible to claim that your sign doesn't have something else in its substratum. If that road appears in a film by Wim Wenders, for example, then all of a sudden what you thought was just a road turns out to be an extremely important social and cultural site.

Clearly the substratum has an intensity to it, would you say that context is less dynamic?

Yes it is, context is usually something that you can list, right? The substratum is context, but it is context with intensities and multiple ones. Coming back to what I said in the beginning; signs are always violent, it's not enough to look at context to understand that violence, you have to look at the substratum, the system of intense effects of the sign across many different and conflicting diagrams.

It seems that "traditional" semiotics, which thinks of signs as a sequence with a set of rules, is better suited to design because it is a discipline of plans, intentions and ideals. The process sign, on the other hand, as a semiotics of contingency and change, seems more suited to unpicking designs. For instance, in one of your more recent essays on process signs you are seeing the process sign being played out as a kind of "critical reflection and democratic scrutiny". Would you elaborate a bit more on the politics of signs?

A sign is always a politicisation and restriction of choices. It is critical scrutiny of the way in which that politicisation takes place that is important. In order to be able to do that the process sign definition is put down formally so you can start to analyse what selection has happened and what diagrams – again, you could call them interpretations but with some caveats – have taken place. This heightened awareness is important, and that's also true for designers, how does a designer stand out, how does a designer do something different? Well it isn't by taking a simple account of meanings and symbols and putting them together, on the contrary, designs that change things do so exactly because they pick up on different intensities and movements, they make a surprising selection. You are always going to be aware that other selections could have happened. You are also always going to be aware that there are many diagrams and that you will prioritise some and not others. A classic example of that is when you are presenting your design to a client, you are very aware that you are showing the good side of it and not mentioning the bad side, even when they ask you what the downsides of the design are, you choose the good downsides. We can think of the design brief as a selection and a sign for the designer, so the designers are already reacting to signs, in fact, their preliminary sketches are diagrams in relation to the brief.

If diagrams are descriptions of signs changing, when are those descriptions happening and how do they take shape?

The diagram, or I should say diagrams, it is always many, are happening all the time. They are the mappings of different effects of the substratum, this is the really controversial or hard to grasp thing because it is a particular view of reality. It means that reality is already always multiple. Do you remember the controversy about the design of the London Barbican, because people kept getting lost in it? If you imagine four people going through the building you might have one who is an expert, one who loves learning about things, one who really doesn't like learning about things, and one who is easily lost. You have immediately four diagrams of the substratum of that sign (the Barbican). You've got one diagram which is: "isn't that brilliant, what a fantastic way to take someone through a building", you've got another diagram that's going: "this is a brilliant game!", you've got one which is: "this is awful, I am starting to feel ill", and you've got one saying: "I'm lost, I am just so totally lost". The diagrams are these multiple things: maps of the multiple effects of the sign and its selection.

There has been a recent emergence of designers thinking about design in contingent and accidental terms but there is a lack of discourse – or what you might call descriptive diagrams – to go with them; mostly what we have are photographs that document the event. Could you offer guidance for this emergent community of designers as they move forward thinking in more reflective and critical terms about what it is they are actually doing?

The idea of the accident needs to be viewed more in terms not of a breaking down but rather as a disjunct of what's expected. Whether something is or isn't an "accidental collage", for instance, is going to be a consequence of how something is taken, not what it is; a photograph is not a record of an accidental collage it makes an accidental collage. This greatly expands what is design and what designers can do. It makes designers much more important and signs much more important because once you realise that everything is operating as a process sign with these potentially very high stakes, then a craft and caution – both in the making and the reading and the interacting with and the criticising and politicising and depoliticising of signs – becomes much more important. I said I wanted to write *A Process Philosophy of Signs* because I wanted to say things about process signs but another reason was because I wanted to show how important signs were. People would say: "it is not the signs that are important, it is the deep meaning". There ain't no deep meaning without the signs.

In a great essay on style you say that "[f]eatures such as font, colour and shape, or epoch, type and manner, are descriptors of rigid states. They fix the sign[...] The sign caused a dimming of our hopes, not the sign was blue." Does this mean I cannot talk about particular formal elements of a sign whilst also accepting the process sign, or are you claiming that I cannot exclusively talk about those formal aspects because they are not an exhaustive definition of the sign? The reason I am asking this is because the thing that worries me about process signs is that I feel unable to return to the artefact of design proper (the poster, for example) without somehow undermining process philosophy, or only using it as some sort of superficial analogy. How can I get at the concrete graphic on a street corner whilst talking about the formal aspects of it and still be committed to a process philosophy of signs?

A Splash and a Stain (Part Two)

It is because the process account isn't an alternative to formal rules, established interpretations, established practices, and so on. It is an extension to and shaking of them. It is an extension to them because it shows where they came from, where they might be going, in how many directions and with what stakes. It's also an extension of them because it increases what they can be. You are not only asking how does what I want to do and understand fit in with these rules and these forms, but also how does what I'm doing break them, shake them, move them, disturb them?

What is the difference between diagramming and free association, such as a Rorschach test or Surrealist poetry?

Any sign will have a series of more overt, or dominant diagrams, because the substratum will have some things which appear to be more or less important by whoever is doing the diagram. But even without looking at it as a sort of analysis or interpretation, the interaction between the sign and something else will have dominant features because of the way the two things are. For instance, a hand and a handle will have a certain set of pressure points, movements, angles, temperature, smoothness, and so on. In that sense, a diagram isn't at all a chaotic thing, it isn't happenstance. This is why the highest level of the sign is democratic. It is about discussion and debate, it features controversies and clashes, but – and this is the important "but" – those aren't exhaustive and they don't have a claim to superior value, they just are. So you could have "these are the five dominant diagrams or interpretations of how a road interacts with a suburb it cuts through" but, because the substratum has everything in it, there is nothing to stop all of a sudden a new diagram coming in and saying it is crucial to look at all of this in terms of how a particular species of snail is going to move from North to South. In that sense, the sign is chaotic, because it is infinitely extended.

In an article on your website about how to diagram signs you say "[e]very sign is a process sign. There is an art to describing their diagrams". What would make a convincing, artful description for you?

This is always going to be dependent on who is reacting to the diagram and the sign, so I will reply to you from my point of view. Diagramming is an art that reveals more than one diagram, that shows the tensions between the diagrams, it's an art that goes beyond the obvious diagrams because those are often going to be the most important ones; they are the ones that are working in the background, or growing in the background, or receding in the background. From my (political) point of view the best diagramming will show the losers, those that are being downtrodden, excluded. This is another reason why you need to move up to the democratic level because you can imagine someone else saying the best diagramming is the one that finds the dominant diagram and tries to make it even stronger. That would be one that responds to statements like: "how are we going to become a leader in the market" or "how can we create the most cohesive society according to our ideals", and so on and so forth. Deep down I would defend mine as art against the other one, but I'm not going to go into that now.

Despite it being broadly accepted now that design is not always problem solving, more often than not students of design see their works as leading to an improvement of the world; they remain solution focused. What is the consequence of this?

There is a great example of this in the 1950s and 1960s when Clement Greenberg tried to establish American Abstract Expressionism as the highest form of painting but also viewed it as a kind of democracy. The problem with that, in relation to process philosophy of events, is that it is heading towards becoming fixed and frozen and therefore perishing

– if you return again to what I was saying right at the beginning of this conversation: the ground is shifting under the sign. An emotional way of saying this is that every designer and every design is always growing old and the way it grows old is by holding to some processes exactly when others are going in opposite directions. You ask me what an art of diagramming and an art of selection would be: it would be how to be as attentive to those other processes as you can be. That really is an art because sometimes it is going to be by ignoring them, sometimes it is going to be by including them, sometimes it will be by bending them, sometimes it's going to be by bending to them and there are no final rules: it's an art, a practice and an experiment.

You define the phrases "no sign should contain a contradiction" and "no sign can make sense unless it is within current social language use" as "stipulations" over the sign. I think these "stipulations" have a connection to how we would normally think of the authoritative role of designers and how we judge the appropriateness and success of a design. How can a sign resist "stipulations"?

The way in which a sign resists stipulations is frequently through paradoxes and contradictions. A contradiction is a shock as well as a logical opposition or a negation. A paradox is something that both makes sense and doesn't make sense. Signs that reveal the limits of stipulations operate in that kind of way. Frequently, disciplines and practices work in exactly that way when they develop and move into something new. To come back to what I said about the art of diagramming, there's not going to be any firm rules about what is or isn't going to be within a discipline. So what will be really important is the way that these graphic events that you describe remain open, because as they become more central, and they will, they themselves will start to separate away and grow old and lose sight of their substratum. It just so happens that now, they are close to a substratum in relation to your interests and mine and other designers.

Going back to the first instance of a process sign in your book, someone is sitting at a kitchen table thinking about a painted white cross on their door. The banality and domesticity of this scene is something close to the heart of this Graphic Events book. Would you say there is a realism to the process sign?

Yes there is a realism but it is a realism in relation to an understanding of the real as many-faceted, mobile, fluid, conflictual, politicised, divided, ever-changing, constantly threatened and enriched by innovation. So we often think of the real as solidity, toughness, endurance, that is not what the real is like at all. The real is instead much more like a hubbub of people when you go into a room; they are milling around, you don't quite know what they are doing or where they are going, you have to start to map what is going on, diagram it. So yes, it is a realism, but it is a realism that is necessarily speculative.

Given that signs are freely made, freely interpreted and open to any sort of "use" – including resistance to the intentions that made them – what is it that stops process signs from collapsing into meaninglessness?

The nature of the sign itself stops it from being meaningless. There will always be the selection, there will always be the diagrams and their intensities, there will always be stipulations over the sign and debate – or at least conflict – around the sign. Meaninglessness in the sense of nothingness, or pure chaos, doesn't exist. What you are going to have are a certain set of relative reactions, affects, emotions, groupings and so on that can be judged as being senseless in the same way that some people look at someone photographing a poster peeling away from a billboard and think it is meaningless – "what are these people doing?" – well actually it does have structure, you just don't see it, or it is not a structure that one reacts to. The whole point of the process sign is that what we would judge as lacking meaning or being chaotic is a relative judgement, which is already a political intervention. You never escape signs.

Your most recent work is on the sublime, do you see any overlap between design, as we have been talking about it here, and the sublime?

What I wanted to show in the sublime book is the way in which the sublime is designed and made. I also wanted to show that the sublime is the design of our highest values; this is something that is (extraordinarily) missed in nearly all discourse about the sublime. Thinkers of the sublime are looking for some absolute truth and highest value, they tend not to think of it as something that is accidental and made with certain sets of consequences, to the point where various people who choose different sublimes whether it is the mountainous sublime, the snowy sublime, the desert sublime, sublime of the abstraction of the mind, or the sublime of the lake district, completely miss the history of those places, they have been staged, cut out: designed. The sublime is manufactured, and the sublime is therefore contingent, it could always be different, it is always covering up many other changes, possibilities and potentials, and back to what I was saying about signs, it is always potentially violent. The worst kind of sign is a sublime that is taken to be the last word about our values while hiding its history – the story of how it was made.

What has changed since you wrote A Process Philosophy of Signs?

The way in which people interact with signs has, quite shockingly, become more crude rather than more subtle. And that is surprising. We have become worse readers of signs.

The way we move through the world, for instance in relation to computers involves a loss of distance and of discomfort, of critical space, because we are making faster use of signs and objects. We are behaving more automatically and more impulsively in relation to our environment and to the way it overflows with signs that affect us. For reasons of speed, ease, control and returns we are not analysing signs as we should. We have become worse readers of signs, it's a big shock to me. It's a bad sign.

Notes:

1.
Risky Signs: Philosophy and Covid-19, www.jamesrwilliams. net, 2020.

2.
A Process Philosophy of Signs, 134.

3Th

The Way We Attend to Things

Returning to the event of Cleopatra's Needle, Whitehead says it is only "[i]f we define the Needle in a sufficiently abstract manner we can say that it never changes".[1] Abstractions are simplifications, they reduce things to make them more stable and tangible than they actually are. Whitehead calls this the "method of extensive abstraction". It describes the transition from vast unthinkable complexity to something simpler, more comprehensible and unit-like. By thinking in terms of this extensive abstraction, it means we can think of events in more exact and reliable terms as "things". But in this transition from confusing inexactness to a refined simplicity there is, as Whitehead says, a "definite loss of content".[2] Generally, we could call this a technique of reducing to determine, or we could call it a process of selecting to grasp.

However, Whitehead does not support just one formal abstraction as an exhaustive and truthful expression of an event; the graphic "thing" has the potential to become something else because its eventfulness supports pluralist, contradictory, paradoxical interpretations (read: abstractions). This is what makes a graphic possible to be both orderly and "monstrous". In other words, abstracting is a way to secure the graphic in our attention, but there are multiple ways to abstract, and further abstraction is unavoidable when we reflect on what has just caught our eye. As such, there is no stable concreteness squatting behind the scenes of the event of Cleopatra's Needle, only more dynamism. For instance, still thinking about Cleopatra's Needle, a physicist may see a "dance of molecules" and an artist may see a "nice bit of colour", a stone mason may see a 224-tonne stone, a drunk passing by may see a place to vomit. Each one of these perspectives offers a reduced awareness of the event called Cleopatra's Needle. As such, to make a transitory graphic event comprehensible there must be a reduction and therefore a loss. But that abstraction is one of many other possible ways of abstracting.

Our lived experiences are abstractions. What we are experiencing are things discerned through an extensive process of abstraction from a mulch of what is potentially discernible. Use these words on the page as an example. If you stop and focus on the last word of this sentence you will only vaguely be able to discern what the other words around it say. We can say that this is one of the ways our processes of comprehension are dependent on abstractions, they are constantly going on. As soon as we point at a graphic and say "look there, at that" we are already abstracting the event to a set of more stable, more determined, more specific, less dynamic qualities.

Abstraction is not "wrong" or inaccurate, it is unavoidable because every experience is a process of selection and exclusion, that is to say: abstraction. It is the overinvestment in particular abstractions as inherently more truthful than others that we need to be wary of. This is what Whitehead calls a "fallacy of misplaced concreteness".[3] It is an attempt to pin down and determine something that is essentially dynamic so that it appears to be unchanging and fixed. That is why, if we take all this seriously, we cannot follow the common reliance on the absolute, the essential, and the truthful unless they begin to mean something radically different. It is why the abstractions we make come to matter. Writing on situated knowledges, Donna Haraway says that with "limited location" and "situated knowledge" we are "answerable for what we learn how to see".[4] This is the motivation to define the graphic as an event, it is a way to provoke this underimagined pluralism and to disrupt what we see and how we learn to see it.

Following in the footsteps of John Constable's interests in "old rotten banks, slimy posts and brick work", Jonathan Miller's book *Nowhere in Particular* is a collection of photographs of stacked pallets, skips, weather-worn surfaces, vernacular graphics, and corrugated shanty iron structures.[5] Near the end of the book Miller refers to Whitehead, saying "[a]lthought we can artificially cut up time into discrete episodes or instants, either by memory or by photography – don't forget that moment when they all pose for a group photograph in the first scene – things actually lead on to one another without any break or interruption". Despite embracing this principle of process and reality Miller goes on to demonstrate a kind of misplaced concreteness himself. Some of his analytical experiments are set on discovering the (supposed) definite fact of subject matters. In one instance, Miller is enamoured by the life-likeness of Botticelli's *Venus*. He studies the "visual modelling" of Venus' left cheek by making a ten by twelve square centimetre mask that cuts out the eye socket, nostril and edge of the cheek.[6] By doing this he finds that there are no "infinitesimally small changes of shading", as he was expecting, but instead claims to see a "more or less uniform" block of colour. By making the "modelling" of the cheek explicit, Miller is overlooking the way that the cheek's existence is dependent on context, in this instance the context of the rest of the painting. In other words, the cheek is not fixed, it is contingent, and Miller demonstrates that as such. The cheek can be both a block of colour and an accurate figurative painting – and also many other things for that matter, feminine, a product of the Italian Renaissance, an artwork among others in the Uffizi Gallery, and following Yuriko Saito, let's not forget about the back of the canvas too. All this is possible because what we are faced with is a dynamic event that withdraws from clear explanation, it is not simply a discoverable thing.

In another instance, Miller claims to understand shadows better by looking through the mesh of a tea strainer to grid the shadow into "simple blocks". He says, "the scene is slightly blurred" but it means that he is not "plagued by the innumerable details of shading". This is another technique to simplify complexity by excluding "excess", in other words, it is a process of abstraction. However, that excess, such as the granular detail of shadows and the implied "modelling" of a cheek in context to a whole painting, make up the potential of what a thing can become. Despite acknowledging that "things actually lead on to one another without any break or interruption" Miller wants to get to the concrete fact of the matter, but from our perspective, what matters is not the (contentious) "fact", rather it is the way we attend to the thing – by masking, being up close, being far away, absent minded, poetic, designerly, lyrical, from behind a tea strainer – this is what really matters when we take the event seriously.

An important thing to remember with the event is that it is not one or the other. It is not either the primacy of the designer's intent or the (supposed) secondary quality of the graphic's life and our felt experiences of it. This is not an argument between the "design as is" and "graphic as seems to be". Rather, they are all part of one and the same eventful nature of graphics. If the question that the graphic event begs is: what do we *feel* to be happening? the answers should be thought of as descriptive rather than explanatory. Just one of many possible abstractions. As such, we should not singularly think of abstraction as an aesthetic process, it is an existential process of experience and it is fundamental to our daily encounters with graphic stuff. It is also one of the ways we can say with certainty that what is essential in the world is the potential for everything to be otherwise. That is to say, what is essential is difference.

So the graphic is not a specific *thing* that is discoverable, if only you look in the right place in the right way. Instead, the eventfulness of the graphic means that it is a general undistinguished happening. It exists in the banal, conjunctive slurry of the everyday and it is made understandable at the abstracting occasion of experience. As such, the graphic event is undifferentiated in the banality of the world, that is, before it "catches" the tail of your eye. The ensuing event of experience distinguishes it as a unique element. It *comes out* as a thing discerned. In this way, we cannot say that the graphic is passive, waiting for an active subject to come and look at it, even posters resist being peeled from the streets.

Notes:

1.
The Concept of Nature: 107.

2.
Ibid, 13.

3.
Alfred North Whitehead,
Science and the Modern World.
Macmillan, 1938 (originally
published 1925): 75.

4.
Donna Haraway, *Situated
Knowledges*: 583.

5.
Jonathan Miller, *Nowhere in
Particular*. Mitchell Beazley, 1999.

6.
This analytical process is
unsurprising, Miller (a trained
physician) hosted a BBC
television programme in the
1970s called *The Body in
Question* that, for the first time
in television history, showed the
dissection of a human cadaver.

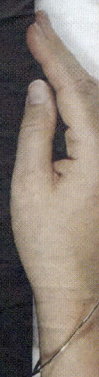

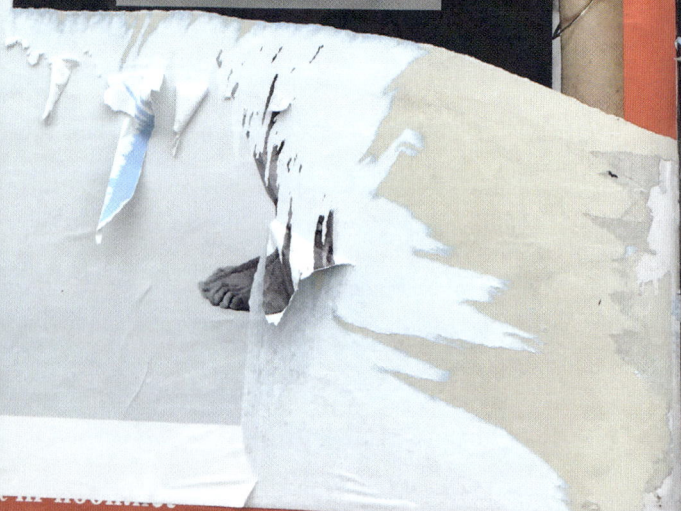

Beautiful, Obliterated

DR.ME and Vicky Carr of Textbook Studio
Interviewed by Nick Deakin

Beautiful, Obliterated

What do you think of the recent fascination in graphic design with collage?

Ryan Doyle (DR): I think it's indicative of the times. Just like the collagists before us, we live in a society overpopulated with images but now people are thinking about collage more as recycling, like it is an ecological thing that happens in the real world, away from the screen. We've just finished a project for Manchester United where we've made everything by hand. We'd seen the competitors had a collage-style too, but it was all digital, which for us was a sad thing to see; this creative process that we love so much being used in such a clumsy way.

What do you think about bigger brands appropriating styles from subcultures? Or is that just the natural way of this commercial business?

How would you describe your working process?

It's different depending on the project. Something I've learnt is that not everything needs a great idea behind it. That has been terribly hard to let go of because that's how I was taught. As a student, competitions and awards were a little more prevalent than they are now and we were encouraged to work in that "smile in the mind" style of graphic design. I still appreciate that tradition but I've learnt that sometimes a purely visual response can work just as well. I still do a lot of research and I collect a lot. Also with regard to the nature of the design process, when you're a student you have this impression that your ideas are the smartest and the most design-savvy because you're a fresh designer and you've just learnt all this lofty stuff about Baudrillard or whoever. But when you start working with people it's very much a compromise, so being able to communicate, listen and change tack is also fundamental to that process.

DR: Bigger brands are hiring younger people. Agencies will have a lot younger art directors that have different tastes from their predecessors so that's naturally going to affect what comes out in the mainstream.

Mark Edwards (ME): We made a collage of an Australian bushfire for *Wired* during lockdown, I'd just assumed it was a fifty year old commissioning editor that we were dealing with. But afterwards when we looked him up it turned out he used to be a student at Leeds Arts University who'd seen us talk there a few years ago. So I agree with Ryan about it being young people's voices coming through.

Globally, we've had tremendous upheaval for the last few years, with wide-spread social instability. Collage is typically thought of as being a critical, counter-cultural creative practice and perhaps a sign of frustrated dissatisfaction, I'm thinking of Hannah Höch, Richard Hamilton, Linder Sterling.

If we are clumsy enough to dissect your practice into two separate strands; on the one hand working with artists on books, websites and exhibitions, and on the other hand your work with Cloudwater brewery, they're two distinctly different audiences. How much do you think about the people seeing your work in the "wild", so to speak?

Regarding the books, they're usually quite niche so it always surprises me the amount of people that have actually had my work in their hands. Whereas if we're designing beer cans for the brewery, unless you're a massive beer nerd, they just get thrown away after they've been used. Although we do occasionally have feedback from stockists, the owner of a bottle shop somewhere will say that the writing is too small and ask us to make it bigger, and then I have to think actually yes I'd better go and stand in a bottle shop and see if it's ok.

Do you think this recent trend in collage is a reaction to what's happening now?

DR: Collage is very affordable, you don't have to buy super expensive canvases and paints or a really expensive computer and software. You can go to a charity shop or order magazines in bulk on ebay, ask your friends for stuff or just tear it from the streets. It's affordable but not skill-less, and anyone can try it.

The work in Cut That Out, 365 Days of Collage and Accidental Collage does not seem to have any political edge, they seem more like fun-loving craft, is that fair to say?[1]

DR: Yes definitely, we try to steer away from making anything too political.
ME: The thing is a lot of our work is escapist, so things that are divisive don't feel right in that context and with there being

Being situated is interesting, standing in the bottle shop with a customer's-eye-view looking at a can through a half closed fridge door. This relates to how we consider there to be an underimagined difference between the ideal intention of a design and the everyday existence of a graphic in the real world. Do you also consider these things to be distinct?

I do because of who engages with them at each stage. When you're working on something isn't it the case initially that you think about what's correct in terms of the classic rules of design, like type, layout etc? Maybe in that stage of the process you're designing for yourself and by extension other designers. The second stage of the process, after it has been signed off, anyone who has a stake in the project – and this, of course, includes the public – make their interpretations, this is separate. The second part is more precarious, it could happen, it might not, and if it does how can you really so many cultural pressures at the moment, it feels weird to engage with them in a playful way.

In a crude sense, collages are abstractions, they take from something, in your case books from charity shops, National Geographic and other magazines from Empire Exchange for example. But Accidental Collage is different, the collages are made by the photographers, while the things they are photographing remain with the world in constant flux.[2] What initially drew you to this project?

ME: It's interesting that you say the photographer makes the collage. The project started when we were travelling to exhibitions and talks, noticing these other-worldly billboards and posters for theatre shows and foreign cinema, torn apart or pasted over. Later I was waiting for my parents in a coffee shop in Bristol and I saw this billboard, took a photo and started the *Accidental Collage* Instagram account. It was

predict who will use it and how they'll react to it. Unless you go and stand beside it and watch everyone looking at it, which is impossible and obviously absurd.

Yes of course, the plurality is endless, anyone doing the same thing will have slightly different experiences. You mentioned type being too small, but that may only be to certain people with failing eyesight, for example, the graphics can also be obscured by condensation on cans and by reflections on fridge doors. These are contingencies that are out of your hands as a designer. In a sense the work is made in cahoots with an unknown public. How, if at all, do you resolve this in your designs?

There's a lot in film theory that I think applies to my design process. I reference Tzvetan Todorov's narrative theory a lot. His idea was that films tend to begin in a state of equilibrium until a subsequent event causes a problem (disequilibrium) requiring early 2020 when I photographed the first few billboards. I'd just been to Amsterdam and there were these beautiful graphics everywhere. After a while, it became a more collaborative project with people around the world photographing decaying posters and sending them to us. It's become a kind of hobby, that's the easiest way of describing it. Eventually we'll make a little publication.

DR: I like the subtle weather worn and battered ones. I think what you're saying about the constant state of flux is interesting, especially the really shabby ones with the glue showing. You walk past them and every time they're different.

ME: There was a huge one really near our studio, it was beautiful, obliterated and torn apart. They'd just ripped the poster off and it took almost everything with it, it was unbelievable.

the characters to find a solution, or maybe not. I think about this sometimes when I'm arranging things on a page.

You share a studio with Eddy from DR.ME, do you have different working processes, what are your conversations like?

We often chat about meaning and whether things make sense. We share different projects or articles, interesting things we've found. I think where we differ is that Eddy and Ryan are less concerned with traditional ways of doing things and we think and respond to things very differently. At a basic level, my first response to a brief would usually be with type, for example, whereas theirs would be image.

Aesthetically, there seems to be a recent fascination with texture in commercial graphic design.

All these things are, of course, outside in the street. Do you think that designers have lost touch with the world outside the studio, do you think that it even matters?

DR: I was driving recently and saw somebody had sprayed this really bright purple graffiti tag and above was the red brick of Manchester. The minute I got home I made a note and ended up using that colourway for a poster. On another occasion, in Italy, I came across a church poster that was red ink printed on fluoro yellow paper. Again, I made a note and in this case used that colour combination for a Manchester School of Art project. I do find galleries inspiring, but thinking that you've got to go and do this properly, official cultural thing to be inspired rarely works. It feels like a cop-out to say it, but just keep your eyes open, or look in…

ME: Unsuspecting places…

DR: I didn't want to sound all: "inspiration is all around you".

ME: Something that we both try to do whenever we travel, for

Are we talking about *Procreate* here? I feel like texture, especially fake texture, has had a massive resurgence. Thinking back to my student days, a lot of people came to design through *Photoshop* and they've learnt to use these effects, cut things out, layer things up, and texture plays a big part in that. Maybe you learn to make things cleaner and more minimal as you go on. It's fascinating to me that it's come back around, especially to this *Procreate* aesthetic with very flat tidied up textures. I think the reason we prefer to employ these aesthetics in analogue, rather than digital, is to give depth and that's not something that the screen traditionally has. It's definitely one of the ways that DR.ME's work has a certain type of energy and dynamism. The images that Eddy and Ryan source have a texture from the quality of print in older magazines, you can see the dots of the printer, these qualities give the print a tangible feel. Maybe a mirror between them and *Accidental Collage* is the organic process, they're rearranging

Beautiful, Obliterated

a talk or exhibition, is to try and find that weird book shop, that little something unusual in a different tongue that shifts your point of reference. The printers in that country will print differently, for example, or use slightly different types of paper. It all just has a different feel, for some reason, and that feeling makes you see in a different way.

In our interview with Patrick Thomas, he mentions that once he started to collect these photographs of street typography and graphics in Berlin it changed the way he would navigate the city. Has Accidental Collage affected you in a similar way?

ME: Yes, I have become a lot more annoying to anyone I'm walking around with, if I see something I'll have to stop and apologise to them while I nip over the street to take a picture of something as I am constantly looking for accidental collages.

things by hand and the billboards are being rearranged by the weather.

Do you think this trend is a reflection of what's happening now socially and politically?

I think it's interesting with texture, particularly with collage, because it is an aesthetic – and now I guess a trend – that is often linked to these shifting political events in the world. I think it's just the processing of all these events making its way into pop culture. It is interesting when clients start to ask for collage, maybe I wouldn't be so impertinent to say "oh have you asked for collage because there's civil unrest?"

You mentioned before that you are a collector, what are you collecting?

If you look at our studio it's a real mess compared to a lot of designer's spaces, it's not a white cube.

Have you found that the search has got more acute?
Thinking about your strange bookshops, gradually the strange
bookshops aren't as strange anymore and you have to look
for something even less familiar and more strange.

ME: I think your eye is constantly adapting, maybe at the
start of *Accidental Collage* I was drawn to things that now I
wouldn't be that excited by. Your eye becomes more attuned
to what it is you're looking at.

With Accidental Collage you are celebrating failures, lost
designs, detritus, things that are on the fringes of design, not
entirely dissimilar to your Fin? project.[3] There is a sort of
humility and candid honesty to this. Why do you think this is
necessary in design?

DR: Interesting you draw a comparison between *Fin?* and
Accidental Collage I've never really thought about it like that.

There are a lot of found objects and things that
are given to us by friends; street signs, bottle caps,
badges, things we found on the floor. I'm a bit of a
hoarder, although I do still collect constantly, I am
trying to be more particular with it. I ask myself: do
I need this cinema ticket, is it more important than
this nice leaf, or this chewing gum wrapper that I've
found? I used to just keep them all.

Do you think it's important as an educator to engage
students in a kind of pedagogy of detritus?

Yes, for two reasons really. One is to observe the
way that things communicate differently. Such as
types of information, the way things are laid out,
different typefaces, point sizes, but also in less
technical ways, such as the way something feels,
like a tear on a ticket stub for example. Secondly,
the idea that as a designer you have to be a bit of
an expert of everything. A challenge I set students
is to try to visualise "nothing" in as many ways as

Beautiful, Obliterated

The reason we did *Fin?* was because when we present work to clients we create so much it seems a shame to only store what doesn't make it on a hard drive. We are aware of the tradition that you shouldn't share mistakes – not to let anyone see behind the wizard's curtain – but we disregarded that and it helped push the studio forward because we couldn't recycle old work, we had to start afresh.

A lot of your work seems to be driven by collections; failed work (Fin?) street graphics (Accidental Collage) pop ephemera (365 Days).

DR: Obviously we collect books and magazines but we don't necessarily collect in the same way that John Balderssari or Peter Blake collect; separate drawers for arms, legs, feet etc., it's a smart idea but we don't do that.
ME: Yes, there's loads of things I collect; records, books, *Apartamento* magazine, which I've fanatically been trying to

they can, such as zero, a hole in the ground, the word "nothing", an empty space, an empty box, the sign that something is missing. You have to engage with the world and how things are signified and what they mean and how things are represented in a non-literal, non-obvious way. To me that's what collecting and observing is for, they are different ways of looking and seeing and being a designer.

Do you see a similar thing happening with Accidental Collage?

I like that it's interactive, that other people are seeing similar things and are submitting their images. If you stand back and look, *Accidental Collage* is a visual essay on the imagery we see on a regular basis, decaying and a little abandoned.

Have you got any tips for undergrads in terms of teaching them how to see? How do you encourage others to look at the world?

find early copies of. Also, just before lockdown I moved to a house in Moss Side that had a derelict alley behind it. We started trying to do it up a little bit and plant things to stop people fly-tipping. Now I've turned into a magpie and anything that looks like a receptacle that could hold a plant I will probably drag it half a mile home and plant something in it. I guess that is a different sort of collecting.

Do you think it's important to engage students in a kind of pedagogy of detritus? You're making use of trash for your alley garden, Accidental Collage is foregrounding condemned signs soon to be replaced, Fin? is resuscitating failed ideas, collage (as you have already said) is seen more now as a practice of recycling.

ME: I think it's good to explain to them that it will be a part of their practice. It's not a weird thing to do. It's just a different way of looking, and that changes how you design.

I think reading really helps in terms of how things are described in different ways. In literary fiction, for example, ten different writers will describe the same event in ten different ways, and sometimes their difference is as subtle as a change in tone of voice.

We have relied on dirty realism in literary fiction to develop our realist account of this typically idealist discipline.[1] When have you experienced this difference between the idealism and realism of graphic design?

We do tend to talk about graphic design with a certain romance away from the grubby hands of real life. As a student one of the reasons I was interested in graphic design was because of the record covers and book jackets. You may have them at home but when they were referred to and discussed in books their criticality was detached from the bedroom carpet. This reminds me of how I

DR: Yes it's interesting what you say about litter, particularly thinking of discarded packaging, colourways, fonts, typefaces, things outside the usual frame of reference. One of my favourite things is shop signs of type made with tape. Things like that are not necessarily something students would think they should be looking at. Why are we into it? I think it's just the naivety, there's an honesty to it.

There's something quite desirable about that amateur effect that is hard for a trained designer to reproduce because it goes against the traditions of design. Is Accidental Collage opposing design in a similar way, like a kind of anti-design?

ME: Yes completely. Graphic design is both exciting and incredibly boring so things that are anti-design are interesting.

Do you feel like part of your own practice is about being aware of what mainstream design is and staying clear of it?

tell a student to explain their ideas, I say: "stick that poster on a bus stop somewhere relevant and give that rectangle some context".

This reminds me of a chapter in The Cheese Monkeys.[2] A tutor drives the class out to a road far from the college campus, gets everybody out and gives them each a marker pen and board before driving off. Their only way home is to make a sign to show passing cars in hope of a lift.

Yes, I was reading something similar recently, about an improvised acting scene where a character had to convince a woman to get off a train with him. They didn't give her part of the script, they just got the actor to come up with his best shot at making this complete stranger get off the train with him. A similar story, regarding a lecturer I know, put her students on a train and told them that when they got to the destination, which was at the other end of the UK, their

DR: Definitely. When we first met at university we were not type nerds or graphic design geeks but we were very much hands-on when making stuff. I think at the time that was very anti-design. That hand-made aesthetic is associated with graphic design now but a decade ago that was maybe not the case. We were anti-traditional design then and to an extent that ideology remains in our studio work. If I'm choosing a typeface, for example, I'm often trying to pick the most uncool typeface I could use for the project.

How do you perceive your role as designers? Would you say you are looking to create coherence, or corruption?

ME: Both, simultaneously!

DR: I think when it's work for ourselves there's definitely more of an element of corruption, but when we have a client we have to create some kind of coherence for them.

dissertation would be finished, then the doors closed and they were off!

What should young designers be worried about?

Automation. I was reading an article by Aggie Toppins who was talking about the idea that designers got really defensive after the invention of the Apple iMac and the tools that were suddenly in everyone's hands.[3] As an industry we had this weird reaction and we attempted to try and "professionalise" everything in this pretentious way. We now have things like *Trendlist* and *Hipster Logo Generator*. *Trendlist* has a poster generator that's already set up with tongue-in-cheek prerequisites. You choose some colours, type and then style categories from the list and it will create a poster for you. So, if computers can do that, what can you, as a designer, do that isn't that? I often have to check that students haven't used *InDesign* or *Google Slides* templates to make work, telling a

Aesthetically there's a jarring quality to all your work that feels intentional. Fraser Muggerridge would probably call that a "knowing wrongness".

DR: Yes absolutely, two or three years ago that kind of "knowingly wrong" work helped us get more recognition. Now a lot of our work is client based so it's been toned down but we still retain a punk rock spirit and we do things now and again to rekindle that.

So in that sense I take it you don't adhere to the celebritism of designers?

ME: Is it Chip Kidd that talks about graphic designers being fancy plumbers? The title of our book *Not Dead or Famous* came from our publisher suggesting we couldn't make it as we weren't dead or famous enough to sell a monograph, but part of that is also a rejection of the designer as a celebrity.[4]

design student not to use templates absolutely baffles me. Can the computer do a better job than you? What are you being employed for? For your ideas and your approach, your brain, but also your expertise in guiding people through projects, print processes, hiring copywriters or illustrators, etc.

What advice do you have for graduating graphic design students?

Why wait around for somebody to give you a job when you can make your own? As a student I was once invited to work in this derelict mill space behind Oxford Road station, but it rained indoors and there were holes in the floor. We shouldn't have been up there really but the landlord was into the arts and happy for us to do whatever we wanted. We built a shed up there and created a little office space. We turned the whole top floor into this giant studio loft apartment. We met a lot of people through that space, Eddy and Ryan of DR.ME amongst

Ryan, you mentioned Robert Brownjohn in Not Dead or Famous. What do you find interesting about his work?

DR: I discovered him through the French publication *Revue Faire*, they highlight a different designer each issue.[5] I read about BJ and his lifestyle and it struck a chord, he wasn't just a title sequence designer, he could draw, he was a photographer, he was a videographer, he didn't pigeon-hole himself and I really like that.

In Graphic Events we are interested in his photographs, particularly when he first came to London in 1961. He was doing what you were describing before; he was in a new place and the different street vernacular was strange and alluring, and so, the camera came out.

DR: Yes, that's exactly what we were doing. You're out of your own city, you're in somewhere new, your whole environment

many others. I try to explain this to students, about networking – that horrible word – it wasn't corporate but networking is what we did. We even ran a film night for a couple of years, and we'd put gigs on and have parties, and people would just turn up and we'd make new friends. Also, don't rush. You don't have to know exactly what you are when you graduate because the industry is constantly changing, so how can you possibly know where you fit? I think people want to hire the difference, not the similarity.

What do you think is needed in graphic design education?

Helping students to help themselves. A focus on producing independent thinkers and people that have confidence. I think we're moving away from this thing in design education where experts teach skills to unskilled people. Teaching should be about facilitating new ways for the design subject to be understood and practiced and challenged.

changes and it's instantaneously inspiring.

ME: Yeah absolutely, that idea of being in a different place and seeing things in a different way totally changes your axis of understanding. This is the sort of inspiration that a gallery, for instance, will rarely match.

You contributed to Erik Brandt's Ficciones Typographika 1642, a project where designers submitted work which was then pasted onto a billboard outside Brandt's home in Minneapolis. The five year project was then documented in a book.[6] What was your approach to the work?

ME: That *Ficciones* project feeds into the stuff we've found interesting over the years, like the continual process of making things, like *365* and *Fin?* and *Accidental Collage*, something that's ongoing and constantly growing. Weirdly, one of our pieces was a type experiment called *JOY* which turned into a book we did with my mum who's an artist.

Notes:

1.
Term coined by Bill Buford of Granta magazine to describe a literary movement. "Dirty Realism is the fiction of a new generation of American authors. They write about the belly-side of contemporary life – a deserted husband, an unwanted mother, a car thief, a pickpocket, a drug addict – but they write about it with a disturbing detachment, at times verging on comedy. Understated, ironic, sometimes savage, but insistently compassionate, these stories constitute a new voice in fiction". *Granta 8: Dirty Realism*, Summer 1983.

She'd seen it and liked it and wanted to use it for the cover of a book about tapestry weaving.

What was it she liked about it?

ME: It was partly the odd typography but also because it was a photograph of a billboard in the street with its surroundings. Seeing it pasted up, makes you think differently.

What should young designers be worried about?

DR: AI is alarming. I find that quite worrying, robots doing graphic design.

Is this another reason why we should be moving away from mainstream ideas of graphic design?

2.
Chip Kidd, *The Cheese Monkeys: A Novel In Two Semesters.* Scribner, 2003.

3.
Aggie Toppins, *We Need Graphic Design Histories That Look Beyond the Profession.* Eye on Design, eyeondesign. aiga.org/Sar9f, June 2021.

DR: It may make for an interesting future, as maybe people will move away from computers and go back to setting type by hand and collage as there are things a computer won't be able to do to the same degree. It may foster a new trajectory if commercial graphic design is in the hands of AI, people will naturally react to that.

What advice do you have for students of graphic design?

DR: I always quote Jay-Z's *My 1st Song*: "treat everything like it's your first project", that way you'll stay humble.
ME: I think supporting your local scene is always a good thing to do. Go to local gigs and shows, buy your friends artwork, put on exhibitions, make small publications. It's the way we started, and it helped so much in those early years.

Notes:

1.
DR.ME. *Cut that Out: Contemporary Collage in Graphic Design*, Thames & Hudson, 2016. *365 Days of Collage* was a year long project by DR.ME which entailed creating a new collage every day between 2014 and 2015. *Accidental Collage* is an instagram account curated by DR.ME which shares "discoveries of accidental collage from around the world".

2.
See James Williams, *A Splash and a Stain*.

3.
Fin? is a zine made by DR.ME collating unfinished and unrealised work. It is published digitally once a month and as a print edition twice a year.

4.
DR.ME, *Not Dead or Famous Enough Yet*. Waiting Room Press, 2020.

5.
Étienne Hervy and Natasha Leluc, *Revue Faire N° 10 — A line: Robert Brownjohn*, 2018.

6.
Ben DuVall, Paul Schmelzer, Erik Brandt, *Ficciones Typografika 1642: Typographic Exploration in a Public Space*. Formist, 2019.

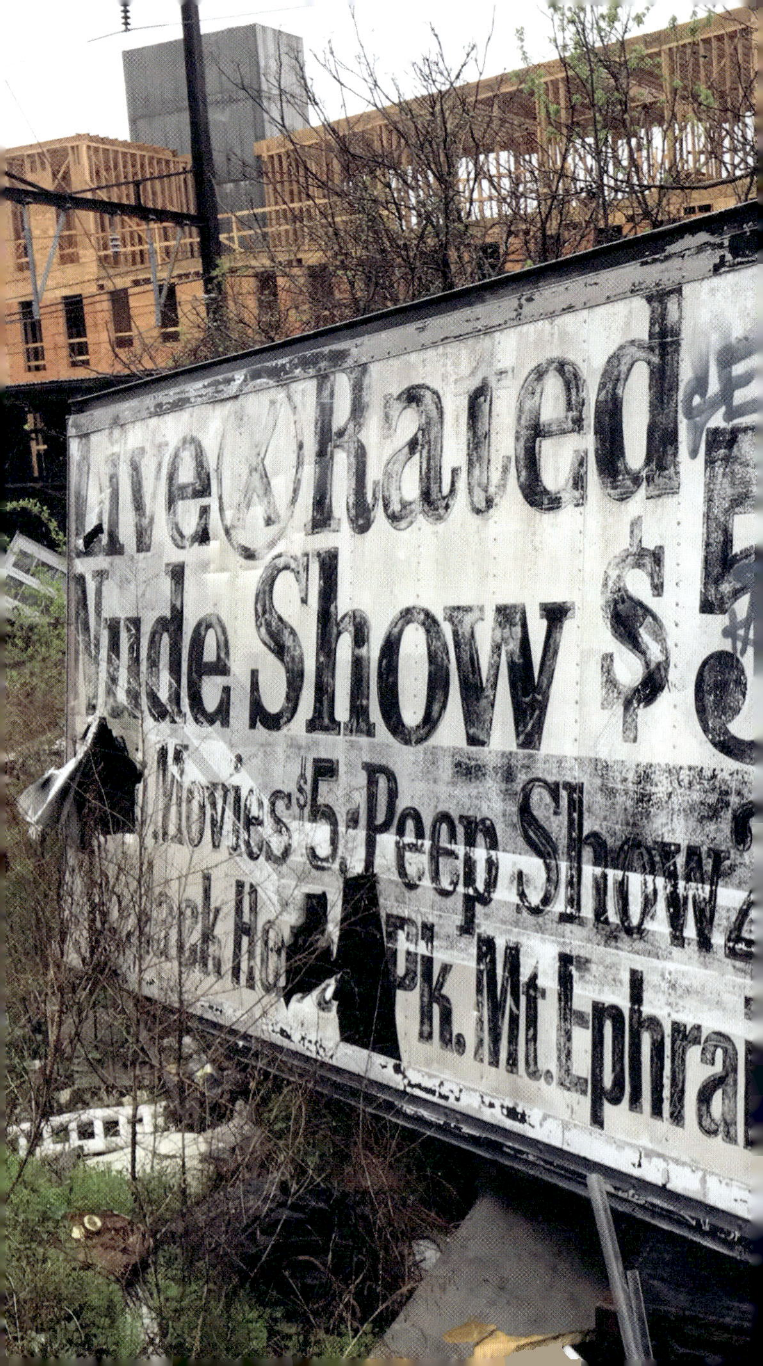
Live X Rated
ude Show $
Movies $5. Peep Show
Pk. Mt. Ephra

Transformative Abstractions

Transformative Abstractions

In the early 1960s, graphic designer Robert Brownjohn photographed quotidian London street graphics. He snaps an "E" that has come loose on a "The Vintner Liqueurs" shopfront sign; tipped over, looking drunk, it leans on its neighbouring "N". He sees "Dubonet", in capitals, on the trim of a collapsed umbrella, the concertina folds warping the letter forms. He finds a poorly hand-drawn sign behind the surface waves of rippled glass, barely readable: "Snacks at the bar always ready". Brownjohn's photographs show the spontaneous, novel life of graphics-in-the-world. He says:

> "The things they show have very little to do with Design, apart from achieving its object. They show what weather, wit, accident, lack of judgement, bad taste, bad spelling, necessity, and good loud repetition can do to put a sort of music into the streets where we walk".[1]

His street-level encounters with graphics are literally not straightforward, you can imagine him leaning into, crouching over, and bending back to photograph these bits of graphics. In other words, part of what makes the picture is his destabilized, expanded perception of the immediate environment and in doing this he finds graphics existing in complex, unanticipated ways, that is to say: as events. The *élan* of the photos, as such, is in the motion blur, tipped orientation and occasional fuzzy focus. These are the qualities of an irregular, but nonetheless embodied experience of graphics. Brownjohn is not acting like an egoless "transparent eyeball", in the sense that he is being nothing but seeing everything.[2] Instead, he is where he is and he sees what he sees on "the streets where we walk".[3] It is in this way that Brownjohn's encounters with graphics are concretely situated in a distinctly different way from those in *Learning from Las Vegas*.

In this instance, we are using the word "situation" as if it were a relation with an intensity, rather than meaning

either present or absent at one position or another. It ranges from the more or less abstract (drawn away from a place) to the more or less concrete (together with a place). We can imagine two registers of situatedness. Firstly, the situation of the pedestrian person experiencing the graphic. In this instance, Brownjohn is a tourist in London, a heroin addict, an alcoholic, someone getting in the way of other pedestrians. Secondly, the situation of the graphic itself, in terms of its specific place and position, above a shop front, on a folded umbrella, behind rippled glass, and so on. In this way, we are taking into account the idiosyncrasy of experience and the peculiar contingencies of the graphic when we are thinking about the situations that make up an event. Brownjohn's photographs mark the traces of a graphic's behaviour, he frames them in a way that lets the graphic grow out into the excesses of its environment. Borrowing from Suzuki, again: Brownjohn sees the graphic and the graphic sees Brownjohn. The graphic event, as such, is Brownjohn-with-graphic, concretely continuous together.

In contrast, since 1987, designer Ed Fella has also photographed everyday street graphics.[4] Unlike Brownjohn, however, he isolates graphics from their immediate

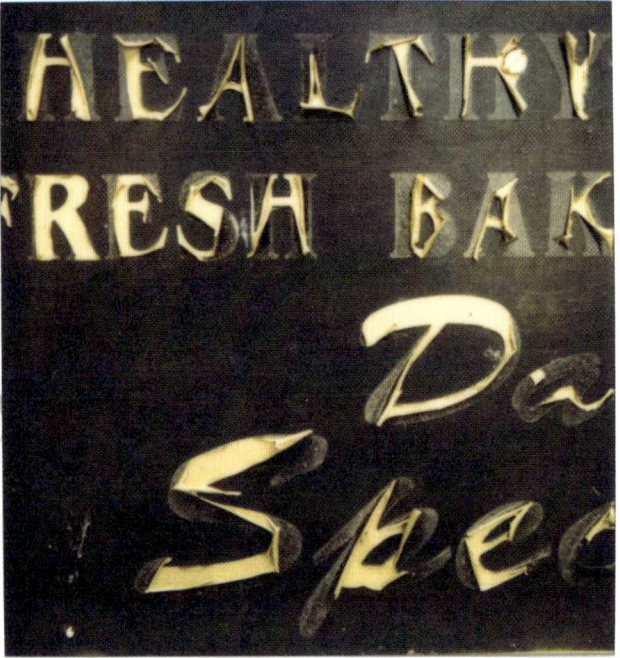

environment by zooming in, or perhaps more accurately: closing out. His photographs register something almost craft-like in the lyrical quirks of ad hoc, vernacular signs messily inked on cardboard and hastily brushed across shopfront windows. He focuses analytically on specific qualities of the graphics; letters striated by split, weathered wood grain, the midday shadows cast by unilluminated neon signs, the sag in large banners pulling the spines, stems and axes of letters out of shape, and so on. Looking through Fella's impressive collection of photographs gives us the feeling of being one big eye, opened wide; he takes in so much detail at the micro-level that the rest of the world around the graphic – what we could call the deep milieu, in this context: the concrete and the contextual at the macro-level – rarely passes into view.

This way of perceiving everyday graphics is more abstract than concrete because Fella appears to be separating the graphic apart from the whole. He directs himself towards the complex interiority of the graphic at a more formal, functional level than we see in Brownjohn's photographs, for instance. Fella's granular level of attention means that the peripheral world falls away, which leaves his perspective and the position of the graphic without a sense of concrete place. However, we know that this is only how things appear to be because Fella is already in and of the world before he is photographing these graphics. There must have been a moment of finding (*trouvaille*), approaching, sustaining attention, framing (closing out), focusing, developing (on polaroid) and finally walking on. The point is that the graphic's situated context and Fella's embodied experience are not drawn into the discourse because in his photographs the design – that more reliable, formal structure of principles – eclipses the contingency of that experience.

It feels like Fella's photos are trying to find use, or make use, of these overlooked graphics. He is trying to bring these seemingly superfluous details back into design, back into the "order of the notable".[5] As such, with Fella's photographs, we do not get to see the fullness of the graphic as it relates to the unstructured areas beyond its edges because the crop cuts out what is extraneous to it. The photographs lose – or perhaps "overcome" – the unintended and indeterminate relations between a graphic and its situation; the graphic is estranged from its lived condition, it has no bearing in the real world other than its quaint vernacular. Arguably, Fella's photographs are more abstract than concrete because he is being faithful to the formalities of his discipline of design, in other words: design is regulating his experience. Whereas, Brownjohn's photographs self-admittedly "have very little to do with Design".[6]

The abstract and the concrete, as we are using them here in these photographic examples are two different kinds of attention to graphics – they are two different ways of encountering, reflecting, recalling – and they constructively make the graphics in their encounter. That is because abstraction is transformative; it stretches and extends out from the concrete, it is not split and broken away from it. As dynamic events, graphics are concrete and therefore integrated in the whole, they are never simply floating bits of stuff. This is an impetus of James Williams' *A Process Philosophy of Signs*, it is about relating the seemingly separate sign back to the "substratum" of the whole.[7] Because Brownjohn is at a slight distance from the graphics, it is enough to show his process of choice, selection, reduction, and singling out. In other words, we could call this his embodied process of abstraction, he sees the graphic as found-in-the-world. Conversely, Fella's narrowly focused attention is probably because he is wanting to use (in some capacity) the graphics he is documenting, in the same way that Corita Kent wanted to use hers so she would "cut out context" using the finder to literally narrow her focus on a select area.[8] Brownjohn is not using these images, at least not directly, he is seeing himself as part of a world of graphics, he considers how he is in the way of traffic and pedestrians and so on. This is the unfamiliar way of being a designer in the world, namely, by being pedestrian.

As such, Brownjohn is encountering and disclosing a graphic's discontinuity with design in a way that Fella cannot, which is why Fella's photographs must exclude the excesses that appeal to Brownjohn. Returning to Brownjohn's photo of the "The Vintner Liqueurs" sign with the dislodged "E", for example. The shop front sign makes up only the bottom half of the photo, above is a white wall, in the middle a sash window is open with net curtains slightly apart. Of course, this is inconsequential to the sign-gone-wrong that must have originally struck Brownjohn's eye, but still, it is part of the graphic's situation, and perhaps even more importantly, it is part of Brownjohn's *framing* of experience. In other words, his perspective is not restricted to design.

When we think about graphics in the abstract – like Fella, but also like the histories, collections, and portfolios previously described earlier on – we lack a sense of place and position, but we preserve the primary importance of the design. We should not forget that designing is about defining significance through reduction; to de-sign is to *reduce* to sign. However, if we insist on the individual and partial perspectives that are always already there in those everyday places, a more pluralistic and contradictory understanding of graphics, one that surpasses their design, is made necessary.

Notes:

1.
Robert Brownjohn, *Street Level*, in Typographica no. 4, December 1961.

2.
Ralph Waldo Emerson, *Nature*. James Munro & Co., 1836: 13.

3.
Brownjohn, *Street Level*.

4.
Edward Fella, *Letters on America: Photographs and Lettering*. Princeton Architectural Press, 2000.

5.
Roland Barthes, *The Rustle of Language*. Translated by R. Howard, University of California Press, 1989 (originally published 1984): 142.

6.
Brownjohn, *Street Level*.

7.
James Williams, *A Process Philosophy of Signs*. University of Edinburgh Press, 2016.

8.
Corita Kent and Jan Steward, *Learning by Heart: Teachings to Free the Creative Spirit.* Bantam, 1992.

NEW
HEAVY DUTY
GIANT
LAUNDRY SAK

ONLY **50**p

INSERT **1 × 50**p

Signs of
the Everyday,
Every Day

by Teal Triggs

Roman Mars and Kurt Kohlstedt, co-authors of *The 99% Invisible City*, suggest that hidden stories are revealed through "the everyday objects that are invisible because of their everydayness" and go on to say that they "refer to the invisible parts of things you *do* notice".[1] Mars and Kohlstedt explore the city through "unnoticed" design and architectural objects, highlighting a ubiquitous cityscape of unseen signs: utility codes, sidewalk and roadway markings, and so on. They tell us what is behind the objects, the stories of how something is made or who made it. This is a process for decoding the city. As a design historian, objects certainly hold my fascination, but equally, I feel the story of an object is made richer and more mysterious by exploring the experiences the object affords within its context. My favourite example is the unfamiliar familiarity of New York City's urban landscape, a city I have been visiting since 1975. This is where I recently began to take a forensic approach to documenting photographically an urban narrative of graphic designs with focus on the everyday. [Fig. 1]

I have an interest in the narratives of the everyday and those which are told from uncanny juxtapositions, close detailing, and formal compositions. My intent as a photographer has not been to use the image and its accompanying text to show what is known about places and objects, but to offer spaces for imagining what is *not known*. In the act of opening this arena, my process became more exploratory, experimental, and playful. The immediacy of an experience shared is encouraged by the Instagram social media platform. The platform is used to document things that I see around me, though the process of what I capture emerges from a more intuitive form of note-taking and observing. The results hopefully offer new ways of seeing and a "sense of being" within the world. At the same time, I am asking: in what ways might we explore a city in terms of everyday encounters, and what of its visible and imaginary traces? [Fig. 2] [Fig. 3] [Fig. 4]

The first official lockdown in England began on 23rd March 2020. Free movement around London, where I live, was severely restricted. Those who had online access worked from home and connected via a network of digital screens. For most, all human contact outside of a designated "bubble" was virtual. It meant I needed to choose a digital platform so I could reach out to friends, let them know I was okay, and pretend there was some sort of normalcy. I used hashtag phrases to describe my mood: #reflection #stillness. Documenting the #thingsthatisee from my picture window became an emotional outlet. At once my position as a global citizen became spatially fragmented whilst also giving rise to a "co-located presence" for my pandemic experiences.[2] [Fig. 5]

In March 2020, I began a daily ritual of walking twice a day, as per government regulations. I rarely ventured outside of a one mile radius from my house in South London. Posting one photograph every day was an act of resistance against an enforced existence of self-isolation within the confines of a familiar domestic interior. At the strictest period of lockdown, we were told how far we could travel and how much time we could take for exercise each day. Posting a daily image was my way of creating a routine. This simple act provided a marker of time. My journey was articulated through what cultural theorist Michel de Certeau refers to as "citations" – the mapping of graphic signs and detailed observances.[3] Noticing signs offered a point of regularity giving rhythm to each day. [Fig. 6] [Fig. 7] [Fig. 8]

My daily walks on Clapham Common purposefully followed the well-trodden paths of the neighbourhood's residents during lockdown. The resulting pathways were worn into the Common's landscape; they had widened out due to recent overuse. Pedestrian movements had transformed them, in what de Certeau calls a process of giving "shape to spaces".[4] Joggers and walkers alike continue to carve out new routes through the path's adjacent grass, which Mars and Kohlstedt discuss as a "desire path", a process made visible. The American urban planner, Kevin Lynch, defines "paths" as "the channels along which the observer customarily, occasionally, or potential moves".[5] In contrast, desire paths emerge out of wanting to "take a path less travelled"; they are non-linear and operate in defiance of imposed systems of urban planning.[6]

Prior to the pandemic, this kind of shape-changing in an urban landscape was rooted in desire. Mars and Kohlstedt suggest that we "create a personal desire path" of "spontaneous trails" which often trace the "shortest distance between two points".[7] The shared path through a grassy area is an example of what Mars and Kohlstedt propose as the idea of "collaborative placemaking" which occurs when more than one person traces a similar "desire path". Of course, this process of tracing equally suggests an act of "collective disobedience".[8] They represent an inherent tension found between citizens and planners in the design of the built environment. At a time of social distancing, where people seek an extended and necessary safe space in which to walk, desire paths may become the dominant norm of a post-pandemic environment.

It was along this pathway made visible, but also my many paths which remain invisible, that I have been documenting my trace. Lynch speaks of how people observe the city while moving through it.[9] He says "the environment suggests distinctions and relations, and the observer [...] selects, organises, and endows with meaning what he sees".[10] The city is awash with images of signs that are both formal (street signs) and informal (handmade signs). As material markers, they represent actions; for example, signposting ways to navigate, establish orientation, and/or provide direction. As I move through the neighbourhood, I am documenting the graphic language of the everyday through the materiality of graphic communication. These paths often speak to "the absence of what has been left behind".[11] My images are often shot tightly cropped, where the viewer is asked to respond to a detail of the object which is bereft of its wider environmental and social contexts. The image creates a kind of intimacy, drawing us in to consider the objects' formal properties, materials, production process, and graphic style. Equally, the image prompts a space for asking questions of how we index our own positions and identities and how we "interact with semiotic systems of the world around us".[12]

Instagram was founded as a photo and video sharing application building on people's desires to network and disclose their social experiences in relation to places, people, things, and situations. As a location-based mobile media application on our smartphones it allows us to record our movements through time and to document the routes taken. In an article about the effects of location-based mobile media technologies Jordan Frith and Jason Kalin argue that Instagram and other mobile digital devices "represent new practices of place-based digital memory".[13] They continue, "to extend current research of mobile media as the interface of the everyday, we are interested in day-to-day activities of mobile media users, those activities that fit within the rhythms and habits of everyday life and that become practices of digital memory."[14] These are sites which allow researchers to focus on communicating understandings of place, but also allow for the process of archiving images and texts as digital memory. [Fig. 9] [Fig. 10]

What is at risk if we do not have digital memory of signs, graphics, designs as they exist now? Why should we remember these things? Why develop our own "urban narrative"? These questions have to do with history and the way in which historians write the narratives of our past. The past is gone, but fragments remain. Historians will piece the fragments together to make a plausible story. Social media is part of this process as an "archive" offering "new kinds of storage space" whilst representing and transmitting the digital traces of our personal lives.[15] Hashtags are used to index the images, in a process akin to the visual typologies preferred by graphic designers.

Signs of the Everyday, Every Day

The media theorist Wolfgang Ernst writes in his book *Digital Memory and the Archive*, that "the function of the archive, as of art, is to hold unlikely things".[16] Instagram, for me, holds the everydayness of graphic objects in a way that can be quirky, unusual, playful, and always in dialogue with the viewer. Since March 2020, I have taken pictures and uploaded one per day, a ritual of early morning or late afternoon practice. Most of these images were taken on my daily walks and posted around the same time every day to capture the attention of colleagues from a wider audience of designers, artists, architects, writers, and academics. My intent was to ensure, as much as possible, an authenticity for a shared, and inherently medially generated experience, between myself and my followers. Random moments that hold my memories and thoughts, reflect my moods, anxieties, or small joys of the everyday, in my daily walks around the neighbourhood with signs of the everyday. My every day is mediated through an ongoing documentation of these places and their traces. Our "sense of being" in the world remains relational to our past, the present and increasingly, toward an uncertain future.

On 19 July 2021 London re-opens. As the city is transformed into its post-pandemic guise, I hope the ordinary and mundane objects and experiences of my everyday walks will not lose their fascination.

[Fig. 1] November 15, 2015. A brisk walk on Sunday morning in New York City. My eye is drawn to the iconic Chrysler Building which peeks out from mid-town's surrounding skyscrapers. It's a scene out of Gotham City. A street crossing light signals for a man to cross the empty boulevard, the figure is a visual clue of the city's architectural scale.

[Fig. 2] October 17, 2017. My travels took me back to Montreal after nearly two decades since my last visit. Though parts of the urban landscape had changed, the homemade signs had not. The visual delights found in irregular spacing of handcrafted numerals and letters, each with their own distinctive form guided by the range of vernacular materials used in their making. The illustrative scene silhouetted in blazing red, of the tow truck dragging behind it a broken-down automobile. What a pleasure to see the hand of the sign maker in this advertisement for parking services.

[Fig. 3] June 21, 2018. I stared out of my hotel window for what seemed hours onto the streets of Porto. Zebra stripes, parallel lines and circular signs contributed to the unique character of this Portuguese seaside city. A second glance revealed heat-worn cracks in the painted white lines and wonky street sign. On this trip my walks were more purposeful – back and forth to a conference venue.

[Fig. 4] December 21, 2018. I've always held a fascination with signs. My father was a graphic designer, and I grew up in Austin, Texas exposed to its unique hand painted and neon signs visible on almost every building and street corner. South Congress in particular, became a mecca for hotels and shop owners to take a playful approach to this form of street advertising. On my last visit back home for the Christmas before the pandemic, I made a point of sharing some of these visual gems for friends back in London.

[Fig. 5] March 17, 2020. The days at the start of the pandemic were marked in my photos by the changing skies seen from the top of my house and my picture window. I held on to the dramatic shift in the spring weather conditions expressed by early golden lit sunrises, midday cobalt blue skies and billowy clouds, and frequently, the dark underbelly of thunderclouds.

[Fig. 6] April 14, 2020. I looked up only by chance to see the materialisation of an immaterial shadowing of the number forty. The long-awaited springtime sunshine had enlivened the mundane nature of house numbers, resulting in an impromptu typographic installation.

[Fig. 7] June 30, 2020. Walks are cathartic. They liberate you from this new immersive world of digitality and screens. We have been catapulted into another kind of reality. A mantra emerges "another world is possible". Store fronts of disused buildings hit by the economic downturn, transform into public poster galleries, bringing life to the neighbourhood once more. I wonder, what are the ways in which we will experience a sense of place once again, in post-pandemic life?

[Fig. 8] April 13, 2021. All points will eventually intersect. Two lines and a sign meet the edges of the street and paving stones. The urban landscape reveals the everyday in surprise compositions in unexpected places.

[Fig. 9] 17 June, 2021. Forty-two has significance someone commented in the posting box. Douglas Adams in *The Hitchhiker's Guide to the Galaxy* (1979) reported that "42" is the answer to the "ultimate question of life, the universe and everything". And so, it remains today.

[Fig. 10] 27 June, 2021. Signs, codes, colours, grids. A language of utility engineers emerges within the urban landscape as fleeting spray paint indicates something underneath, not on the surface; a map of a subterranean world.

Notes:

1.
Roman Mars and Kurt Kohlstedt, *The 99% Invisible City: A Field Guide to the Hidden World of Everyday Design*. New York: Hodder & Stoughton, 2020: ix.

2.
Rowan Wilken, Lee Humphreys, Erika Polson, Roger Norum, Saskia Witteborn, Germaine Halegoua, Jordan Frith, Jacob Richter, *Digital Placemaking*. Panel presented at AoIR 2020: The 21st Annual Conference of the Association of Internet Researchers, 2020.

3.
Michel de Certeau, *The Practice of Everyday Life*. Translated by S. Rendall, Berkley: University of California Press, 1984 (originally published 1980): 120.

4.
Ibid, 97.

5.
Kevin Lynch, *The Image of the City*. Cambridge: The MIT Press, 1990 (originally published 1960): 41.

6.
The 99% Invisible City, x.

7.
Ibid.

8.
Su Ballard, Zita Joyce and Lizzie Muller, *Networked Utopias and Speculative Futures*, in The Fibreculture Journal: Digital Media + Networks + Transdisciplinary Critique, Issue 20, 2012: 6.

9.
The Image of the City, 41.

10.
Ibid, 6.

11.
The Practice of Everyday Life, 97.

12.
Ron Scollon and Suzie Wong Scollon, *Discourses in Place: Language in the Material World*. Routledge, 2003: x.

13.
Jordan Frith and Jason Kalin, *Here, I Used to Be: Mobile Media and Practices of Place-Based Digital Memory*, in Space and Culture, August 2015: 2.

14.
Ibid, 5.

15.
Jussi Parikka (Ed), *Archival Media Theory*, in Wolfgang Ernst, Digital Memory and the Archive. Electronic Mediations, vol. 38. University of Minnesota Press, 2013: 3.

16.
Wolfgang Ernst, *Digital Memory and the Archive*. Electronic Mediations, vol. 38. University of Minnesota Press, 2013: 83

DEVONSHIRE
NO VACANCIES

St. Michaels
VACANCIES

VACANCES

Double
Four

42

4C

The Discerned and the Discernible

The Discerned and the Discernible

To get a better sense of the graphic event, we need to stick with this tension between the abstract and concrete a little while longer. There's not a clear contrast between the abstract and the concrete because they are related, albeit with varying stretching depths of relation. One is not better than the other, or even more preferable, it is just that right now in discourses of design, the abstract is more dominant.[1] The risk of this dominance is that everyday experience, in terms of unclear, indeterminate, curves of activity, will increasingly be subordinated to the anticipated and preconceived – the clear, simple, exact and mechanical – even if the former (which we can think of as graphics) and the latter (in this case design) are at odds. So the graphic event is a way of generating resistance to the supposed simple, unmysterious ways in which graphics are made knowable. Speculatively, the graphic event demonstrates and validates the potential of viable alternatives.

This is a way of thinking critically about abstraction. Alfred North Whitehead describes the process of abstraction using two curious terms: the "discerned" and the "discernible".[2] Firstly, the discerned, he claims, are things that have "their own individual peculiarities".[3] We can think of the discerned as the things that lure designers like Ed Fella and Robert Brownjohn into taking photos of graphics; the grime caught in the counter of an "O" on a brass sign, irregular descenders of letters scratched into windolene, the low, winter sun flared in shop windows distorting signs. These are particular things *discerned*. Whitehead goes on, "the entities of this [discerned] field have relations to other entities which are not particularly discriminated in this individual way".[4] These are the *discernible*; they are the elements closed out of Fella's photographs but *discernible* in Brownjohn's. Whitehead elliptically describes them as "merely a 'something' which has such-and-such definite relations to some definite entity or entities in the discerned field". For instance, the window above "The Vintner Liqueurs" sign in Brownjohn's photograph is *discernible* as a general "something", but it is not part of the particular character of the "E" that we primarily *discern*, it just has "such-and-such definite relation" to it. The discernible are the aspects that we are only vaguely aware of but are not yet directly perceiving. As such, the discernible "lack further definition" because it is the "particular character" of the discerned, the "E" in this instance, that draws our attention. However, the distinction between the discerned and the discernible is not an abrupt division. It has, as Whitehead puts it, a "ragged edge". He uses a room to illustrate this idea of the ragged edge.

Beyond the discerned confines of a room, Whitehead imagines, there is also an outside exclusion of the discernible. However, "the junction of the interior world of the room with the exterior world beyond is never sharp", for example, sounds seep through the walls, shadows are cast through the windows, smells draft through the vents, light leaks beneath the doors.[5] As the definitive clarity of the supposed unitary composition of the room is distorted by the flux of the excluded and the included, the absolute distinction of the "discerned" is compromised by the constant presence of a "discernible". If we think about graphics in these terms we can see how the design – as the discerned *par excellence* – has a "ragged edge" in the everyday and, therefore, how recognising and attending to extraneous, discernible details dynamises the rigid solidity of the design itself.

Returning again to street photographs of graphics, and continuing with this more specific sense of the concrete and the abstract, we can think of what passes into frame in terms of the discerned (abstracted) and what is outside of the frame as the discernible (concrete). In *Eye Magazine*, Rick Poynor writes about designer Wojciech Zamecznik's street photographs, he says they have "a preoccupation with the ways people relate to spatial settings formed by the built environment".[6] Zamecznik would include passers-by in his photos of street graphics, as well as the surrounding environment, drawing attention to how graphics are resident in the world and how the neighbouring aspects of weather, people, substrates, buildings, adjacent posters – in other words: the discernible – all contribute to the contingent makeup of those street graphics, despite being incidental details. This is also what we see in Teal Trigg's brief essay *Signs of the Everyday, Every Day*. In Whitehead's terms, they are drawing attention to what is "merely a 'something' which has such-and-such definite relations to some definite entity or entities in the discerned field".

If design synonymously means plans, intentions, choices, things made with a deliberate sensibility, then the things that Zamecznik photographed included the satellite aspects of those designs; they are the unintended parts of a design, they are the parts that had originally been excluded from that design, and they are reintroduced by the photographer that takes one step back from the graphic he photographs to let the deep milieu of the undesigned pass into frame. Designer's reduce to sign – we know we have already said it, but it is worth repeating – regardless of style, designers exclude and abstract, it is a fundamental tenet of de-signing. However, once a graphic design is freely situated in everyday life it is in a peculiar possession. Discerning these details is important for us to consider this realist account of graphics and challenge how we typically come to think of graphic designs.

We can feel this most vividly in Georges Perec's *An Attempt at Exhausting a Place in Paris* where Perec makes notes on "conventional symbols" and "fleeting slogans" in complex association with other (supposedly) arbitrary things: "a rather big chunk of sky [...] some sort of basset hound".[7] In this way, we cannot think of designs as containers that hold graphics still, graphics have their own impulses. Instead, the design is just one of many abstractions. Perec also knows this, because he acknowledges that the way he attends to these events changes what they are, in other words: they are not predetermined or fixed. He says, "I'm drinking a Vittel water, where as yesterday I was drinking a coffee (how does that transform the square?)".[8] This way of thinking, perhaps a low, "infra-ordinary" kind of thinking, is underappreciated in critical graphic design discourse because – as James Williams argues in our interview with him – it is not part of the reliable, structuralist tradition of semiotics to think of these unstructured seemingly irrelevant things.[9] But isn't it a more convincing, realist account of our daily encounters with graphics?

Notes:

1.
Iain McGilchrist gives curious reasons for this at a broad cultural scale. See *The Master and His Emissary: The Divided Brain and the Making of the Western World*. Yale University Press, 2009. In his latest book *The Matter with Things: Our Brains, Our Delusions and the Unmaking of the World*, McGilchrist argues there are no substances, only patterns and habits.

2.
The Concept of Nature. Cambridge University Press, 1964 (originally published 1920): 49-98.

3.
Ibid, 49.

4.
Ibid.

5.
Ibid, 50.

6.
Rick Poynor, *Posters for the People*, in Eye Magazine, 2019.

7.
Georges Perec, *An Attempt at Exhausting a Place in Paris*. Translated by M. Lowenthal, Wakefield Press, 2010 (originally published 1975): 6.

8.
Ibid, 30.

9.
Louis Aragon's *Le Paysan de Paris* (1926) is littered with these supposedly arbitrary thoughts provoked by encountering the excesses of modernity. Despite Aragon being a Surrealist, the novel can be read as if it were the confessions of a realist.

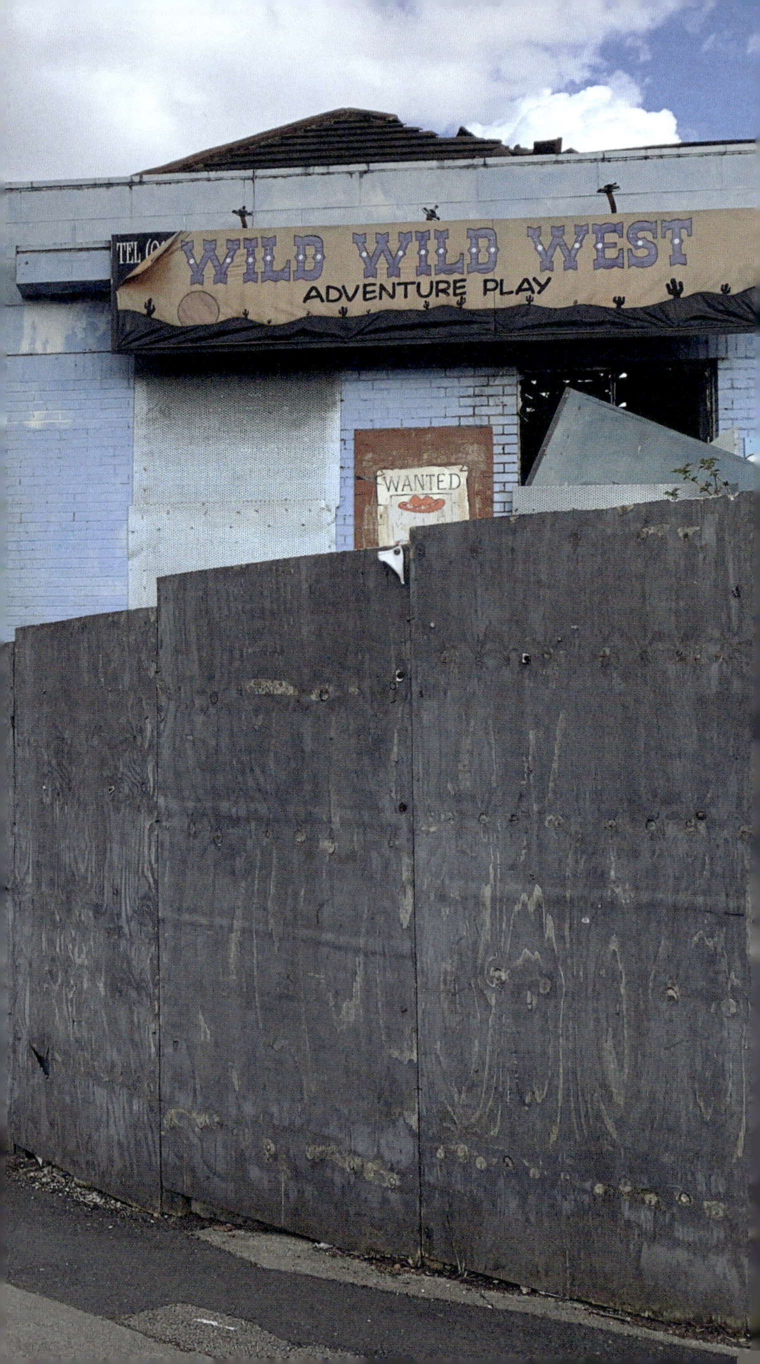
TEL (0
WILD WILD WEST
ADVENTURE PLAY
WANTED

The Trivial the Clumsy and the Insignificant

In the opening to an essay on *Objective Literature*, Roland Barthes describes a large neon sign outside the Gare Montparnasse that is designed to read: *bons-kilomètres*. The sign's lights are broken, "several letters of which are regularly out of commission".[1] Barthes thinks the "extremely complicated, [and] somewhat unstable" sign is a good object for the 1960s *nouveau roman* author Alain Robbe-Grillet. Robbe-Grillet thought of himself as a realist. In fact, he claims, "[a]ll writers believe they are realists".[2] He says it is the common ground of the classicists finding reality to be classical, the romantics romantic, naturalists natural, and surrealists surreal. "Each speaks of the world as he sees it, but no one sees it in the same way".[3] This is a fitting definition for what we think of as realism in relation to the graphic event too; different perspectives drawing contradictory descriptions of the same graphic. In this way, we can imagine Robbe-Grillet looking at the broken *bons-kilomètres* sign and making "exclusive descriptions of 'surfaces'".[4] But we can also think of Brownjohn finding nothing much of design there, just "accident", and James Williams diagramming a process sign, and we can think of Fella closing in with his polaroid on the terminal of one flickering letter, and so on. These are things that are happening in a way unjustified by design. So the sort of realism we are meaning here, from the literary point of view, concerns the way the world is as it appears to us and the ways that we represent (de-scribe) those experiences.[5]

It's possible for these different descriptions of the same sign to be viable because we are not assuming there to be any stable essence at the core of the event. Also, we are not prioritising the transcendent, rational order of design over the imminent, idiosyncratic experience of these pedestrian encounters. This is why, as we have said, returning to Whitehead's example of Cleopatra's Needle, a physicist may look at the monument and see a "dance of molecules" and an artist may see a "nice bit of colour", and so on. As such, the contour of this literary-inspired realism is without a hard-line matter-of-factness. Ultimately, it was that matter-of-fact, positivist realism of *Learning from Las Vegas* that eclipsed other goings on from being in any way relevant. When we say that the graphic event is a realist account of graphic designs, we mean it provokes us to seek out and embrace alternative discernible details that we otherwise overlook; it is a realism that is a digression. In this way, it is a realism that is not part of the continuity of a design, it is a way to be inclusive of differences that have otherwise been underimagined in design discourse.

Inheriting realism from this more literary perspective means that when we talk about realism we are referring mainly to descriptions of experiences, and more specifically what the limitations of those descriptions are. As Robbe-Grillet sees it, this sort of literary realism is about "advancing in ways as yet unknown, in which a new kind of writing becomes necessary".[6] In this context, being a realist means being open to what appears now to be real and taking it seriously, even if it contradicts what you think *should* be real. What is important here is that the realist's job is not to dutifully reflect reality in the most realistic terms possible because with that sort of realism we would just end up back at the almost-but-not-quite-life-likeness of embalmed animals that we began with at the start of this book. Instead, our emphasis of realism is on creative constructions of reality. What we make of something, what we feel to be going on; that is what we think of as realism. As such, this is a realism that does not rely on the "realistic illusion", whereby the most valuable reality is remotely, somewhere out there, yet to be revealed. In the same way, Robbe-Grillet distinguishes between the novelist that describes the things they see, and the novelist that "sees the things he invents". He claims, "I do not transcribe, I construct".[7]

With this emphasis of construction, as opposed to transcription, in realism, the thing that *comes out* of the everyday and draws our attention is not something that appears to be true or real in the traditional, proper sense. Instead, as we have shown, it is the error, the mishap, the mistake. It is not the thing that "rings true" but instead the thing that "rings false" that catches our attention, such as the broken sign Barthes describes at the Gare Montparnasse. Robbe-Grillet illustrates this with Franz Kafka's diary entries, it is worth quoting in full:

> "Thus, even in Kafka's diaries, when the writer notes down what he has noticed during the day in the course of a walk, he retains merely fragments which are not only without importance, but further, which seem to him cut off from their signification, hence from their *verisimilitude*: the stone abandoned for no good reason in the middle of the street, the bizarre gesture of a passer-by, incomplete, clumsy, not seeming to correspond to any function or precise intention. Partial objects, detached from their use, moments immobilized, words separated from their context, or cross-conversations, whatever rings a little false, that lacks 'naturalness' – it is precisely this which rings truest to the novelist's ear".[8]

These things of "no good reason" that are "incomplete", "clumsy" and "cut off from their signification" call back to Whitehead's notions of the "discerned" and the "discernible". The discernible, which we can think of as real, pure potential is not limited to things traditionally associated with the discipline of graphic design, such as the potential choice of typeface, colour, line weight, etc. What is discernible is everything that makes up the living reality of the graphic, which may not necessarily be design-related at all. For instance, a hangover, honking car horns, the sudden release of air from the storage reservoir of a braking bus, the smell of acrid piss, these could all be discerned to make up the graphic event of a Paris metro sign more than its Art Nouveau style or the biography of Hector Guimard, for instance. The vast potential of the discernible is lost when we only think of graphics as isolated bits of stuff, faithful to their designs that exist somehow apart from the rest of the living world, as if graphics were nothing but the "verisimilitude" of their design. But when we appreciate a graphic as an event – an event with "no good reason" – these seemingly arbitrary details of experience become viable aspects of the graphic. To give another example, we could discern that the typeface of a metal sign is Helvetica, but when we look at it in detail we may notice that there are discernible chips in the crux of the "T", or a ding in the tail of a "Y", features that Max Miedinger would not accept in his *designs* for Helvetica. It is by being attentive to the independent impulses of a graphic, rather than prioritising and overextending the authority of its designs, that brings us to the actuality (the realism) of the ongoing graphic event.

To further clarify, being drawn to details is not the same as looking for simple or reductive clarity. Instead, counterintuitively, details reveal what John Ruskin calls "doubtful forms". In volume four of *Modern Painters*, Ruskin says "[w]hat we call seeing a thing clearly, is only seeing enough of it to make out what it is".[9] That is to say, we can have vivid experiences but not necessarily clear understandings. Ruskin imagines how indistinct the shapes of an embroidered handkerchief and an open book would appear from half a mile away, he calls it "the point of mystery for the whole of those things". Walking closer to them they can be recognised but the book cannot be read and the embroidery cannot be traced, and that process of attraction, walking closer, and recognising the objects is part of the vivid experience, but it is not, as Ruskin goes on to show, somehow making the object more (simply) clear. At this point, Ruskin says, "The mystery has ceased to be in the whole things, and has gone into their details". Getting closer still to the objects, the text can be read and the embroidery traced but the fibres and threads cannot be seen. Ruskin goes on: "We take both up and look closely at them; we see the watermark and the threads, but not the hills and dales in the paper's surface, nor the fine fibres which shoot off from every thread." From here, we are at the limits of our senses after walking over to the thing and holding it up close, and closer. There is, however, still "mystery" but it is in another (fourth) place "where it must stay, till we take a microscope, which will send it into a fifth, sixth, hundredth, or thousandth place, according to the power we use". Ruskin is zooming in to see (and see again) mystery in the possibility of more discernible detail that disrupts the limited sense of discerned wholeness.[10] In this way, these are details that cannot be reduced to function in (or for) design exclusively. As such, everything is of a depth, but never "the depth", never the essential bottom of it all, or the absolute uppermost limits. Considering this in terms of graphics – perhaps walking along a street, rather than across Ruskin's field – by noticing and describing idiosyncratic details of real experience, we are never exposing the essential, material interiority of the graphic, instead, what we encounter are more surfaces and the potential for more vivid experiences.

There is a politics to taking these sorts of (mysterious) details seriously. Modern realist novels would often have seemingly trivial descriptions of details of everyday life. Barthes notes that these bits of detail have traditionally been left out of structural analysis because they are considered "superfluous" to structure. "[F]rom the point of view of structure", says Barthes, these details are "scandalous". However, as Barthes goes on to argue, for an analysis to be worthy it should be exhaustive and "account for the totality of its object".[11] As such, when accounted for in analysis, these "luxury" and "scandalous" details serve a purely representational order because, from a structuralist perspective, there must be a use for the useless.

Jacques Rancière says that this sort of analysis concludes that "[t]he usefulness of the useless detail is to say: I am the real".[12] Semiotically, this is what Barthes calls "the reality effect". However, when Barthes claims that the descriptions of details are only there to show that the realist scene is really real, Rancière claims Barthes' "modernist and structuralist presuppositions" are overlooking a "rupture with the representational order".[13]

Rancière says "[t]he purported 'reality effect' is much rather an equality effect".[14] It concerns, he suggests, "the equality of all beings, all things and all situations open to being seen" and that "clutter" of stuff doesn't leave space for the refined, "harmonious development of a plot".[15] Relating this back more explicitly to the graphic event, it means that seemingly irrelevant (and constructed) details of graphics are open to being seen without needing to be held together, or validated as significant by the logic of the structure – that is to say the plot – of design. As such, by using the concept of event to provoke realistic accounts of graphic designs, we (as pedestrians) are disrupting the boundaries of what is proper to the plot of design by intensifying the idiosyncratic, local detail. It is in this realism that we see the event-like normality of graphic designs disturbing the normalised image of the graphic as design.

For instance, in a short documentary series *Typo-safari* designers are filmed walking around city streets and talking about the typography they encounter. In each instance, the designers talk about the things they know – the anatomy of type, the anecdotal history of the signs, biographies of designers, and so on – which is to say they are talking about the design of the type. But they never refer to what is happening at that moment, as they are being filmed, or mention the seemingly superfluous material, physical qualities of the graphics: the flakes and blisters of old painted signs, metal sheet signs with brittle layers of browning iron, cheap black vinyl signs flayed in the middle and curled at the edges. We could say that they are talking about what they know to anticipate from their encounters with designs, rather than what they feel to be happening then and there. In this way their perception is structured by their commitment to the grander plot of design at the cost of their own independent, grounded experiences. Their passionate descriptions are in line with the order of the design. What they have missed is

the "texture of the real" in the ways the graphics go on living beyond the intention of their designers.[16]

It is not just about who gets to say what is and is not real or what should and should not be valuable, but also what is and is not included (discerned) in these aspects of reality. The point is that the detail's being there and the encounter with them matters. Take Jeff Wall's 1999 photograph *Morning Cleaning*, *Mies van der Rohe Foundation, Barcelona* as an example. In Wall's photograph, inside the pavilion, at the back of the room, in the shadow of the morning light, a cleaner has spread suds across its tall glass panes. He bends over a cadmium yellow bucket, its casters sit in a small puddle on the travertine marble, there are two well-used cleaning rags hanging over the back of a white leather-upholstered and chrome Barcelona chair, also designed by Mies van der Rohe for the pavilion. At a surface level the cleaner's bucket, blue trousers, and plain white t-shirt complement the rich red velvet drapes, the aqua-tint of the glass he cleans, and the green trees that reach above the outside marble wall. But the cleaner does not belong to the opulent modernist design in the same way that for William Gilpin vulgar peasants and workers do not belong to picturesque landscapes. It is this disregarded part of the ideal design that interests us; the way that it is always penetrated and obscured by a (really real) realism. The cleaner is not part of the sensible narrative in the way the marble, and the chairs, and the drapes are. But his being there makes a difference, it is a difference to design, a striation in the sensible.

Notes:

1.
Roland Barthes, *Critical Essays*. Translated by R. Howard, Northwestern University Press, 1992 (originally published 1962): 13.

2.
Alain Robbe-Grillet, *For a New Novel: Essays on Fiction*. Translated by R. Howard, Northwestern University Press, 1992 (originally published 1963): 157. In David Shields' book *Reality Hunger* he quotes Émile Zola saying something similar: "every proper artist is more or less a realist according to his own eyes".

3.
Ibid, 158.

4.
Ibid, 150.

5.
This is quite different to what realism usually means in a philosophical context, which is the way that the world exists beyond our being there or knowing about it.

6.
For a New Novel, 158.

7.
Ibid, 161-163.

8.
Ibid, 163.

9.
John Ruskin, *Modern Painters Volume IV*. John Wiley & Sons, 1843: 58.

10.
This brings to mind Robert Hooke's "micrographia" from 1665 and his images of the needle tip, razor's edge, and full stop.

11.
Roland Barthes, *The Reality Effect* (originally published 1969), in The Rustle of Language, Translated by R. Howard, University of California Press, 1989. (originally published 1984): 141.

12.
Jacques Rancière, *The Lost Thread: The Democracy of Modern Fiction*. Translated by S. Corcoran. Bloomsbury Academic, 2016: 55.

13.
Ibid, 58.

14.
Ibid, 68.

15.
Ibid, 63.

16.
Ibid, 66.

We thank John Walter for his un
mmitment and energy, which hav
nd pleasurable exhibition to orga
grateful to the artists who have e
given special attention to their con
he following: Reversible Destiny
Madeline Gins) have refurbishec
chitectural plans for *Arcade House*
he USA (special thanks to Peter Katz
Benedict Drew is reformulating a
many of his previous interests v
Duggie Fields has allowed us to sho
have not been exhibited for some t
en extremely generous in organisi
orks by Louise Fishman from the
ngrid Nyeboe has been instrument
photographer Jonathan Bassett mad
o capture Hundertwasser's buildin
lped with the rediscovery of classi
shown in recent years; Tim Spoon
of his exhibition, *The Voice of N*
rteadmin): all of the works by Ni

A Knowing Wrongness

by Fraser Muggeridge

With designers using the same tools, visual references, and production techniques, how can new graphic designs have elements of bespokeness or feel uniquely creative?[1] I wonder if a "knowing wrongness" of typographic experiment and print processes could lead to new forms of typographic practice. I am asking this question in my research at the Royal Melbourne Institute of Technology (RMIT) and it is also part of my design practice.

It is clear to see that the advance of readily available technology and the general awareness of graphic design over recent years has enabled anyone with basic software knowledge and little training to be competent at making a piece of visual communication. Designers and non-designers throughout the world are all using the same easy-to-use software and have access to the same new fonts. This, in combination with work being lifted and regurgitated from the internet with little or no concern for context, can lead to a uniform blandness with everything looking the same after a while.

The drive for perfection in design production means that individuality is in danger of being lost. In this post-postmodern world, better typefaces are being produced, combined with higher and higher resolution images, printed on modern, cleaner, more accurate presses with overall l ess and less human intervention. Clean is the norm. This kind of minimal aesthetic is certainly the most dominant one in mainstream graphic design culture. Here we see a contemporary coffee shop, "The Commission" at London Heathrow airport; clean, minimal, a familiar sight on the high street.

Contemporary typeface design has reached not only the highest quality in terms of technological advances and drawing quality but also the largest choice. With typography being at the heart of what I do, choosing typefaces is an important and increasingly difficult part of the job. The history of the font, its visual appearance and feeling are all important qualities that I take into account when choosing

a font. But I often struggle to use these new fonts. I think a leading factor is that they are perfect, with a machine-like quality, lacking the idiosyncrasies present in hot metal composition. Also, just using them straight out of the tin almost feels too easy, as if I don't have much to do. The hand of the type designer may be visible, but what about the hand of the graphic designer? Is it now being lost, or perhaps overshadowed by metaphors for things they aren't actually doing anymore? It seems that the hand of the graphic designer has been replaced by the digital cut and paste generation.

My recent design work reacts against this contemporary backdrop by intentionally setting myself apart from the mainstream. I create original work that intentionally shows evidence of the graphic designer's hand in manual and digital productions. Using type design software the "wrong" way, or using software developed for other uses, and coupling this with a process-driven art practice approach, has in some part led me to a new way of thinking about graphic design and its production.

For instance, at first glance this double page spread looks like a normal, straightforward, well considered book made to certain high standards. But when we zoom in, you will notice that the typeface is in fact two typefaces alternating between each other. We have Palatino by Herman Zapf and Trump Medieval by Georg Trump. If you look at the "R"s in "territory" and the "D"s in "addresses" you will see that they're ever so slightly different. This can be done relatively easily by making a hybrid font that uses the "contextual" feature in *OpenType* software to automatically alter the font when typeset. These interruptions of "wrongness" are a recurring theme in my practice.

Manipulation of existing fonts really started to take shape in the late 1980s when graphic designers, as opposed to type designers, could open and edit digital fonts, chopping bits off, adding bits from other fonts, and so on. Layered, punk, new wave typography was in its heyday when Rick Poynor's influential book *Typography Now: The Next Wave*

Oceanic peoples. These traditional w
ks, were regarded as a means through
icate with the living. We might not be
ad through Ozbolt's 2014 series of por
nich the sitters are disconcertingly ma
e motifs – which also reappear in *The*
sculpture, and in *United we stand* (2(
st totems – are symbolic again of the
:al territories, to embrace multiplicitie
in his work.

non-sense that Ozbolt's characters inh
lly. The artist also focuses on the elem
:o egregious or traumatic that they de
zi-era Germany are one such example
emporary traumas he addresses in oth
ill, in the aftermath of the First World
rn. Compare the foreboding landscape
New World (1918) for example, with O.
oth paintings, Nash's in oil, Ozbolt's in
space. The trees in Nash's work – pai
on to the British artist's time in the tr
bolt's landscape is more lush, but the
ose used in his expanding foam sculp

was published in 1989. Around this time, Max Kisman created Fudoni, a mix of Bodoni and Futura. Jonathan Barnbrook's Prototype, released in 1995, is another combination of sans and serif and upper and lower case. Fuse, from 1991, is Neville Brody's and Jon Wozencroft's experimental publication on fonts and typography, it showcased and distributed experimental, illegible, conceptual typefaces to a wide desktop publishing audience.

In their focus on the
by which we come
something, they also
a process of epistem
Like Cocker's essays,
words and objects
sentences classical.

Continuing this anti-tradition of type design, in 2013 I designed Megafont, which is a typeface made up of 52 different typefaces, all being of similar grotesque but each unique for uppercase and lowercase characters. Aligning each letter to the x-height gave the typeface some kind of uniform evenness that, in turn, contrasts with its "wrongness" in ever so slightly different microspaces of weights, character shapes, ascenders, and descenders. Megafont was made for *MAN AARG!* a publication by David Berridge, published by X Marks the Bökship described as "a jumbled exercise in reading about writing and writing about reading". I followed Megafont with a serifed version too, called Century Megafont. Similarly constructed of 52 versions of Century typefaces, but with an added feature of randomness within each letter, again made possible with 26 sets of contextual alternatives. If you look, the "T"s are different in the example.

These Megafonts, in their various incarnations and reincarnations, bring a certain unequal, uneven and unresolved texture to a piece of work. A flicker on the screen and a flicker on the page reminiscent of letterpress printing with all its faults and misprints or, let's say, "wrongness". In many ways, it looks as if the text has been handset and printed badly. By intensifying chance and embracing the unforeseeable, as the designer, you don't know what letter is going to come next. In this way, the typeface comes alive. Recognising the life of type like this means that what I am describing is a kind of type designing without designing type.

For example, another form of what we could call "type hacking", as a knowing method of wrongness, is to alter individual letterforms or parts of the letterforms themselves. Radical Essex is a font made for a modernist architectural project in the UK. It was created by turning all the curved points of Helvetica from round to straight, and then jumbling them back together again.

St Louis Return' begins its
at saw Burroughs' sixth birt
p style with an incomplete k
s and immediately problem
t of the text: '(ticket to St L
who is the third that walks k

Another example of this is transposing the counters of one typeface to that of another. In this instance, swapping the counters of Futura Book with Futura Bold and Futura Bold Condensed. Again, this creates an uneven effect when used to set text, partly because of the counterintuitive design (i.e. unclean, impure, disorganised) but also because the letters that don't have counters are left unchanged.

In 2015 I worked with the artist Fiona Banner creating a typeface constructed from a blend of all the typefaces that

Helvetica Regular	ABCDEFGHIJKLMNOPQRSTUVWXYZ & abcdefghijklmnopqrstuvwxyz01234567890
All bezier curves removed	ABCDEFGHIJKLMNOPQRSTUVWXYZ & abcdefghjklmn◇pqrstuvwxyz0123456789
top half removed	ABCDEFGHIJKLMNOPQRSTUVWXYZ & abcdefghijklmn◇pqrstuvwxyz0123456789
bottom half removed	ABCDEFGHIJKLMNOPQRSTUVWXYZ & abcdefghijklmn◇pqrstuvwxyz0123456789
random removed	ABCDEFGHIJKLMNOPQRSTUVWXYZ & abcdefghijklmn◇pqrstuvwxyz0123456789

she uses in her work. We called it Font. It was made using the interpolation tool in type design software, which is supposed to be used as a tool to blend a bold and light weight of a typeface to create a regular weight typeface. Using this software intentionally wrongly by blending a serif typeface with a sans serif typeface, and using a badly designed free font, produced this new bastard form of aesthetic ugliness.

Working with Giorgio Sadotti, another artist, we developed the conceptual typeface HIDE. It has letters within letters. The first line shows an "A" within an "A", which is simply an "A", followed by a "B" within an "A", and so on. This font, like the others, has 26 variations. We also made SPLIT SWISS,

delles nim ania volectas nusanisquis quae adi du
ol orporei cillest oremporem hil ium im nempe de
sequosa ndemolor autem quatustint offic tem h
verovid quo quis sequam quodit evelende most fu
sperion natentinte qui officturi consequid quia v
sum estrum alit quae dolupta quam sequatiae lib
Jgia sunt aspe ne eum vellendus enim doloreptas
n non rent, iscilla utatiur, conem eostiosaped ut (
a quidi a nonsenis aut omnimilitae cumquis secer
nse sa quat ad quatur? Qui ut idel ium dolupie n
m voluptatum, tet remolut landi invel ius senimp
icien damusam si sam exceserferis enia conseru

simply a font called Swiss split in half and ROLL FONT, a font rolling around a cylinder. These typefaces are barely legible and in many ways all wrong. It's a new way of creating fonts. Rather than designing particular aesthetic letterforms, the font is created through the design of a framework and system that is then played out.

Writing & Illuminating, & Lettering by Edward Johnston first published in 1906, talks about the essential skeleton form of a letter. Recent online type design software, such as *Prototypo*, uses this notion as the basic form for the creation of do-it-yourself typefaces. I was curious to see if I could reverse this process and theoretically re-draw the skeleton of existing fonts, which of course is an essential structure that has never really existed. I chose Akzidenz Grotesk, a relatively monolinear sans-serif that, through its process of being designed, has undergone very small adjustments to every curve to form its character and produce an even rhythm when set as words in sentences. I was interested in erasing these perfecting optical alterations that have been made to sans-serif typefaces. I did this by acting as if their phantom

WHAT
IS
ROLLED
IS
MOVING

SRY JJ

Grotesk

skeleton was actually real. The system I used was simply to draw down the middle of each letter; the magenta line is exactly the halfway point of the font. Plotting the midpoint of each stroke like this resulted in an uneven baseline.

This new scaffold form can then be re-stroked to create any desired weight that has certain characteristics of the original Akzidenz Grotesk font but with new characteristics that are a consequence of this process. As such, a new typeface has been created. This is typeface design without actually drawing the letters based on visual judgement. In the context of contemporary graphic design's aesthetic values, there would be a temptation to optically correct the unevenness and the irregularity of this typeface, but to me, that is what makes it interesting, it is the way (as I said before) it comes alive.

There is this robot drawing machine that paints in watercolour any image that you vectorise and feed into it. *Stipplegen*, its software, maps a continuous line for the brush to follow (as opposed to how *Adobe Illustrator* would create a series of trace lines). I noticed that each time the task was performed a different path would be drawn, so I wondered what would happen if you applied this to a letter form. The software is creating the letter "A" as a continuous path. Each time a different path is generated, therefore each

ABCDEFGHIJKLMNOPQRSTUVWXYZab
cdefghijklmnopqrstuvwxyz01234567890

ABCDEFGHIJKLMNOPQRSTUVWXYZab
cdefghijklmnopqrstuvwxyz01234567890

ABCDEFGHIJKLMNOPQRSTUVWXYZab
cdefghijklmnopqrstuvwxyz01234567890

ABCDEFGHIJKLMNOPQRSTUVWXYZab
cdefghijklmnopqrstuvwxyz01234567890

ABCDEFGHIJKLMNOPQRSTUVWXYZab
cdefghijklmnopqrstuvwxyz01234567890

time there is a different letter "A". These can all be saved as vectors and then imported into type design software as multiple alternative characters, which can be used to create a typeface with an infinite number of variations. Again, this is type design without designing type.

Mimeographica Aphabetica, was an exhibition at the Whitechapel Gallery in 2014, it was the result of a series of workshops exploring the possibilities of stencil lettering systems and mimeograph printing which is a form of stencil duplicating. Here I drew through both the upper case stencil and lower case stencil at the same time to create this abstract font. The letterforms were cut by hand as paper stencils, printed on basic stencil duplicator and shown with the printer as part of the exhibition's installation. These abstract letterforms moved from typographic to graphic, from text to image, through a revival of a stencil production and stencil print processes.

Somesuch Stories is a recent book that takes on board typographic principles of hierarchy and arrangement, but uses all of them at the same time in an unexpected and expanded manner: centred, justified, ranged left and ranged right all on one page. These risky combinations of arrangement make

sense due to the book's theme of the dispersed and the experimental nature of the publisher, combined with my ambition to always try to do something new to push this discipline. A rigorous execution of microspacing and typographic rigour, which is always present in the work, creates a tension of typography dos and don'ts existing at the same time.

Similarly, *Shonky: The Aesthetics of Awkwardness*, combines a knowingly wrong approach in both form and letterform. Sixteen fonts (one font for each section of the book) were designed with the online font tool *Prototypo*. Using parameters sliders that affect all the letters at the same time, as opposed to individual ones, it is something like pushing all the controls on a music mixing desk to their extreme to create a distorted sound. Each typeface is distorted within a different parameter: curviness, serif width or serif arc. Each paragraph of the book is set in a rotating sequence of these sixteen fonts, mixed with a daring centred arrangement throughout the book, setting a fitting "shonky" atmosphere.

My strive to create bespoke and unique outcomes in terms of form and letterform through unconventional methods of process and production, coupled with a consistently inconsistent knowingly wrong approach, is a way to make real alternatives to the now so called "café normal" in graphic design.

Notes:

1.
Transcript and images from presentation at *Typography Day*, Sir J. J. Institute of Applied Art, Mumbai, 2018.

Shonky

The Aesthetics of Awkwardness

Edited by

John Walter

With a contribution from

Zoë Strachan
& Louise Welsh

Hayward Publishing

Conclusion

Conclusion

In 1985, graphic designer Paula Scher attended a seminar on graphic design education at the Maryland Institute of Art. In an article for AIGA the following year, Scher says she felt shame, boredom and anger because "the speaker is supposed to be talking about graphic design, not quantum physics".[1] She felt that academics with a sense of "professional inferiority" were being pompous with their applied "theoretics". Holding on to graphic design's conservative, rationalist and functionalist traits, Scher argues for "meaningful discussion", "clear explanations" and "tangible results" rather than baffling theories of graphic design. She asks, frustrated, "where is the graphic design?"

Scher explains how she asked seven of her favourite, award winning designers to define "semiotics" – a process of studying signs that is often associated with brow-furrowing neologistic writing.[2] Scher claims her contacts struggled or outright refused to give a definition. She goes on to suggest that if they were asked how a symbol works, they could have given concise and informed explanations. Scher seems to be proposing that designers should only – and perhaps can only – concern themselves with things comfortably familiar to design because being concerned with anything else could undermine the designer's competence. Perhaps what Scher is presenting in her brief article is the preference for "theoretics" to be more like kinds of insular, deductive, instrumentalist investigations of designs by designers, which should not be peculiar to the design discipline as we have come to know it, but should instead conform to the practicing (read: pragmatic) designer's lexicon.

Therefore, we can assume that the kind of theoretical considerations that Scher prefers begin with design and end with design and do not question the assumed category of Design itself.[3] This is presented as a kind of hard boiled, resolute version of design theory that is solely focused on what we (need to) know about graphic design in its common use. The unknown, hesitant, and unclear, as such, are reluctant risks in this kind of thinking about design because it makes the materials that design uses to understand itself unfamiliar. This avoidance of the unknown for the sake of self-preservation leaves design with an "odour of decay", to borrow a phrase from Friedrich Nietzsche's genealogy of morals. We are back in this familiar place where a graphic is only its design as a matter-of-fact. But as we have shown, a graphic is more than a straightforward evocation of its design. As designers, we should be hesitant of our certainties, we need to introduce new perspectives so that we can re-view what we anticipate to be meaningful because difference challenges what we think we (can) know about something as a matter of definite fact.

Historically, the way to challenge rigid doctrinal order has been to undermine things that are traditionally considered to be unchanging by exaggerating their more or less conditional qualities. In doing this, seemingly fixed things are shown to be more radically contingent and more openly plural than previously thought. For example, in the nineteenth century Friedrich Nietzsche argued vehemently for a genealogical understanding of morals. He reframed morality as something made up of transient historical ideologies as opposed to timeless God-given values. In this way, Nietzsche was not arguing against false claims to a true morality, and therefore calling for a more accurate, more properly true version of moral values; Nietzsche's critique is not about colliding one substance with another harder one. Instead, he undermines the notion of "Truth" as any sort of discoverable thing. In historical context, following on from Nietzsche's nineteenth century secularisation of Truth, circa 1917 nuclear reactions proved the divisibility of the supposedly indivisible atom, and circa 1925 the Copenhagen interpretation of quantum mechanics argued for the indeterminacy of matter, around the same time Whitehead's philosophy pushes against "the fallacy of misplaced concreteness" by critically unpacking the "scientific doctrine of matter".[4] In each of these instances, the notion of a bottom level unchanging structure, such as atoms (maybe pixels and pigments are the designer's equivalent), or a higher level order, such as God (or perhaps in this context a transcendent designer), is undermined by the forceful potential of difference.

It is this uncertain flux of nature that may be discouraging Scher from quantum physics because it undermines the authoritative structures of design; at the depth of discipline, design isn't able to bottom out at the level of a meaningful, rational foundation and at the depth of the everyday it is diffuse without any sense of targeted purposive end. As such, what Scher is resisting being brought into conversations of graphic design is a kind of embrace of non-wisdom, or unknowing, or contradiction. It is similar to what we have already referred to a few times with Cleopatra's Needle. For argument's sake, let's say there's a poster stuck on the monolith. Scher would approach the poster and consider its design qualities, such as its colours, typography, treatment of images, layout, etc., and a quantum physicist may walk by and see the poster as a "dance of molecules". For Scher, a designer should not, and perhaps cannot, see the value of the scientist's perspective of the poster as a "dance of molecules" because it seemingly has little to do with design, there are no "clear explanations" and "tangible results" from this perspective. And more to the point, the scientist's perspective – and a semiotician's perspective too – admit to a graphic's unbounded surplus. It's likely that Scher is not actually opposed to quantum physics itself but rather what it represents; a multivalance of difference and a willing embrace of indeterminacy and uncertainty. As such, this is why, when faced with something unfamiliar and unknown that admits graphics have the ability to withdraw from design, that Scher asks (and read this now in a worried, concerned tone of voice, rather than an irate one) "where is the graphic design?"

It is curious that Scher did not ask "how" is this relevant to, related to, in tension with, challenging, contrasting, etc., graphic design. "Where" is a question that is seeking, looking to grasp, determine, state as ultimately here or not here. Alternatively, asking "how" has degrees, it is a way in which a thing does something, it is not something that can be grabbed and held onto, it is a process that can only be (partially) understood through the act of description because for it to sustain its most fundamental quality (of dynamism) it cannot be understood by holding it still. So what is at risk if we take the coming together of quantum physics and graphic design seriously? Or, for that matter, if we take seriously the everyday and graphic design, or pluralism and graphic design, or indeterminacy and graphic design, in other words: the graphic event. It is certainty that is at risk; the possibility of "having" knowledge.[5]

As we have shown, whilst the graphic has been designed, it is nonetheless inexhaustible by the knowledge and language of design discipline and process itself, just as equally we can never fully know the graphic from the perspective of the pedestrian, the scientific materialist, or the street cleaner either. In context to realism, as we have described it, there is no reason why in design discourse one of those perspectives should sustain a higher level of value over any other. Of course, there is an authority in the voice of a designer when talking about design (we would call it subject-specific knowledge) but it leaves little room for difference, agonism, contestation, conflict, etc., if it is the only one talking when graphics are the subject of conversation. The graphic event, as such, works as a conceptual detour out of design-conventional ways of perceiving and representing graphics. Of course, we know that graphics have at some point been designed, but they live on beyond the intentions of those designs.

Momentarily bracketing design and experiencing the graphic as an event is a way of being vigilant about the inevitable surplus of design in the same way that we have described the relation between what Whitehead calls the "discerned" and the "discernible". It is important to notice these things happening because our seeing them and being aware of them makes us observant in ways that do not fit to the structures of given designs. That is to say, what the graphic is and what it could be (and is becoming) are brought into a closer embrace through immanent everyday experiences. This is what makes the graphic event a confusing, mixing, mingling process. The event is provoking us to consider what it would mean for graphics to be irrational, which is to say, in some sense, adversarial to design (if we still have to think of design as a rationalist discipline). It is a way for us to connect, and relate, and live at the level of personal experience and feeling with graphics without having to couch that experience in a design vocabulary. This may mean that one of the ways we come to experience graphic designs is not as something that we know in an instant, as something familiar that we glance past, but instead as something that we need to attentively live with. As we have hinted at with the drawing, pulling, attracting *acts* of the event; there is something possibly more theatrical to graphic design that has been overlooked in its discourses.

Obviously, the concept of the graphic event is not reinventing graphic design to be something else, rather, it already is radically different from what we normally think it to be; it has always been doing something (else). This is why the way that we *attend* to graphics is so important. The danger is that experience – in terms of unclear, indeterminate curves of activity – will increasingly be subordinated to the anticipated and preconceived, the clear, simple, exact and mechanical, even if what is intended (designed) and what is experienced (graphically) are at odds. So the graphic event is a way of generating resistance to simple, clear, fixed, unmysterious ways in which graphics go on existing. It is about being prepared to live with the never-entirely-knowable. This is why there is a distinction between the normality of graphics in life which may be indifferent to design, and the normalisation of graphics in (and for) design. Time needs to be given in the discourse of design for the counter-perspective and contra-experiences of the dramatists and the tragidists to speak about design from a more graphically-oriented perspective.

Patti Smith's *Year of the Monkey* is probably one of the most thought provoking and unacknowledged texts for graphic designers since James Williams' recent *A Process Philosophy of Signs*. Smith describes episodic encounters with signs that draw out lived and fabulated experiences, rather than descriptions of clear fragments. She shows everyday graphics, and what Williams would describe as "process signs", to be spontaneous and unbounded by the rational ideal intentions of design and even the anticipations of regular day-to-day experiences. From Smith's account, the graphics are not things to be seen or content to be had, they are moments to live through. She records them in vignettes that do not call back to designs because what she is describing are event-like, chance happenings. They are graphics alive that give life (such as in melancholy daydreams) to other stories and relations. The graphics Smith describes are billboards, shopfront notices and street signs, but they exist as part of an imminent and withdrawn deep milieu; amongst other things, seen and unseen. It is from what we would consider to be Smith's realist perspective that she can describe signs to have "supercilious tones" and to be "kinetically trailing".[6] What Smith shows us as designers is an exaggerated experience of familiar things, the whole book is an intensifying of signs that do not arise from a reliable structure and are not delivering their (supposed) intended meaning. Reading Smith alongside Larkin and Dylan – and to an extent Brownjohn – there is an emerging sense of the lyrical and the poetic, and even the tragic and the dramatic.[7] It is difficult to say if this has any inherent "value" to graphic design but that should not mean that it is dismissed so quickly.

The graphic event is not simply about mobilising descriptions of details in design, it is about cluttering and complexifying design for the sake of not knowing (Fraser Muggeridge), being alert (Patrick Thomas) and taking difference seriously (James Williams). This is the disensus necessary for a more open, critical discourse of graphic design. This is why the idiosyncratic perspective of the pedestrian is so important, more than staffage, we must change how we orient ourselves as pedestrians (not just designers) to have "[…] a heart / That watches and receives" and get back to graphics in the world. But we should not forget, this is an awkward reorientation and disorderly process. Whilst these are private unworded experiences, there is something spectacle-like happening in public view. Drifting into the ragged edge of the not-yet-discerned and barely-discernible, we are getting in the way of the regular and routine as we defamiliarize and reorient ourselves in public space.[8] Franz Hessel was bothered he looked like a criminal, aimlessly wandering in *Walking in Berlin*, he calls it the "suspicious nature of the observer". Design theorist John Chris Jones felt embarrassment photographing the "obviously 'odd'" in St Ives. As a "sky-gazer" Virginia Woolf was ill and in the way of a "disconcerted" public as her attention lingered on the often passed by scenes of the day to day. Brownjohn imagines being knocked down by a car, staring up at buildings and signs from a stretcher; the only way to notice anything above "road, pavements, and the first two floors". Even Richard Maybe, one of the early writers of ecologies on city fringes, felt conspicuous looking through his binoculars at wildlife on high streets.[9] This is the embodied part of the curves of experiences of the graphic event, it's clumsy, awkward and in the way of usual goings on.

The pedestrian should be a newly subversive point of view in design discourse. Perhaps we need to ingress this underimagined point of view as a way to be agonistic and provoke difference. We can see in recent design discourses that the public (read: non-expert) has been cut from emergent critical modes of design – the speculative, the relational, the ambiguous, the ontologically processual – for the sake of precision and exactness in rational design procedures. But the graphic event is not a procedure, it is graphic design's living, existential condition. It is not something that has a "use", or an inherent value, or solution. This is what we mean when we have said that designers should not be working *out* contingency, or somehow *using* contingency, but *living* with it. As such, we are wary of defending the graphic event by presenting it as something that can have capital in design practice, as if knowing of the event may make a design ideation process more fruitful, authentic, or original.

The graphic event insists we stand grounded in the present to cultivate new experiences of graphic designs that are drawn out by the "little bit of detail", and informed by the specific parameters of context. This is how we override the dominant order of the structured and the rational to regain the lost atmosphere of feeling in representations of graphics in design discourse. Be mindful, and receptive, ask yourself: what do you feel to be going on? Remember, this is a question we are asking from a place that is away from the book, the app, and the traditions of the discipline. We are on the street, at the asphalt-level, and what we come to experience may have little to do with design. We need to foster many new ways to talk about design to generate a critical mass of difference in discourse. It is precisely because graphic events are problematically difficult to understand and explain that they need to be introduced into design-discursive representations of graphics. As a catalyst for curiosity, the graphic event offers a new atmosphere for critical enquiry into graphic design. The graphic event makes new, risky, contingent, monstrous perceptions of design necessary.

Conclusion

Notes:

1.
Paula Scher, *Back to Show and Tell*, in AIGA Journal of Graphic Design, Volume 4, Number 1, 1986.

2.
For a graphic designer's introductory guide to structuralist semiotics see Sean Hall, *This Means This, This Means That: A User's Guide to Semiotics*. Laurence King, 2012.

3.
We see the same thing in a recent publication by designer Henry Hongmin Kim too. See *Graphic Design Discourse: Evolving Theories, Ideologies, and Processes of Visual Communication*. Princeton Architectural Press, 2017.

4.
Alfred North Whitehead, *Process and Reality: An Essay in Cosmology*. Macmillan, 1929.

5.
Along these lines, in *A Knowing Wrongness*, Fraser Muggeridge plays with the idea of the typographer as tinkerer, hacker and system maker, rather than the diligent doer of known processes of production.

6.
Patti Smith, *Year of the Monkey*. Bloomsbury Publishing, 2019: 80-95.

7.
There have been calls for poetic and lyrical thinking in graphic design before now: Steve Baker, *A Poetics of Graphic Design?* in Visible Language 28, 1994: 245-245. Terence Rosenberg, *The Reservoir: Towards a Poetic Model of Research in Design*, in Working Papers in Art and Design 1, 2000. John Chris Jones, *Designing Designing*. Bloomsbury Publishing, 2021. (originally published as *Essays in Design*. John Wiley & Sons, 1984). Daniel van der Velden, *Lyrical Design*, in Design Dedication: Adaptive Mentalities in Design Education. Valiz, 2020. And it is also worth remembering François Dufrêne, Burhan Doğançay, Isidore Isou in this context of the semiotically unfixed and graphically unusual.

8.
Peter Buwert, *Defamiliarisation, Brecht and Criticality in Graphic Design*, in Modes of Criticism 2: Critique of Method. Onomatopee, 2016: 25-38.

9.
There are more examples of these navigations of urban spaces as a-typical practices in Lauren Elkin, *Flâneuse: Women Walk the City in Paris, New York, Tokyo, Venice, and London*. Chatto & Windus, 2016. And in Rebecca Solnit, *Wanderlust*. Granta, 2014.

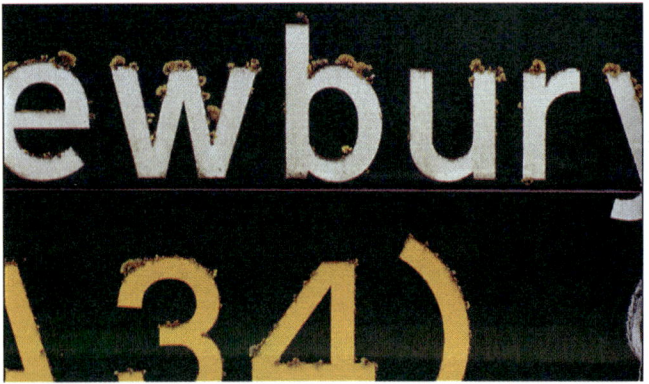

Acts of Address

Postscript
by Johanna Drucker

Acts of Address

This volume brings the discussion of graphic works as temporal and spatial events into clear focus. The multifaceted approach makes a clear case for the importance of taking location and context into account. Historical dimensions of both time and space factor largely in the pieces in this collection as they call attention to the ways graphic objects live in the made world. While the claims to universality and autonomy, so central to modernism and its aesthetics, have long been set aside, they sometimes linger almost unnoted. At the most basic level, this insular approach generally means that the development of a design (usually on a computer screen) isn't conceived as a social object. Also, as several authors here point out, designed artifacts are again lifted out of context when displayed in pristine gallery spaces, or are buffered by wide empty margins in a print publication. This means that the lived experience of these graphics is very often absent, ignored, unrecoverable. By contrast, the photographs and essays throughout this collection pay serious attention to the circumstances of encounter. This attention to "process" and "event" argues convincingly for seeing graphic works within the conditions of their place(s) in the world. This shift introduces accountability for what designs *do*, not just what they are in formal terms.

Such considerations lead to thick and rich investigations of the life cycles of graphic objects. Things read in different ways according to their circumstances. Some are immediately conspicuous, they are "discerned", to use the language of these texts. Others age, becoming out of sync with their surroundings. Their language becomes quaint. Styles become historic or nostalgic. In their becoming, paint peels, paper wrinkles, neon blinks and flickers, wood cracks and metal buckles. The physical changes and cultural shifts participate in different kinds of historicizing processes. A hand-lettered advertisement for a five-cent peep show or one painted on a brick wall advertising horse feed, now next to a paved parking lot, are more than aging relics of another age. They are parts of broken circuits of communication in which the "receiver" is no longer present. That is to say, those who would have recognized themselves as the target of that interlocutor, the implied "you" of the written speech acts, are no longer part of the body politic or public presence. The addressee is absent. The locution – the literal utterance or speech act – is dislocated in historical or cultural time and space. The concept of a locution is central to the study of language as a social activity, embedded in systems of power that are in part enacted through performative statements.

Social subjects change over time, as individuals and as collectivities. The banishment of claims to universality of form, so important for historicizing the very modern aesthetic that wished to transcend specific circumstances, is now complemented by a recognition that the person spoken to or addressed by an image or a text receives it according to their own socially situated identity. Even the signs mounted by the city or municipality posting parking regulations, noting evacuation paths, or indicating one way streets have a valence within certain sectors of the population that they do not have in others. Each individual receives the address according to the degrees of security or vulnerability they carry with them in public space. The most fundamental mode of address, "hey, you," positions each of us differently within the field of communications. This example was first used by Louis Althusser, who suggested that when uttered by a policeman on a street, it had multiple meanings and valences depending on the receiver.[1] Within the varied demographics of contemporary urban life, the impact of being hailed by a policeman can readily be understood as dependent on how one sees one's identity in relation to many systems of power, repression, state violence, and perception under the law. Althusser was using the example to demonstrate his concept of "interpellation", the production of what he termed "subject position". His larger point was that all locutions (utterances) are located, the "address" of their recipients is a specific part of the "event" that takes place when they occur.

Thus, the concept of "address" serves to signal location in several domains, each of which contains an allusion to the specificity of where the receiving subject is positioned. Locution as location has many aspects, such as place, time, and eye line. The power enacted by a view cone is always reciprocal. When a sign can be seen, it is also seeing its viewer. These positions are strategic. The events it enacts are those of surveillance and control as well as of effect and communication. The surreptitious glance, the ducking head, and turning away from a communication in an act of self-protection are all responses to the recognition that we are positioned as subjects of that vast network of enunciations that structures the spaces we inhabit. There are as many modes of address that exist as there are receivers of communication. They proliferate with infinite variety and specificity. Words in the world, images in a site, seen and viewed, are powerful enactors of those subtle and not-so-subtle aspects of power that permeate human culture and its workings. The "address" of a graphic event is thus another dimension of its dynamic, a transactional spacetime as well as a fluid social location within which the locution takes place.

The critical move in these essays marks an important shift from thinking of graphic works as objects to understanding them as events. Perhaps one marked feature of this collection is that the authors are critics *and* practitioners, educators *and* working designers, historians *and* documentors of the work in the world. This demonstrates a crucial synthesis of what, in an early generation, might have been a divide between theory and practice. Now the domains of critical reflection and production are intimately linked. This suggests a commitment to keeping a framework in place for considering the situatedness of design work within cultural and material conditions from its initial conception. As part of this awareness, we can include attention to how graphic events exist within the systems of address that locate the reception of every locution as a dynamic social act.

Notes:

1.
Louis Althusser, *Ideology and the Ideological State Apparatus*, in Lenin and Philosophy and Other Essays. New York City: Monthly Review Press, 1972: 174.

Photo Credits

6, James Wise (Sweat of the Gods).

10, Angelo Bramanti (Paper Vandalism).

18, Chris Ashworth.

24, Tony Brook.

32, Janet Hart.

42, Joseph Hughes (Typography is Real).

52, Jim Sutherland.

60, Malcolm Garrett.

70, Matthew Turner (Life without Billboards).

73, *Car View of The Strip with Robert Venturi and Denise Scott Brown*, 1968, photograph by Steven Izenour.

78, Haarkon.

90, Erik Brandt.

98, Mark Edwards (DR.ME).

118, Peter Woodall (Hidden City Philadelphia).

121, Robert Brownjohn, London Street Level BW 0072.

122, 123, Edward Fella.

128, Andy Altman.

146, Zeynep Aktuna (Hey Chuck).

152, Hannah Platt.

160, Jeff Wall, *Morning Cleaning, Mies van der Rohe Foundation, Barcelona*. 1999. Transparency in lightbox. 187.0 x 351.0 cm. Courtesy of the artist.

164, Sample from *Shonky: The Aesthetics of Awkwardness*. Catalogue design by Fraser Muggeridge studio.

182, Jacques Villeglé, Quai d'Ivry, 27 Novembre 1989, photograph by François Poivret.

194, *Robinson in Ruins*, ©2010. Patrick Keiller and the Royal College of Art. Images Courtesy of the Filmmaker. Licensed by BFI National Archive.

Contributors

Dr James Dyer is senior lecturer of Graphic Design at the University of Huddersfield.

Nick Deakin is senior lecturer of Graphic Design at Leeds Arts University.

Professor Alex Coles is Professor of Transdisciplinarity at the University of Huddersfield.

James Williams is Honorary Professor of Philosophy and member of the Alfred Deakin Institute for Citizenship and Globalization at Deakin University, Australia.

Professor Patrick Thomas runs Patrick Thomas Studio and is professor of communication design at ABK-Stuttgart.

Fraser Muggeridge runs Fraser Muggeridge studio and is visiting lecturer at The University of Reading.

DR.ME is the collaborative art and design practice of Ryan Doyle (DR) and Mark Edwards (ME).

Vicky Carr runs Textbook Studio with Chris Shearston.

Professor Teal Triggs is Associate Dean in the School of Communication at the Royal College of Art.

Professor Johanna Drucker is the Breslauer Professor of Bibliographical Studies and Distinguished Professor in the Department of Information Studies at The University of California.

Colophon

Onomatopee number: 223
Title: Graphic Events
Subtitle: A Realist Account of Graphic Design
Authors: James Dyer and Nick Deakin

ISBN: 9-789493-148666
Editors: James Dyer and Nick Deakin
Graphic design: Totally Okay
Text editor: James Dyer
Advisor: Professor Anne Massey
Printer: Kopa
Fonts: Messina Sans, Cooper Black.

Made possible thanks to the generous support of The
University of Huddersfield's School of Arts and Humanities
and Leeds Arts University. With special thanks to Dr Rowan
Bailey and Freek Lomme.

Onomatopee Projects
www.onomatopee.net

Graphics have a way of living that is often awkward and unplanned. We see it when they are ripped from walls, littered on streets and faded in shop windows. We wouldn't say they are that way by design, however this everyday difference between graphics and their designs is underimagined in critical discourses. Graphic Events intensifies this difference in a montage of original essays and interviews that coax graphics into unfamiliar dialogues.

Including

Alex Coles
DR.ME
Johanna Drucker
Fraser Muggeridge
Textbook Studio
Patrick Thomas
Teal Triggs
James Williams